"Democratic politics is a glorious, dangerous, and ever-changing game. These short commentaries are insightful, easily read, and just as lively as the game itself."
Alasdair Roberts, University of Missouri

"A brilliant effort by one of our most prolific writers to engage us in the public dialogue so urgently needed in a world of Trumps, Brexits and other populist challenges."
Melvin J. Dubnick, University of New Hampshire

"This a book that the interested reader can read a couple of chapters of before bed or on the train and get insight, enlightenment and an occasional smile. It captures many of the issues and discontents facing many democracies and begins to talk about how they might be addressed."
Gerry Stoker, University of Southampton and University of Canberra

"An extremely unusual, accessible and innovative way of getting across crucial messages not only about the importance of democracy but how it affects a whole range of aspects of our lives. I hope that people will find it as entertaining and intriguing as I do."
Rt Hon, the Prof Lord Blunkett

"A very elegant collection of concise comments on contemporary politics – witty, thought-provoking and a great read."
Mark Bovens, Utrecht University School of Governance

"An accessible series of thought-provoking posts, Flinders draws on political science to bring a fresh interpretation to many of today's most topical political events."
Claire Ainsley, Joseph Rowntree Foundation

"What an engaging and FUN book! Flinders' thoughts are accessible, challenging and insightful. A must-read not just for politics academics but for anyone interested in the apparent 'madness' of our contemporary democracy."
Angelia R. Wilson, University of Manchester

"A skilfully crafted succession of humorous, scholarly and thought provoking insights into contemporary democratic politics and more ... should most definitely be on the coffee tables of all serious politicos."
Rosie Campbell, Birkbeck University

What kind of
DEMOCRACY is this?

Politics in a changing world

MATT FLINDERS

First published in Great Britain in 2017 by

Policy Press
University of Bristol
1-9 Old Park Hill
Bristol
BS2 8BB
UK
t: +44 (0)117 954 5940
pp-info@bristol.ac.uk
www.policypress.co.uk

North America office:
Policy Press
c/o The University of
Chicago Press
1427 East 60th Street
Chicago, IL 60637,
USA
t: +1 773 702 7700
f: +1 773-702-9756
sales@press.uchicago.edu
www.press.uchicago.edu

© Policy Press 2017

British Library Cataloguing in Publication Data
A catalogue record for this book is available from the
British Library

Library of Congress Cataloging-in-Publication Data
A catalog record for this book has been requested

ISBN 978-1-4473-3762-1 paperback
ISBN 978-1-4473-3992-2 ePub
ISBN 978-1-4473-3993-9 Mobi
ISBN 978-1-4473-3991-5 ePdf

Cover design by Policy Press
Front cover image: Donald Trump and Boris Johnson
embrace on Gloucester Road, Bristol
Printed and bound in Great Britain by
CMP, Poole
Policy Press uses environmentally
responsible print partners

With thanks to all the graffiti artists whose artwork
appears in this book. If anyone thinks their copyright
is involved in this publication, please contact Policy
Press.

In 'Before you open the post', an extract from
'Postcard' is reprinted by permission from Collected
Poems (Coffee House Press, 2013). Copyright ©
2013 by Ron Padgett.

In '1st post', an extract from 'Threshold' by R.S.
Thomas, from Poems of R.S. Thomas (University of
Arkansas Press, 1985) has been reprinted. All efforts
were made to obtain permission.

In '2nd post', an extract from In Defence of Politics by
Bernard Crick (1962) is reprinted by permission from
the Crick Centre.

In '5th post', an extract from 'The revolution will not
be televised' by Gil Scott-Heron (1970) has been
reprinted. All efforts were made to obtain permission.

In '5th post', lyrics by Scroobius Pip from the song
'Thou Shalt Always Kill' by dan le sac vs Scroobius
Pip were reprinted with permission.

Contents

Before you open the post...

It is not easy writing
someone a postcard.
The size and shape
of the card cut you
down to size…. (Ron Padgett,
'Postcard', Collected Poems, 2013)

'The politics of postcards' is not a common topic of conversation or academic study. And yet, history reveals that for a large part of the early 20th century, postcards were probably the most commonly used means of political communication. In their heyday they fulfilled the role of email, text message and telephone call, and even today, specialist marketing companies help political parties and candidates to craft and design the most effective campaign postcard. The postcard was easy to produce in large numbers, relatively cheap to distribute to a mass audience and offered a simple platform on which to make a straightforward argument. From subtle vintage postcards through to the more aggressive 'target–print–mail' postcards of the 21st century – not forgetting the existence of a historically rich and constant seam of satirical political postcards – the postcard has enjoyed a powerful democratic space somewhere between the poster and the pamphlet. To talk of postcards in a vaunted age of 'digital democrats' and '24/7 instant communication' might appear somewhat antiquated, even quaint, but the resilience of the postcard as a political medium, as a mode of mass communication, in both developed and developing countries around the world, suggests that there is something quite special about this form of interaction. ("Everyone loves to get a postcard!" my mother used to say as she encouraged, coaxed and forced me into writing countless postcards to friends and relatives during family holidays around the UK.)

To understand 'the politics of postcards', however, and specifically what endows them their special qualities as both *an expressive act* and *an act of expression*, there is a need to look beneath their physical form, their instrumental value and their mass-produced messages. An argument could be made – indeed, *will* be made – that the deeper value of postcards and their political significance lies in the nature of the writing they commonly capture and in their … simple brevity. To write a postcard is therefore to unwittingly strip down one's thoughts and engage in a possibly more honest and direct form of writing. The paradox here is that if politics is defined through the dominant contemporary lens of negativity, then political writing would itself be automatically associated with mendacity, falsehoods and half-truths. To make this point is to work within the contours of George Orwell's famous essay of 1946, 'Politics and the English language', and his argument about political language making 'lies sound truthful and murder respectable, and to give an appearance of solidity to pure wind.' Orwell sought to encourage concreteness and clarity instead of vagueness, and in many ways the brevity of the postcard encourages honest precision. Put slightly differently, the paradox of postcards is that their physical form promotes straight talking (possibly, straight *writing*), and through this, arguably offers a more honest and engaging account: 'Weather poor, hotel terrible, having a good time, missing you loads.'

The argument, first developed in French by Blaise Pascal in 1657 and later popularised by Mark Twain in a letter of 1871, that it can take longer and be harder to write a shorter letter than a longer one, speaks to the demands of stripping down one's thoughts and clarifying one's arguments; far easier to avoid such strenuous and potentially risky endeavours by hiding one's views within a sea of knowledge claims, counter-claims and caveats. The link between this argument, those of Orwell and contemporary scholarship is provided by Michael Billig's caustic *Learn to Write Badly: How to Succeed in the Social Sciences* (2013), but my argument here is really about the manner in which postcards by their very nature command a certain sense of clarity and precision, possibly even honesty, and certainly a sense of timelessness. This may not, of course, be the case in relation to modern mass-produced campaign literature for the simple fact that they are neither written from one person to another, and nor do they have any subjective or personal quality. They are thin and shallow pieces of card. They are an element of modern machine politics that too often focus on telling you what is 'wrong' with the opposition's candidates or other parties, and too little about what is 'right' about the actual sender of the card. The same might be said for the pre-printed postcards distributed by a vast range of special interest organisations and pressure groups to their members on the basis that, with the addition of their signature, they should be dispatched (first class) to the relevant politician. This represents a significant shift in the use and abuse of political postcards as they were traditionally used to promote a specific argument, candidate or vision rather than as a tool of political warfare within an increasingly grubby form of 'attack' or one-dimensional politics.

We might, then, separate political postcards into a number of discrete forms. There are Big 'P' political postcards of the sort sent by candidates and parties, which in modern times tend to be blunt, impersonal and cosmetic and may, as a result, form one small element of a wider story about the rise of disaffected democrats, critical citizens and the professionalisation of politics. Although apparently precise and direct in terms of tone and style, I am confident that Orwell would have much to say about these Big 'P' political postcards and their murky relationship with the English language in terms of honesty. Against this one can imagine a second category of small 'p' political postcards that may be written from a mother to a son, a daughter to a granddaughter or from one friend to another as a means of nourishing and demonstrating the existence of a relationship. These will be warm and personal

and offer a degree of emotional depth or meaning – even if it is just of the 'Weather poor, hotel terrible … missing you loads' variety. The important point, however, is that they remain 'political' in the small 'p' sense of the term due to the manner in which they convey information and feelings, while also brokering a relationship. Postcards in the small 'p' sense are therefore an element of 'everyday politics' by which we make sense of the world around us and interpret change. (The absurdity is that political parties increasingly try to use technology in order to increasingly personalise their campaign literature, to make their Big 'P' postcards look and read like small 'p' postcards from a friend or neighbour.)

The point is that postcards frequently allow souls to escape. There is a therapeutic quality to writing in general, and in writing postcards in particular, which stems very much from the traditional context in which they were written. The small 'p' postcards with which this introduction (and book) is predominantly concerned tend to be conceived and born

from a position of personal and professional distance. Put simply, postcards are generally written on holiday when the author has space for reflection away from the pressures of day-to-day life. It is this notion of 'headspace' or 'distance' – rarely acknowledged but vital for the genre – that arguably gives postcards their personal – indeed, political – *value*. The fragments of thought, the messages between the lines, the issues left unspoken, the achievement of closeness while acknowledging separation, make the postcard if not a great neglected literary form then definitely one worthy of appreciation. This is an argument that has been made with great insight by Esther Milne in her *Letters, Postcards, Email: Technologies of Presence* (2010), but the link with this book is that I consider each of the 60 short articles or essays very much as 'postcards' from myself to the reader. They were never originally written on card, garnished with my thoughts in no more than 50 words; there was no picture of a landscape or bawdy cartoon on the reverse; and no annoying hunt for a stamp and letterbox in a place one hardly knows and is unlikely to visit again. But as a literary form they were intended very much as open letters to offer authentic thoughts, honest reflections and short provocations on a range of issues that each in their own way share a focus on sense, self and society. Digitally distributed and read by people around the world, what each attempts to do is engage with the reader by rejecting the styled performance that accompanies academic writing, replacing it with a new playfulness based around informality, intimacy and 'artful conversation'. They are therefore intended to be a cross between postcard writing and conversation that draws inspiration from the insights of Brenda Danet's *Cyberpl@y* (2001), particularly in relation to the cultivation of new forms of creativity and dialogue.

Although concerned with exploring the boundaries of society, politics and democracy, they are very personal in style and tone. They engage in a form of translation that is therefore quite risky for academics, just as it would be for a politician or anyone else. To put one's honest views and interpretation on

the internet is to invite critique, confrontation and even attack. There are also more subtle challenges in the sense of attempting to capture complex or multi-levelled debates within a style of writing that is both accessible and broadly enjoyable to read. That is not to say that writing for a large global audience is synonymous with 'dumbing down', but it is to acknowledge that just as there are no simple solutions to complex social challenges, it is also sometimes difficult to capture the central essence of those complex challenges in simple terms. Something may be 'lost in translation' and that 'something' is likely to be used by those critics – often hiding behind online anonymity – to tear you apart. But as Bernard Crick emphasised, politics is not for the faint-hearted. It is also not all bad in the sense that one of the most pleasing elements of having written and published these posts – online and offline – over the last 36 months is that I have been delighted with both the quality and quantity of the positive feedback and messages I have received. Letters and postcards have been gathered, debates have been initiated, politicians and parliaments

have requested more information, and schools have invited me to speak. Dare I say that one or two previously 'disaffected democrats' might even have been encouraged to re-engage and 'step back into the arena' that is the messy world of democratic politics.

And yet, to be brutally honest, my aim has never really been to alter behaviour or change public attitudes. The aim of writing these and then posting them off into the wider world for whoever might be interested to read them was really simply a way for me to try and understand exactly that wider world itself. In his wonderful book *The Sociological Imagination* (1959), C. Wright Mills writes about 'the trap' and 'the promise' with a verve and style that reflects his own incredible sociological imagination. 'The trap' is one I have felt myself to be ensnared in at many points in my life, and revolves around a sense of ever increasing social change, a sense of loneliness in a crowded world. C. Wright Mills captured this sense of dislocation with typical raw eloquence,

Nowadays men often feel that their private lives are a series of traps. They sense that within their everyday worlds, they cannot overcome their troubles, and in this feeling, they are often quite correct: What ordinary men are directly aware of and what they try to do are bounded by the private orbits in which they live; their visions and their powers are limited to the close-up scenes of job, family, neighborhood; in other milieux, they move vicariously and remain spectators. And the more aware they become, however vaguely, of ambitions and of threats which transcend their immediate locales, the more trapped they seem to feel.

'The promise' of the social sciences in this context was to help men and women understand their position in the world, and their capacity to act and shape their relationship with a broader social system that could too often appear remote and uncontrollable. For Mills, however, 'the promise' of the social sciences would only be achieved when scholars moved away from the 'abstracted empiricism' and 'grand theory' that had, in his opinion, undermined the social relevance of the social sciences. There is, then, an intellectual heritage that binds the work of C. Wright Mills and Bernard Crick around a focus on accessibility and action. In the intervening half-century since Mills' *Sociological Imagination* and Crick's *In Defence of Politics* were published, however, the scale, impact and visibility of 'the trap' has increased while 'the promise' of the social sciences to offer some sort of broader social anchorage or understanding has arguably decreased. Indeed, what is interesting about both books is that their arguments about the professional responsibility of social scientists to the broader public and their related arguments about impact, relevance and engagement beyond the lecture hall and seminar room could almost be intellectual manifestos for the contemporary 'impact agenda' that is arising in many parts of the academic world. Wright Mills and Crick were advocates of a model of 'engaged scholarship' that is now in great demand. 'It is a writer's responsibility to orient modern publics to the catastrophic world in which they live', Mills wrote in the *Columbia Alumni News*, 'but he cannot do it if he remains a mere specialist. To do it all he's got to think *big!*'

'The politics of postcards' is therefore that they, just like letters or other forms of personal writing, provide a space for honest reflection and engagement. The recipient might, to some extent, play a secondary role to that of the author's primary need to set down his or her own thoughts or ideas on paper (or on screen), but that in no way detracts from the personal or social value of such correspondence. One only needs to glance through the pages of Wright Mills' *Collected Letters and Autobiographical Writings* (2000) or the short essays and commentaries that Bernard Crick published over the years in *The Political Quarterly* (edited by Stephen Ball and published as a collection in 2015 under the title *Defending Politics*) to comprehend the value of the small 'p' type of writing that both scholars excelled in, and that this collection attempts to emulate. Both fulfilled Orwell's ambition to turn political writing into an art form, and both believed that the study of politics could not (and should not) be separated from the activity of politics itself. But what is also interesting, although generally not acknowledged, is the existence (or emergence) of a clear pattern, the emergence of a set of arguments or the gradual development of a clear ideological journey within these letters, notes and commentaries. Put slightly differently, it is possible to trace the intellectual evolution of a person through their personal papers, which may not be possible through the analysis of their formal public works. As such, one of the most fascinating elements for an author in collecting together a set of apparently fragmentary texts published over several years in a variety of outlets is exactly how those fragments rapidly reveal their embedded and interlocking characteristics. Like disparate strands of material that can be woven together to form a strong fabric, so, too, can the posts presented in this book be pulled together into a coherent narrative that reflects, from a range of positions and perspectives, on both the innate nature of democratic politics and on the changing nature of democratic governance in the 21st century. Indeed, what they combine to focus attention on is not simply *what kind of democracy we have*, but also what *kind of democracy we want*.

And yet, thinking about 'what we want' instead of 'what we have' has not been helped by the dominance of problem-focused political science or a media that believes only bad news sells. One of the 'problems with democracy' is certainly that it has become shrouded in a blanket of negativity. This dominant 'politics of pessimism' risks creating a vicious spiral of cynicism that sucks the positive energy and potential out of all democratic activities. The result is disengagement, distrust and the constant interpretation of each and every decision or result as further evidence that politics is failing, and that politicians are not to be trusted. And yet, positive change can occur. From South America to Eastern Europe, the final decades of the 20th century were dominated by transitions from dictatorship to democracy and, although never quite at the pace we might like, or in the exact form we might like, positive democratic change and transition is a constantly occurring process. Many of the posts in this book are testament to this fact, and in many ways this book is focused on capturing the ebb and flow of democratic politics in terms of successes and failures, fire and ashes. In order to capture this great variety – from shark fishing to satire and from sleepwalking to storms – the structure of this book divides the collection into six main sections that roughly move the focus of discussion from the very broad to the more specific, and from traditional democratic politics to more innovative forms of democratic expression.

The first section brings together a number of posts that focus on the art of living in the 21st century in the sense of exactly this search for meaning, anchorage or rootedness that Wright Mills captures in his notion of 'the trap'. Through a focus on dislocation and distance and through risk and the notion of reconnecting, this opening section sets the context to many of the more specific themes and issues raised in later posts.

As such the second section focuses on the rise of democratic dissatisfaction, and floats the politics and management of public expectations as a way of understanding the gap that seems to have emerged between the governors and the governed. Posts in this section look at the nexus between 'old' and 'new' forms of political participation, the emergence of 'post-tribal politics' and the role of education as a potential 'glue' with which to bind an increasingly fragmented society.

The third section continues to engage with many of these themes, but through a more applied focus on recent developments in the UK. This includes the Scottish referendum on leaving the Union in 2014, the subsequent debate about democratising the English regions, and the referendum on the UK's membership of the European Union in June 2016. In many ways what this focus reveals is exactly those wider tensions, democratic dysfunctions and embedded

power relationships that this opening essay has at least tried to bring to the fore. Posts therefore explore the existence of 'constitutional anomie', or what more simply may be referred to as 'a mess'; the reluctance of the government to innovate in terms of democratic engagement; and the emotions and excitement of actually orchestrating a major democratic experiment.

This emphasis on orchestrating politics leads to a focus on the conductor and the nature of those brave or foolish personalities who step into the arena themselves. It is for exactly this reason that the fourth section involves a set of posts that focus on a range of personalities and political leaders in order to try and gauge exactly what makes a successful politician and – more specifically – why it appears to be possible to detect the emergence of a phase of cosmetic, celebrity, performative politics (or political claims). This leads into a set of questions concerning the nature of political life and how individuals cope with the stresses and strains of a profession that Ashley Weinberg's *The Psychology of*

Politicians (2011) suggests should come with a government health warning.

And yet, one of the main aims of this collection is to encourage the reader to think differently about democracy and about how they might engage with it. Democratic politics is not and should not be about politicians and votes. The spectrum of democratic activities is very broad, with conventional voting and party activity at one end, and more radical, sometimes painful, examples of democratic activism at the other. The aim of the fifth section is to try and engage with this broader terrain through a focus on arts and activism. Posts in this section therefore focus on the contemporary role of music festivals as new democratic spaces, on parks as new arenas of collective civic endeavour, on the power of poetry and satire and on the role of architecture in terms of the physical manifestation of a specific approach to how to 'do' politics.

This architectural focus is carried over into the sixth section's collection of posts, specifically on the emergence of a new form of post-truth, post-facts politics that find form in 'attack ads' and the statecraft of spin doctors. This takes the form of posts on the politics of gun control and the measurement of truth claims and credit claims, on the blunders of governments and on the distribution of blame.

This focus on 'blame games' and 'blame boomerangs' leads to a final focus on the public understanding of politics and the need to promote not simply 'more public engagement' in politics, but 'more *informed* public engagement' in politics. This emphasis on political literacy – the non-partisan citizenship education promoted by Bernard Crick – raises questions about exactly the link between the study of politics and the activity of politics discussed above. The final section therefore includes a set of posts that reflect back on the role of the university professor of politics in the 21st century, and the need for greater vision, dangerous minds and creative rebels. What these posts combine to draw attention to is the emergence of a transformative phase in human history, that is,

a stage in which representative democracy appears exhausted and under attack from both the left and the right, a democracy that has somehow defaulted on its role as a counterweight to the primitive forces of the market, a democracy turned inside out and upside down, a *deranged democracy*. It is for exactly this reason that the final post in this collection rather ominously invites the reader to 'Listen to my chronicle of a death foretold', and welcomes them to 2017, 'the year of living dangerously'.

The concluding essay – 'A special delivery' – explores this notion of a 'deranged democracy' in more detail as part of a considered and contemporary response to the question, 'What kind of democracy is this?'

Note to the reader: All of the posts included in this collection are available online (with permission obtained), and all sources are provided.

Life, feral politics and fell running

Local protest on Gloucester Road, Bristol

1

Fire and ashes: Success and failure in politics

Politics is a worldly art. It is a profession that is founded on the ability to instil hope, convince doubters and unite the disunited – to find simple and pain-free solutions to what are, in fact, complex and painful social challenges. In recent months a small seam

of scholarship has emerged exploring public attitudes to politics and politicians through the lens of Daniel Kahneman's work on behavioural economics and psychology. 'Think fast' and the public's responses are generally aggressive, negative and hopeless; 'think slow' and the public's responses are far more positive, understanding and hopeful. Such findings resonate with my own personal experience and particularly when I founded a 'Be Kind to Politicians Party' as part of a project for the BBC, it was amazing how many people I was able to recruit in a fairly short time.

The aim of telling this tale is not to make the reader feel sorry for politicians, or really to defend them or their profession. The 'aim' – if there really is one – is to promote the public understanding of political life and to steer it away from over-simplistic representations

of sleaze, scandal and self-interest. (P.J. O'Rourke's *Don't Vote! It Just Encourages the Bastards* suddenly springs to mind.)

Admitting to the pressures and dilemmas of political life is rarely something that a politician dares acknowledge while in office, but political memoirs and autobiographies frequently admit to the anguish created by a role that is almost designed to ensure a decline in mental wellbeing. Job insecurity, living away from home, media intrusion, public animosity, low levels of control, high expectations, limited resources, inherently aggressive, high-blame, low-trust, etc…. Why would anyone enter politics? Exploring the pressures placed on individuals as politicians – we often forget that politicians are individuals – is a topic that a small seam of scholarship has explored, with Peter Riddell's *In Defence of Politicians (In Spite* of Themselves) (2011) providing a good entry point to a more scholarly and complex field of writing, where Gerry Stoker's Why Politics Matters (2006) and David Runciman's Political Hypocrisy (2010) form critical reference points.

But what has so far been lacking is a political memoir written by an academic that reflects solely on the paradoxes and dysfunctions of democratic politics. That is, until Michael Ignatieff penned Fire and Ashes: Success and Failure in Politics (2013) as something of a cathartic process, post-political recovery project.

Until 2006 Michael Ignatieff was a hugely successful and acclaimed academic, writer and broadcaster who had held senior positions at Cambridge, Oxford and Harvard. After 2006 he was an elected member of the Canadian House of Commons, and from 2009, Leader of the Liberal Party. Ignatieff was therefore an academic schooled in the insights of the political and social sciences who made the decision to move from theory to practice. 'What drew me most was the chance to stop being a spectator,' Ignatieff writes, 'I'd been in the stands all my life, watching the game. Now, I thought, it was time to step into the arena.'

Despite its title, the deeper insights of his book are less about success or failure, fire or ashes, but about the manner in which the demands of democratic politics appear to almost oblige individuals to adopt a certain way of being that grates against the ideals and principles that led them to enter politics in the first place. Put slightly differently, the political hypocrisy that is so often detected by the public, ridiculed by the media, and even attacked by opposition politicians who are spared the dilemmas of power is arguably systemic failure in nature rather than representing the failure of specific individuals.

The reality of modern attack politics, of 24/7 media news, of the internet, of all those elements that come together to form 'the system', is that an individual's freedom to actually speak openly and honestly is suffocated. The energy and life – possibly even the hubris – that propelled an individual to enter politics can be very rapidly destroyed by a systemic negativity and cynicism that means that spontaneity must be surrendered to a world of sound bites and media management.

But to end at this point – to blame elements of 'the system' – in the hope of explaining the rise of anti-politics would be wrong. There remains a deeper tension at the heart of democratic politics that takes us right back to Bernard Crick's classic In Defence of Politics (2005) and a focus on the essence of compromise. Democratic politics is – when all is said and done – an institutional structure for achieving social compromise between contesting demands. And here lies both the rub and the real insight of Ignatieff's experience: the worldly art of politics requires that politicians submit to compromises in a world in which compromise is too often associated with weakness and failure. Moreover, specific sections of society must be made to feel that they are special and that their demands are not being diluted when in fact they are, due to the harsh realities of political life. To a certain extent, the hypocrisy, half-truths and fake smiles become essential due to the simple fact that no politician can please everybody all of the time. Democratic politics is a crucible for compromise.

But for the individual who enters politics with a very clear mission, the need for compromise and conciliation – combined with an environment based on aggressive 'fast thinking' – can be soul destroying. 'As you submit to the compromises demanded by public life, your public self begins to alter the person inside,' Ignatieff notes. 'Within a year of entering politics, I had the disorientated feeling of having been taken over by a doppelganger, a strange new persona I could hardly recognize when I looked at myself in the mirror…. I had never been so well dressed in my life and had never felt so hollow.'

The 'hollowing out of the state' is a topic that has received a huge amount of academic attention, as is the 'hollowing out of democracy', but could it be that the 'hollowing out of politicians' demands at least a little consideration within debates about 'why we hate politics'? Ignatieff is, however, nothing if not resolutely positive about the beauty of democratic politics and the capacity of politicians. His aim – like a lot of my writing – is not to put people off stepping into the arena, but to help them enter the fray better prepared than he was. Better prepared in the sense of understanding the need to 'play the game', in the sense of being worldly and sinful, while also remaining faithful and fearless at the same time.

On reflection

Since writing this little piece back in December 2015 so much has changed. Levels of anti-political (and therefore anti-*politician*) sentiment have increased all around the world. Populist 'non-politician politicians' have managed to secure office on the back of public frustration, and my main thought two years later is that the title of Michael Ignatieff's memoirs – *Fire and Ashes* – does provide something of a metaphor for the broader democratic project. Professor Ignatieff is currently President and Rector of the Central European University in Budapest, and is grappling with the challenge of leading a liberal institution in an illiberal country.

2

Down and out in Bloemfontein

One of the most interesting elements of Bernard Crick's *George Orwell: A Life* (1980) is the debate concerning Orwell's attempts to understand and experience the reality of poverty. This relationship with poverty as a lived experience, notably between 1928 and 1931, stemmed from both a basic need and an intense intellectual curiosity. Orwell admitted to this rather sensitive balance when he wrote in a preface to *Animal Farm*, 'I sometimes lived for months on end amongst the poor and the half criminal elements who inhabit the worst parts of the poorer quarters, or take to the streets, begging and stealing. At that time I associated with them through lack of money, but later their way of life interested me very much for its own sake.'

These experiences were subsequently published in 1933 with his first full-length work, *Down and Out in Paris and London*. Four years later, *The Road to Wigan Pier* drew on his time living with a range of people in Wigan, Barnsley and Sheffield, and laid bare the bleak living conditions, the social impact of poverty, the warmth of the working classes and the existence of a North-South divide. Orwell's writing and imagery – 'the monstrous scenery of slag-heaps, chimneys, piled scrap-iron, foul canals, paths of cindery mud criss-crossed by the prints of clogs' – revealed more than a thousand contemporary social surveys could ever show about the state of modern society. It was with Orwell's approach to the art of political writing in mind when a newspaper headline in the *Daily Mail* caught my eye over the recent festive period, 'Luxury shantytown where rich can pretend to be poor…'[1]

In what can only be described as the zenith of bad taste, a fake South African township has been built with the explicit intention of allowing the rich 'to experience the grinding life of the poor.' The delights apparently include an unlicensed alcohol bar, a 'long-drop' toilet and shabby shacks complete with rusty, corrugated iron walls and roofs. What would George Orwell have made of this contemporary manifestation of 'poverty chic'?

14

I know there is a long tradition of the middle and upper classes visiting poorer areas to observe 'how the other half lives' (and vice versa). Towards the end of the 19th century wealthier people regularly visited poor suburbs such as Whitechapel and Shoreditch in London with little thought to the ethics of ogling those born into want and squalor. Towards the end of the 20th century a whole new field of poverty or 'township tourism' emerged with a more explicit ethical twist. While some observers emphasised that most of the (generally rich, white and educated) slum tourists were motivated by curiosity and a need to place their own lives in perspective, others were less sanguine, and voiced strident concerns regarding voyeurism, exploitation and the risk of re-packaging poverty into a marketable form of entertainment. If the 'luxury shantytown' is to be believed, then the 21st century appears to be witnessing a new and more profound form of poverty tourism in which the aim is not so much *to observe* but *to experience*.

What rubbish! You cannot experience poverty for a weekend or a fortnight. Poverty is not poverty if you can leave the streets and return to the bosom of your home at any point. Orwell understood poverty as he lived through his pen, and during the early years of his career he spent years writing 'novels and essays that no one would publish.' Absolute poverty is an individual and social condition where individuals cannot 'opt in' or 'opt out' at will. Marie Antoinette did not experience poverty when she retreated to her Petit Hameau, a rustic retreat in Versailles, to don peasant frocks and pretend to be poor. You cannot have poverty without the pain or without the fight, and therefore to be truly 'down and out' is to sever the way back to a more comfortable existence. Anything else is empty and contemptuous *gesture politics*.

For those thinking twice about their planned trip to the 'luxury shantytown', there is no need to worry. There will be no grind, no fight, no pain. The three-bedroom 'shacks' that cost per night half of what most South Africans earn in a month (and would pay the rent on an ordinary shack for six months) are apparently located within a private game reserve. Instead of taking the risk of being raped or beaten in the night walking to the communal toilets, guests can enjoy hot and cold water, patterned felt blankets, Wi-Fi and underfloor heating – all in the luxury shantytown where the rich can pretend to be poor. Can there be a more brutal or cold embodiment of Orwell's 'boot stamping on a human face'?

But what does this really tell us about the relationship between the über-rich and the über-poor? Why does this tale of capitalist angst actually matter? How does it fit within either a narrative or a wider comment about democratic politics?

It tells us that for all the achievements of democratic politics in terms of reducing want, squalor and disease in many parts of the world, its primary failing has been in not curbing the growth of inequality. The statistics on this are clear and relatively well known. From the mid-1940s until the 1970s incomes grew rapidly and at roughly the same rate up and down the income ladder. From the late 1970s middle- and lower-level incomes stagnated while higher-level incomes enjoyed significant growth. In the UK, for example, in 2013 the richest 1% of people took home nearly 15% of the income compared to 6% in 1979. In the US the wealth gap is more extreme, with the top 10% possessing nearly 80% of all financial assets. Although hairs can be split, the historical data would seem to suggest that on a global level the rich have become richer and the poor have become poorer. The state has failed to act as a counterbalance to the more predatory, aggressive and exploitative elements of the market. Could it therefore be that the gap between the very rich and the very poor has grown so severe that a market for 'poverty porn' has emerged in order to provide the former with some form of social anchorage, however shallow and meaningless?

My message is simple: we can change the world, but only if we recognise that we have an economy based on exclusion and inequality. Some people are 'down and out' in Bloemfontein or Rio de Janeiro, or even London, because they were born into a system that entrenched certain inequalities that would shape their life chances. They are not animals in a zoo to be gawped at or mimicked.

On reflection

The slum tourism industry has boomed since this piece was originally published in January 2014. The only thing that has really changed is the number of slum tours that are now on offer. South African townships must now compete with high-price low-risk tourist trips to the favelas of Rio, the slums of Mumbai and New Delhi, or even the skid rows of LA, Detroit, Copenhagen and Berlin. Not surprisingly the fact that slums are now 'cool' has itself become the focus of academic attention, and in this regard, Fabian Frenzel's *Slumming It: The Tourist Valorization of Urban Poverty* (2016) provides a wonderful analysis of the motivations and consequences of slum tourism, not just for the areas involved, but also for the voyeur. And yet what is arguably more interesting is the mass marketisation of poverty porn based not on visiting but on viewing. Fly-on-the-wall reality TV now allows viewers to enjoy the pleasure of seeing others in pain as they lose their house, car or possessions. 'Can't Pay? We'll Take It Away!', 'The Sheriffs Are Coming' and similar programmes provide in-person poverty porn direct to your sofa. It's not just the market preying on the poor, but also the poor preying on the poor: poverty and crisis accepted as little more than cheap entertainment. Getting bored with house repossessions and families thrown out onto the street? Don't worry, the production companies have managed to make some XXX extreme poverty porn specials just for you! You couldn't make it up – 'The Final Demand Special', 'The Benefits Special' and even 'The Christmas Special'. What would Orwell think?

3

Reveries of a solitary fell runner

New Year is a time to reflect on the past and to consider the future – or so I am told. Put slightly differently, it is a time *to think*. Is it possible, however, that we may have lost – both individually and collectively – our capacity *to think* in a manner that reaches beyond those day-to-day tasks that command our attention?

The sheer pace and speed of life, the challenge of somehow stepping outside the storm in order to gain some sense of where you are going (and why), a capacity to pause and think, has arguably become an increasingly precious commodity in an ever busier world. This is reflected in the changing nature of higher education and the imposition of pressures and expectations that have arguably combined to squeeze out the space for scholarly thought and reflection. Fifty years ago the founding professor of the Department of Politics at the University of Sheffield, Sir Bernard Crick, used to insist that *all* students and *all* members of staff would 'walk out' together in the Peak District every Wednesday afternoon in order to nourish both physical and intellectual health. The realities of scholarship in the 21st century leave little room for such endeavours (ie, some space to think).

In 'taking strength from the hills', Bernard Crick's attitude had much in common with those expressed in 1782 by Jean-Jacques Rousseau in his *Reveries of the Solitary Walker*.[1] As a fell runner I appreciate 'the pleasures of going one knows not where', and as a writer I understand the manner in which physical activity and a sense of remoteness 'animates and activates my ideas'. 'I can hardly think at all when I am still; my body must move if my mind is to do the same', Rousseau wrote. 'The pleasant sights of the countryside, the unfolding scene, the good air, a good appetite, the sense of well-being that returns as I walk … all of this releases my soul, encourages more daring flights of thought, impels me, as it were, into the immensity of being, which I can choose from, appropriate, and combine exactly as I wish.' These words capture almost perfectly exactly why I run.

So where can we rediscover that time to think? The hills and valleys provide exactly that escape, that sense of isolation, that passing moment of release from the instrumentality of grinding social conformity, from the pressures of daily life that many crave but so few appear to be able to achieve. A deeper account of the reveries of the lonely fell runner or walker might engage with Sigmund Freud's[2] *Civilization and Its Discontents* (1930), with its focus on the idea that a fundamental tension exists between the conformity and control demanded by civilisation and the instinctual freedom demanded by individuals. Freud therefore leaves us with a core paradox that takes us not just *back* to Rousseau, but *forward* to more recent works such as Alain de Botton's *Status Anxiety* (2004), Barry Schwartz's *The Paradox of Choice* (2005) and Oliver James' *Affluenza* (2007) in the sense that the social and economic structures that we have created to protect ourselves from various risks (squalor, want, disease, etc) seem unable to make us happy. The growth of research and writing on the 'science

of happiness' in recent years therefore reveals (or more accurately *recognises*) a longstanding fault line in modern life.

Although Alfred Wainwright (the British fell walker, guidebook author and illustrator) would have given short shrift to such 'scientific' pretensions, he was undoubtedly a man who understood the need to draw inspiration and energy from the hills. The paradox that Rousseau reflected on and that caused Wainwright such angst was the realisation that by drawing attention to the reveries of the solitary walker – to the raw and simple beauty of the fells and peaks and moors – they risked destroying the very peace and tranquillity that the countryside provided. And yet, in their writing, both Rousseau and Wainwright could not conceal the pleasures of escaping – albeit temporarily – the trials and tribulations of modern life. Indeed, at the beginning of his poem 'Sylvie's Walk' ('L'Allée de Silvie', 1747), written nearly 30 years before he began *Reveries of the Solitary Walker*, Rousseau wrote,

As I wander freely in these groves,
My heart the highest pleasure knows!
How happy I am under the shady trees!
How I love the silvery streams!
Sweet and charming reverie,
Dear and beloved solitude,
May you always be my true delight!

With these words in mind, let a lonely (but happy) fell runner offer you a Happy New Year in which you find the space to *think*.

On reflection

Can it really have been four years to the day since I wrote this little piece? This is really about the art of thinking in a world that is increasingly loud and chaotic. I cannot help but think that over the past few years there has been a (fittingly) quiet revolution in the growth of endeavours and pastimes that are thought to facilitate a little creative space. A cultural phenomenon – how can the success of the 'Great British Bake Off' on television, the growth of microbreweries,

the surge in demand for allotments, the revival of sewing bees and pottery 'throw downs', be understood in any other way? Gardening, brewing, cooking, etc are simplistic endeavours. Fell running is known as an almost Spartan sport in terms of kit – trainers, shorts and vest, and 'off you go'. They can be social or solitary pursuits, there are a few basic rules, but they also exercise the senses – the smell of fresh bread or yeast, the feeling of wet clay between fingers, the sound of birds hiding in the hedgerow…. That sense of achievement in actually making or growing something yourself from raw ingredients – be they seeds or eggs or milk or clay – or running over a mountain that touches the clouds. There is also a natural generosity in these activities – the over-production of food, beer or vegetables often leads to sharing around friends and neighbours, whereas fell running always ends in a pub or a café. They all provide just a little space and time to … think.

4

Feral politics: Searching for meaning in the 21st century

Could it be that conventional party politics has simply become too tame to stir the interests of most citizens? With increasing political disaffection, particularly among the young, could George Monbiot's arguments about rewilding nature and the countryside offer a new perspective on how to reconnect disaffected democrats? In short, do we actually need feral politics?

Feral:[1] In a wild state, especially after escape from captivity or domestication.

My wife and I like to play a game. She insists I am not allowed to read 'work' books about politics during weekends or holidays; I respond by searching out the best political writing that happens not to have an obviously political title. The benefit of this little game of domestic power politics is that I am frequently forced to read books that would otherwise never have made it to the top of my 'must read' pile. One such example is George Monbiot's *Feral: Searching for Enchantment on the Frontiers of Rewilding*[2] which I devoured last week, and like all good books, it left my mind buzzing not just in relation to the specific focus and arguments of the book, but also in relation to its broader relevance.

When stripped down to its basic components, *Feral* is a treatise about re-engaging with nature and rediscovering our landscape by restoring and rewilding our ecosystem. This process might range from changing farming and fishing methods away from a hegemonic monoculture through to reintroducing certain animals such as wild boar, lynx and wolves to certain parts of Western Europe. Unlike the bleak pessimism of a great deal of environmental writing, Monbiot charts a way out of ecological decline by allowing nature to return to a wilder, less predictable, form. This new positive environmentalism offers a way to reconceptualise the world around us – to redefine the art of living – in relation to the physical landscape. But it also offers much more. The problem was that for at least a week I couldn't quite put my finger on what exactly this 'more' element was or why it mattered. And then the party political conference season opened in the UK and everything became clear.

In essence, George Monbiot's book is not about boar and bears, but about the art of living in the 21st century. It is about how we live our lives, how we define what matters and whether, deep down, we are satisfied by a world based around ever increasing consumption. Simply put, it seems we are not satisfied. The World Health Organization[3] rates clinical depression as one of the main health challenges for the 21st century, while in the UK the most common cause of death among young men is suicide.[4] To rewild or turn feral is not therefore just about reconnecting with the landscape; it is also about reconnecting with yourself.

'We still possess the fear, the courage, the aggression, which evolved to see us through our quests and crises, and we still feel the need to exercise them. But our sublimated lives oblige us to invent challenges to replace the horrors of which we have been deprived,' Monbiot argues. 'We find ourselves hedged by the consequences of our nature, living meekly for fear of provoking or damaging others.' This resonates with Sigmund Freud's arguments in *Civilisation and its Discontents* (1930) that 'civilisation' (Western modern civilisation) was a trade-off in which one cherished value (individual freedom) is exchanged for another (a degree of security). The tension between a deep need for instinctual freedom – wildness, adventure, risk, those qualities that make life worth living – and the conformity demanded by society was the root, according to Freud, of widespread social discontent. Émile Durkheim's[5] classic 1897 work on social anomie[6] and suicide came to not dissimilar conclusions about the evolution of modern life. And yet, the contemporary relevance of this seam of scholarship only became clear when watching the party conferences. Has there ever been a more depressing display of the death of politics in the sense of a failure to promote fresh ideas, to inspire belief or hope, to offer new choices or to dare to stand out from the pack? Is it any wonder that surveys suggest 18- to 25-year-olds are withdrawing from politics? To them politics simply doesn't matter, and if the party political conferences are anything to go by, it's easy to see why they think this.

My argument is not, of course, that politics doesn't matter – it matters far more than most disaffected democrats seem to realise – but at the same time it would be naive to deny the existence of a serious disconnection between the governors and the governed. Might an argument about rewilding not therefore apply to the political realm? Could there be an as yet unmet need for a slightly wilder political life – a desire for a fiercer, less predictable and more varied political ecosystem? Just as both the land and sea suffer from a hegemonic monoculture – captured perfectly in the term 'sheep wrecked' – so politics seems trapped within a similarly narrow hegemonic ideological framework where the parties offer variants of the same pro-market model. Can anyone show me the creative rebels or the big ideas or the politicians who are simply willing to tell the public that there are no simple solutions to complex problems?

The danger of using the metaphor of 'rewilding' or encouraging the evolution of feral politics without some accepted boundaries is that it risks unleashing a range of social forces that once freed cannot so easily be controlled or channelled. Put slightly differently, there are many parts of the world where politics seems far wilder, but I doubt whether those countries or regions offer great inspiration for those seeking a more contented or meaningful life. If they did, why would hundreds of thousands of refugees risk their lives attempting to seek out a new life in Western Europe, North America or Australasia? Could it be that the notion of feral politics risks throwing away centuries of social progress and that democratic politics is, by its nature, slow, incremental … domesticated (ie, Max Weber's[7] 'slow boring of hard boards')?

I'm not convinced. Political choices are rarely black or white, and my sense is that the public have an appetite for 'big ideas' that dare to question the robotic and instrumental nature of modern life. George Monbiot's book provides a glimpse of what some of these ideas might be.

▬▬▬▬▬▬

On reflection

As the previous post revealed, I am a fell runner. Not a good fell runner, but I can huff and puff over the fells with the best of a community of runners in which anyone weighing over 60kg is labelled 'a fat boy'. Running out in the wilds is how I cultivate a little thinking space and maintain an attachment to the simple pleasures of life. But it's deeper than that. There is a psychological driver behind my forays into the hills. I want to return to a wildness in which I can respond to Sigmund Freud's theory in *Civilisation and its Discontents* about the human need for adventure. In many ways I want my own life rewilding, and that is why George Monbiot's

book hit such a deep chord when I wrote this piece in October 2013. In the intervening four years the concept of 'rewilding' has certainly been popularised and widely discussed, but action on the ground remains sparse. It is true that wild boar have been released in Scotland, bison in Romania, beavers in Denmark and lynx in Germany, but progress remains very slow in a broader political environment in which economic development and growth remains central. Indeed, one of the most worrying elements of rewilding has been the growth of ecotourism. Take a 'Bison, Bear and Chamois' safari in the Carpathian Mountains, or be part of the growth in 'Wolf Observation Tourism' in Finland, Northern Spain or Yellowstone Park. Rewilding as part of a new economic ecosystem….

▬▬▬▬▬▬

5

Sharks, asylum seekers and Australian politics

We all know that the sea is a dangerous place and should be treated with respect, but it seems that Australian politicians have taken things a step (possibly even a leap) further. From sharks to asylum seekers, the political response appears way out of line with the scale of the risk.

In the UK the name Matthew Flinders will rarely generate even a glint of recognition, whereas in Australia Captain Matthew Flinders (1774-1814)[1] is (almost) a household name. My namesake was not only the intrepid explorer who first circumnavigated and mapped the continent of Australia, but he is also a distant relative whose name I carry with great pride. But having spent the past month acquainting myself with Australian politics, I can't help wonder how my ancestor would have felt about what has become of the country he did so much to put on the map.

The media feeding frenzy and the political response surrounding shark attacks in Western Australia provides a case in point. You are more likely to be killed by a bee sting than by a shark attack while swimming in the sea off Perth or any of Western Australia's wonderful beaches. Hundreds of thousands of people enjoy the sea and coastline every weekend, but what the media defined as 'a spate' of fatal shark attacks (seven, to be exact) between 2010-13 led the state government to implement no less than 72 baited drumlines along the coast. Australia's Federal Environment Minister, Greg Hunt,[2] granted the Western Australian government a temporary exemption from national environment laws protecting great white sharks, to allow the otherwise illegal acts of harming or killing the species. The result of the media feeding frenzy has been the slow death of a large number of sharks. The problem is that of the 173 sharks caught in the first four months, none were great whites,[3] and the vast majority were tiger sharks, a species that has not been responsible for a fatal shark attack for decades.

The public continues to surf and swim, huge protests have been held against the shark cull, and yet the Premier of Western Australia, Colin Barnett, insists that it is the public reaction against the cull that is "ludicrous and extreme", and that it will remain in place for two years.

If the political approach to sharks appears somewhat harsh, then the approach to asylum seekers appears equally unforgiving. At one level the Abbott government's 'Stop the Boats' policy has been a success. The end of July 2014 witnessed the first group of asylum seekers to reach the Australian mainland for seven months. In the same period last year, over 17,000 people in around 200 boats made the treacherous journey across the ocean in order to claim asylum in Australia. 'Operation Sovereign Borders' has therefore 'solved' a political problem that many people believe simply never existed. The solution – as far as one exists – is actually a policy of 'offshore processing' that uses naval intervention to direct boats to bureaucratic processing plants on Manus, Nauru or Christmas Island. Like modern-day Robinson Crusoes, thousands of asylum seekers find themselves marooned on the most remote outposts of civilisation. But then again, out of sight is out of mind.

The 157 people (including around 50 children) who made it to the Australian mainland last week exemplify the harsh treatment that forms the cornerstone of the current approach. After spending nearly a month at sea on an Australian customs vessel, they were briefly flown to the remote Curtin Detention Centre, but when they refused to be interviewed by Indian officials, they were promptly dispatched to the island of Nauru and its troubled detention centre (with its riots, suicides, self-mutilation, etc). Those granted asylum will be resettled permanently on Nauru, while those refused will be sent back to Sri Lanka (the country that most of the asylum seekers were originally fleeing via India). Why does the government insist on this approach? Could it be the media rather than the public that are driving political decision-making? A recent report by the Australian Institute of Family Studies found that the vast majority of refugees feel welcomed by the Australian public but rejected by Australian political institutions. How can this mismatch be explained? The economy is booming and urgently requires flexible labour, the asylum seekers want to work and embed themselves in communities, the country is vast and can hardly highlight over-population as the root of the problem.

There is an almost palpable fear of a certain type of 'foreigner' within the Australian political culture. Under this worldview the ocean is a human playground that foreign species (ie, sharks) should not be allowed to visit. The world is changing as human flows become more fluid and fast-paced – no borders are really sovereign any more. And yet, in Australia, the political system remains wedded to 'keeping the migration floodgates closed', apparently unaware of just how cruel and unforgiving this makes Australia look to the rest of the world. What would Captain Matthew Flinders think about this state of affairs almost exactly 200 years after his death?

From sharks to asylum seekers, Australian politics seems 'all at sea'.

On reflection

The irrationalities of democratic politics are arguably the core theme that connects all of the posts in this book: the over-reaction of politicians in relation to some issues and their under-reaction in response to others. The issue of shark attacks and shark protection provides a wonderful example of the role of politicians as the intervening variable between the public, on the one hand, and perceived risks to the public, on the other. It also provides a link to the focus of the previous posts due to the manner in which shark fishing was outlawed in many parts of Australia, which led to a rewilding of many parts of the Indian Ocean and a boom in ecotourism based around shark watching. The problem was that attracting large sharks close to boats filled with hoards of excited people demands that huge quantities of food – 'rubby-dubby' or mashed fish – is put into the water. The sharks, possibly not surprisingly, learn to associate the sounds of humans with food, and as a result, there has been an increase in shark attacks since this piece was published in August 2014. However, the actual number of shark attacks worldwide is tiny – less than 100 – but the response of politicians in Australia has been predictable – a re-setting of baited drumlines that will kill large numbers of small sharks but very few, if any, of the large sharks that may have been responsible for recent attacks.

6

The smart fork and the crowding out of thought

One of the critical skills of any student of politics – professors, journalists, public servants, writers, politicians and interested members of the public included – is to somehow look beyond or beneath the bigger headlines and instead focus on those peripheral stories that may, in fact, tell us far more about the changing nature of society. It was in exactly this sense that I was drawn recently not to the 'War in Whitehall'[1] or Cameron's speech on the UK's future relationship with the European Union,[2] but to a story about the launch of a 'smart fork',[3] the 'smart' feature being the existence of a shrill alarm that would inform its user if they were eating too quickly. This, I have quickly realised, is just the latest in a long stream of innovations that seek to nudge individuals towards making better choices about the way they lead their lives (eat less, save more, drive more slowly, etc). And so it turns out that the 'smart fork' is just one of a great series of new innovations that seeks to deliver a form of liberal paternalism by somehow reconciling individual freedom and choice with an emphasis on collective responsibility and wellbeing. My favourite among these innovations was the 'smart trolley', a supermarket trolley with sensors that beeped (and flashed) at the errant shopper who succumbed to the temptation to place a high-fat product in their trolley.

There was something about the idea of a smart fork, however, that I found particularly disturbing (or should I say, 'hard to swallow', 'stuck in my gullet', 'left a bad taste in my mouth', etc?). My mind jumped back to Michael Sandel's[4] argument that 'the problem with our politics is not too much moral argument but too little…. Our politics is over-heated because it is mostly vacant.' My concern with the launch of the 'smart fork' is that it arguably reflects an unwillingness to deal with the moral arguments that underlie the obesity endemic in large parts of the developed world. If Sandel's concern about the imposition of market values is that it could

26

'crowd out virtue', then my own concern is that the behavioural economics revolution risks 'crowding out thought' in the sense that new technologies *may* provide little more than an excuse or displacement activity for not accepting responsibility for one's actions. In the 21st century do we really need a computerised fork or shopping trolley in order to tell us to eat less food more slowly, or to buy less high-fat food and to exercise more?

The smart fork therefore forms little more than a metaphor for a society that appears to have lost a sense of self-control and personal responsibility. This, in turn, pushes us back to broader arguments concerning the emptiness of modern political debate and to the relative value of the public and private sectors. As Alain de Botton argued in *Citizen Ethics in a Time of Crisis*,[5] we could ask whether individual freedom has really served us so well as the leitmotif[6] of modern life. 'In the chaos of the liberal free market we tend to lack not so much freedom [but] the chance to use it well', de Botton writes. 'We lack guidance, self-understanding, self-control … being left

alone to ruin our lives as we please is not a liberty worth revering.' Slavoj Žižek paints a similar argument across a broader canvas in his provocative work *Living in the End Times*.[7] 'The people wanted to have their cake and eat it', Žižek argues, 'they wanted capitalist democratic freedom and material abundance but without paying the full price.' He uses an advert on American TV for a chocolate laxative – 'Do you have constipation? Eat more of this chocolate' – to mock the modern public's constant demand for results without ever having to suffer unpleasant side effects.

Although hidden far beneath the front-page headlines, the story of the launch of the smart fork (in Las Vegas, need I say more) highlights the existence of an underlying problem in the sense that most politicians appear either unwilling or unable (possibly both) to tackle the issue head on. Between 1980 and 2000 obesity rates doubled in the US to the extent that one in three adults (around 60 million people) is now clinically obese, with levels growing particularly among children and adolescents. In this context it

may well be that individuals require – even want – not a *nudge* but a *shove* or a *push* towards a healthier lifestyle. If this is true, it is possible that we need to revisit certain baseline assumptions about the market and the state, and not simply define the role of the latter as an inherently illegitimate, intrusive and undesirable one. To make this point is not to trump the heavy hand of the state or to seek to promote some modern version of the enlightened dictator, but to inject a little balance into the debate about the individual and society. Is it possible that we 'hate' politics simply because, unlike those unfeasibly self-contained, sane and reasonable grown-ups that we are assumed to be by liberal politicians, most of us still behave like disturbed children (or political infants) who simply don't want to take responsibility for our actions or how they affect the world around us? Or, to put the same point slightly differently, if the best response we have to the obesity crisis is an electric fork, then in the long term, we're all *forked*.

On reflection

To some extent 'smart' seems to have become
the dominant adjective of recent years.
When this piece was first published back in
February 2013, the role of technology and
its link to behavioural economics was only
just emerging, but now there seems almost
no facet of human life that cannot be 'smart'.
Smart forks now exist within a new universe
of Fitbits, i-Phones, Google glasses, etc.
Obviously everyone needs a smart TV and
smart meters – smart *this*, smart *that* – but
the social and political implications of the
availability of increasingly sophisticated
and individually tailored technology are only
just being realised. Very few people, for
example, realise that the watches or bracelets
they wear on their wrists are actually data-
acquiring devices. Even fewer know that major
companies can access and sell that data as
part of an emerging global 'smart grid' based
on 'big data' as a tradable commodity.

7

'Vape' – a word that encapsulates the nothingness of today

There has to be something seriously wrong with the world when the 'Word of the Year' is declared to be 'vape'. What the dickens is 'vape'?! I've never heard of it, none of my kids has ever heard of it – even my students look at me with an unusual quizzical stare. Okay, so there is nothing that unique about the quizzical stare of my students, but the word 'vape' is so ridiculously empty and meaningless that I can't help but think that there is something deeper – and more worrying – going on.

Apparently 'vape' means 'to inhale or exhale the vapour produced by an electronic cigarette or similar device; while both the action and the device can also be known as a "vape"'. Apparently New York banned indoor vaping in April 2014 while London led the world by opening the first vape café – The Vape Lab – just weeks later. But what does the emergence of 'vaping' actually say about the world around us? Does the fact that 'vape' is 'Word of the Year' (of course this has to have its own funky little acronym, so in future it will be 'WOtY') actually matter?

As a boring and over-thinking academic I'd have to come up with some argument that it does matter, and in this case it has to be something to do with how contemporary society attempts to deal with the issue of risk. For many people, vaping was a safe and socially acceptable alternative to smoking; it was cool and trendy; and you could even have funky flavours that made it all such fun. Just like the cake that doesn't make you fat, the exercise that doesn't involve sweating, the laxatives that taste of chocolate (I kid you not) and the 'adventure' holidays that are perfectly safe, 'vaping' offers all the pleasure of smoking but without the pain. And it's this vacuous nature of modern society that worries me. There is an existential quality to 'vaping' that gives it a meaning and relevance far beyond the public carrying of a – if we are honest – rather embarrassing bong. Milan Kundera's *The Unbearable Lightness of Being* (1984) keeps coming into my head, but I have neither the time, interest, nor the energy to explore why. It has to be something about the vaunted erosion of risk in society … but now Freud's *Civilization and its Discontents* (1930) has popped into my head … no one told me that vaping had such intellectual off-shoots, but it seems there is something unquestionably meaningless about 'vaping' that fits within a broader social-psychological fabric.

The other contenders for 'WOtY' (how cool am I?) offer a similar menu of meaninglessness – 'normcore', 'slacktivism', 'budtender' … that each in their own way points to an unbearingly bleak vision of social emptiness. But now the World Health Organization has spoilt all the fun by highlighting the dark side of vaping. Apparently e-cigarettes emit just as many potentially dangerous chemicals as good old-fashioned cigarettes and have similar

passive smoking risks. Could that actually be good news? Do we all really want to live in a sanitised risk-free world? Is it really making us happy? So go on, hold your head high and have a little vape – puff out your chest and puff out some steam! But then again, if you don't like the risks, just stop smoking. Period. That would have meaning.

On reflection
There is something very interesting about the annual 'Word of the Year' due to the manner in which those cunning lexicographers at Oxford University Press tend to be able to select a word that captures a certain social shift. In 2014 it was 'vape', in 2015 it was 'emoji' and in 2016 it was 'post-truth' … can anyone recognise a certain pattern or subtle similarity between these words? Smoking but not smoking, expressing emotions but in a digital form, the evolution of a model of politics in which emotions trump facts … it wants to make me 😠 and makes me want to 😂. It appears that my largely critical blog about vaping and 'the nothingness of today' had little impact on what continues in 2017 to be a booming industry. Increased government regulation, the reduction in the number of places that allow smoking and the decision by insurance companies to penalise smokers more heavily than in the past has had the combined effect of 'nudging' people towards vaping as an apparently safer and more socially acceptable behaviour. Although health concerns exist, for the time being the vape industry is blowing away the tobacco industry in terms of growth.

8

Saints and sinners, politicians and priests

Justin Welby[1] recently used his first Easter sermon as Archbishop of Canterbury to warn of the dangers of investing too much faith in frail and fallible human leaders, be they politicians or priests. Blind belief in the power of any single individual to bring about true change in any sphere, he argued, was

simplistic and wrong, and led inevitably to disillusionment and disappointment. Surely this was the point in the sermon when a member of his flock was duty-bound to heckle, "But what about that bloke called Jesus?!" Unfortunately, good manners triumphed, and the leader of the world's 77 million Anglicans was able to continue his sermon. "Put not your trust in new leaders, better systems, new organisations or regulatory reorganisation", he told the congregation at Canterbury Cathedral. "They may well be good and necessary, but will to some degree fail. Human sin means pinning hopes on individuals is always a mistake, and assuming that any organisation is able to have such good systems that human failure will be eliminated is naive."

Bishop Welby's sermon reminded me of Max Weber's famous essay of 1919, 'Politics as a Vocation', with its warnings against 'infantile' understandings of politics and its emphasis on the complexities of governing and the need to hold realistic expectations of what politics – and therefore politicians – can deliver. 'Politics is', as Weber maintained, 'a strong and slow boring of hard boards', and one might argue that almost a century later the challenges of governing have, if anything, become far greater and more complex. And yet, there was a nagging part of Bishop Welby's sermon that left me disheartened, frustrated and possibly even angry. It was, for me, as if the new Bishop had accepted the advice of Bernard Baruch to 'vote for the man [or woman] who promises the least as they'll be least disappointing'. Surely one of the key social roles of politicians and priests is to inspire, to promote hope, to make their communities believe they can deliver positive social change? Might it therefore be that in warning against 'the hero leader culture' Bishop Welby revealed his own weakness? In the sense that he seemingly does not understand exactly why certain social groups seem so willing to grasp 'quick, easy and gratifying solutions' to even the most intractable problems.

Bishop Welby suggests that people could only escape 'cynical despair' by acknowledging God and trusting in his power, but if you're living in poverty, and face a multitude of social challenges that conspire to limit your life chances from birth, then I can understand why you might fall for the cheap tricks and empty promises of rogue politicians. Put slightly differently, instead of arguing that too many people look to politicians for simple and pain-free solutions to complex and painful problems that simply do not exist, might it not be equally true to suggest that encouraging people to accept human fallibility and to trust in God is just a *different* form of expectation inflation that is almost guaranteed to fail – a 'mere cruelty' of a different kind?

I, for one, am actually quite glad that Barack Obama, for example, did not turn out to be Superman, and Bishop Welby is surely correct that we should not set people or institutions up to the heights where they cannot do anything but fail. But it would be quite wrong to suggest that individuals cannot make a positive difference, or to deny that some politicians have, in fact, delivered on their promises, or that – when all is said and done – democratic politics generally delivers far more than most people seem to recognise. Welby concluded his sermon by quoting the Welsh poet and Anglican priest R.S. Thomas,[2] from his poem 'Threshold', on the human need for communication with God,

I am alone on the surface / of a turning planet. What / to do but, like Michelangelo's / Adam, put my hand / out into unknown space, / hoping for the reciprocating touch?

And yet, once again, my moral soul was irked by such platitudes; I could not help but think that what most humans crave is not so much communication with God, but communication with each other. It is increased social fragmentation that threatens humanity, not some form of existential angst or theological breakdown. My concern is therefore not so much that the public demands too much of politics and politicians, but that at many levels the public's expectations are actually too low. Local elections, for example, are due to take place in the UK in a matter of days but have so far been met with a deafening silence in terms of public debate or interest. There seems little evidence of the blind faith or hero leader culture that Bishop Welby warns against in any of the 36 English and Welsh Councils that will be contested next month. I'm not suggesting that one sermon by the Archbishop of Canterbury has single-handedly dampened expectations that would otherwise have had the local election campaign buzzing across the country, but I am suggesting that the Bishop's position is too simplistic. We actually need more trust in political leaders and more active community engagement at the local level alongside a measured dose of healthy scepticism about what our local political leaders can realistically deliver.

On reflection

Although Bishop Welby gave his address back in May 2013, the core of his argument regarding the need for the public to be a little more cautious about putting their faith in political leaders (and political promises) appears strangely prophetic four years later in light of the rise of populist nationalism in many parts of the world. Bishop Welby's sermon therefore reminds me of a more recent sermon given not by a priest but a King-in-waiting during a December 2016 radio broadcast. Prince Charles used an appearance on 'Thought for the Day' to suggest that the rise of populist nationalism across the world – and notably within many West European countries – had disturbing echoes of the fascism of the 1930s, and warned against the 'horrors of the past' to prevent religious and other kinds of persecution. As many of my later posts illustrate, the issue of populism and social fragmentation has emerged as a key theme within my writing, and it is in relation to the populist 'politician-non-politicians' that Welby's words 'put not your trust in new leaders' appears to have, for me at least, such contemporary resonance.

9

Why satire is no joke any more

What has happened to political satire?

The journalist John Walsh recently argued that 'there is a groundswell of opinion that too many stand-ups are smug, over-paid, potty mouthed enemies of the common people.' By way of evidence he could have cited a recent episode of Radio 4's 'The News Quiz' that described Education Secretary Michael Gove as a 'foetus in a jar' (cue laughter and wild applause). You might just think it's good fun, that politicians deserve everything they get, and satire corrects the shortcomings being laughed at. But what if political comedy and satire contribute to and reinforce those shortcomings? What if the message it really spreads is political scepticism?

It is at this point that comedians and writers scoff at the suggestion that anything has changed, and without fail remind me of the historical contribution of writers such as Daniel Defoe and Jonathan Swift, or caricaturists such as James Gillray and Thomas Rowlandson. All four used their creative and artistic talents to highlight, ridicule and deflate some of the big political notions of their day.

Yet such nostalgic reflections overlook the simple fact that the world has changed, and so has political comedy. The rise of the 24/7 media machine with ever more pressure on ratings combined with the rich pickings offered by mass market DVDs has fuelled a satire that is snide, aggressive and personalised. It is also designed to reinforce the general view that politics is failing.

Satirists often say that their trade is necessary to prick the egos of the powerful. They claim they are vital to the functioning of a democratic society, that they can say what commentary and news cannot. However, a quick journey through recent history shows just how far we have come. In the 1950s the then Chairman of the BBC, Lord Simon, blocked the broadcasting of a light comedy about a fictional Labour minister and nuclear secrets on the basis that "this is not the moment in world history to weaken respect for democracy and the belief in democratic values." Fast forward through the ground-breaking satire of 'That Was the Week that Was' in the 1960s, through to the slightly sharper 'Not the Nine O'Clock News' and 'Yes, Minister' and onwards to 'Spitting Image' and the weekly politician bashing of 'Have I Got News For You' until finally reaching programmes like 'The Thick of It' and 'In the Loop' with their docu-style and non-stop expletives. I'm not alone in thinking that political satire and comedy is heading in the wrong direction. Jon Stewart, presenter of the 'Daily Show' in America, now arguably the leading satirist in the US, has argued "if satire's purpose was social change then we are not picking a very effective avenue."

On this side of the Atlantic, Rory Bremner, Armando Iannucci, Eddie Izzard and David Baddiel have all raised concerns about the increasingly aggressive and destructive nature of modern humour.

I believe in change. I want genuine alternatives. But I want to know what role political comedy and satire might play in producing a new way of organising our society, which brings us to Russell Brand. This cheeky chap was recently interviewed by Jeremy Paxman about his guest editorship of the *New Statesman*.

The way Brand stuffed Paxman was exquisite, yet there was one moment when he let the mask slip. Right at the beginning, when Paxman jabbed him about his right to edit a political magazine, Brand compared himself to Boris Johnson, saying, "He has quite crazy hair, quite a good sense of humour, doesn't know much about politics." The problem is that everyone knows that while Boris may be foolish, he is no fool. He is, in fact, a deceptively polished *über* politician who uses buffoonery as a political self-preservation mechanism. Brand has also pushed buffoonery and comedy to new limits, but he has never dared to step into the political arena. I just wonder if it is a little too easy to heckle from the sidelines, to carp at the

weaknesses and failings of others, to suggest that there are simple solutions to complex problems, and to enjoy power and influence within society but without ever shouldering direct responsibility.

On reflection

P.J. O'Rourke is an American political satirist whose best-selling book is entitled *Don't Vote! It Just Encourages the Bastards* and whose shock-jock antics have been a thorn in the side of American politicians for decades. His next book, however – published in March 2017 – is called *How the Hell Did This Happen? The Election of 2016* and promises to be a diatribe against modern democracy. The flaying of modern democracy has emerged as something of a popular pastime since this post was written back in November 2013, but its core concern about increasingly aggressive political debate being parodied by an increasingly cynical satirical response continues to have traction. And yet, in some ways, recent political events have provided

comedians and satirists with material that they hardly know what to do with. Speaking at the 2016 Cheltenham Literature Festival, P.J. O'Rourke suggested that the election of Donald Trump had almost popped the balloon of satire – "I'm a political satirist … and the election has been completely self-satirising." This is the dilemma and why satire really might not be a joke anymore. It's not that satire is dehumanising politicians in an aggressive and unfair manner but, paradoxically, it may actually be humanising politicians who hold dangerous viewpoints.

'Take the money and run' graffiti near Montpelier Health Centre, Bristol

10

In our name: The ethics of democracy

One of the dominant memories of my childhood is my father shouting, "Don't blame me! I didn't vote for any of them" every time a politician appeared on the television or radio. Despite my complete lack of political knowledge or interest, this constant retort always jarred with me and now, having read Eric Beerbohm's *In Our Name: The Ethics*

of Democracy (2012), I can understand why. My father was, in essence, denying any form of complicity on the basis that non-voting somehow relieved him of all forms of political responsibility. It is this focus on the politics of responsibility and the complex nature of citizenship that Beerbohm so deftly brings to the fore in a superb work of political theory that deserves to be read widely, both within and beyond academe.

'Search for the moment,' Beerbohm writes, 'you came to believe that your state was committing a crime. You suspected this for some time. At some point your suspicion hardened into a belief. Then it dawned on you that you live in and have some modicum of control over a democratic, unjust state.' The 'modicum of control' provides the intellectual and empirical hook on which this book hangs. From the torture of individuals to unjustified

wars to the acceptance of various forms of social, economic or political deprivation – might you be, in some small and indirect way, to blame? Was there a moment in your life when you turned the page or turned your head to deny your power of agency, no matter how limited that power might be in our increasingly large and complex democracies? Is it just too easy to blame those politicians when deep down you know there are no simple or painless solutions to complex problems? Is our idea of citizenship strong enough to implicate you?

The starting point is therefore a simple acceptance that all citizens are born into both a social structure and a political system we did not pre-select. Our involuntariness as citizens arguably ebbs away, like a tide on a shore, as we mature as individuals and are at some point forced to accept (or deny) the office of citizenship.

Whether we like it or not, 'our discrete interactions with political institutions voluntarily tie us to its largesse', Beerbohm suggests, and this can leave individuals feeling almost trapped with a latent form of moral liability that can be both painful and confusing. For Beerbohm, however, the traditional chants of 'Not in my name!' represent the denial of a basic political responsibility that simply cannot be so easily side-stepped. His argument is therefore clear and direct: 'In this book, I argue that there are responsibilities of the democratic citizen that are non-delegable.'

In adopting this novel and provocative position, Beerbohm provides a sophisticated link between the generally micro-specific literature on 'blame games' (Christopher Hood), 'multiple accountabilities disorder' (Jonathan Koppell) and the broad organisational or governance-theoretic literature on 'the problem of many hands'

(Dennis Thompson), and the far broader literature on public disengagement and political apathy. Key reference points in this latter seam of scholarship include Colin Hay's *Why We Hate Politics* (2007), Gerry Stoker's *Why Politics Matters* (2007), Pippa Norris' *Democratic Deficit* (2011) and Yannis Papadopoulos' *Democracy in Crisis* (2013). At base, Beerbohm suggests that it is far too easy for 'disaffected democrats' to heckle from the sidelines while blaming those weary souls who do step into the political arena for the general sins of society as a whole. The author admits that 'the theory of citizenship that I describe and defend here is not likely to induce comfort in readers', but it is for exactly this reason that this book deserves to be read. Taken forward, this logic suggests that in a representative democracy citizens have reason to reduce their 'complicity footprint' through more active participation. How exactly this participation is to be undertaken and channelled into the institutional mechanisms of collective behaviour remains uncertain, but what is beyond doubt is that *In Our Name* is a distinctive and important

contribution, not just to political theory, but also to the political and social sciences more broadly.

On reflection

The notion of a 'complicity framework' almost sends a shudder down my spine. The notion that I might be in some small way responsible for some of the developments that have sent a shockwave through the world – and that will shape that world for years to come – is almost too much to bear. The funny thing is that the ethics of democracy – the core of Beerbohm's thesis – make all of us, to some extent, tainted. If democracies get the politicians they deserve, then we must surely deserve the rise in populist nationalists, Donald Trump and the Brexiteers. 'Not in my name', I hear you cry, but as Christopher Achen and Larry Bartels argue in *Democracy for Realists* (2016), democratic politics has always existed as something of a romantic folk theory that rarely matches the actual human nature of democratic citizens. David van Reybrouck's *Against Elections*

(2016) goes even further: 'Democratic Fatigue Syndrome is a disorder that has not yet been fully described but from which countless western societies are nonetheless unmistakably suffering…. Elections are the fossil fuel of politics. Whereas once they gave democracy a huge boost, much like the boost oil gave the economy, it now turns out they cause colossal problems of their own.' His answer rests on a shift from elections to sortition (ie, selection by lot). This may well bring something different to political recruitment and the nature of politics, but what that 'something' is in precise terms remains unclear. Better the devil you know.

11

The problems with democracy – continuing the conversation into a new year

An invitation from the British Library to give the first in a new public lecture series called 'Enduring Ideas' was never a request I was going to decline. But what 'enduring idea' might I focus on, and what exactly would I want to say that had not already been said about an important idea that warranted such reflection? The selected concept was 'democracy' and the argument sought to set out and unravel a set of problems that could – either collectively or individually – be taken to explain the apparent rise in democratic disaffection.

Such is the world we live in that a lecture is no longer a lecture but rapidly becomes a multi-media 'artefact' and the beginning of a global discussion. I suppose this is probably not quite true of *all* lectures – I've been to quite a few that really do need to be forgotten – but I'm pleased to say that the intellectual ecosystem seems to have exploded in all sorts of ways that I could never

have imagined. Within hours the lecture was available to a global audience via a British Library podcast. Within weeks the lecture was published online by the Oxford University Press journal *Parliamentary* Affairs,[1] and within a month or so the same journal had published a number of response pieces by an array of leading scholars.[2]

I had not given a public lecture at the British Library – I had started a conversation.

It was therefore a source of some delight and contentment when the latest instalment of this conversation appeared online in the form of a University of Manchester blog by a former student of mine, Dr Kevin Gillan.[3] Now some scholars might snort and snuffle at the idea of a former student seeking to challenge his former professor in such an open and accessible arena, but I say "Well done, that chap!" Kevin was always a bit of a livewire, but the way he tries to turn my arguments and ideas upside down and inside out, to get to the basic core of my logic in both an empirical and normative sense, is really a joy to read.

To my relief, Gillan's approach is less concerned with sharpening the knife with which he seeks to butcher my argument but, on the contrary, is concerned with sharpening my argument by bringing in interdisciplinary insights from the sphere of critical social movement studies.

The problem with my 'problems with democracy' from Gillan's perspective is that my analytical lens is too narrow. I stand up and decry the loss of 'what we might call our democratic or political imagination … our capacity to *re-imagine* a different way of living; to *re-connect* with those around us; to *re-interpret* challenges as opportunities or to *re-define* how we understand and make democracy work' (italics in the original), but for Gillan, this argument reflects my own failure to look beyond the standard

framework. 'The political imagination is already being exercised outside of the mainstream,' he argues, 'developments in the alter-globalisation and social forum movements and, latterly, among the *indignadas* of Spain and the occupiers of the public squares across Europe and the US.'

With this basic argument in place, Gillan proceeds to highlight three issues – *representation, institutional change* and *the internet* – that add extra tone and texture to the problems I identify in my original lecture, podcast, article, t-shirt, etc.

It is true that the concept of representation is hardly mentioned in my original lecture, but it is, as Gillan suggests, 'squarely in the sights of those for whom some form of direct democracy … is part of their activism.' The interesting reflection here, however, lies not in simply focusing attention on the concept of representation itself, but in relating this to my original critique of market-driven individualisation and its corrosive impact on collective social values. And yet Gillan reveals

the existence of a parallel paradox in the sense that many of the contemporary critical social movements have their ideological roots in anarchism, although for many protestors, this may be a less relevant grounding than the fact that, for them, it fits with a deeply held respect for the individual as sovereign bearer of rights. This is a line of argument that chimes with William Gairdner's position in *The Trouble with Democracy* (2001), but if anarchist-inspired values and practices have really 'overtaken revolutionary socialist ones in influence in most of today's critical social movements', then *The Trouble with Representation qua* Gillan is that a large proportion of the 'new' politics beyond the mainstream is imbued with its own form of individualism that grates against the logic of democratic collective action.

The issue of institutional change posits an equally thorny problem, as Gillan paints a picture of an increasingly labyrinthine institutional architecture in which functions and responsibilities are spread across many governing levels and within many types of organisation. The topography of this terrain is undeniably dense. In *Walking Without Order*[4] I attempted to map this territory, but the structures are so fuzzy and fluid that I achieved little more than a rough sketch of the terrain. In light of this, the public's shift away from mainstream politics and political parties to a form of issue-based activism can be seen as completely rational. The problem, if one exists, lies not with the public in Gillan's analysis, but in the failure of the dominant institutional structure of representative democracy to keep pace with social and economic shifts. 'So the dominant institutional structure of representative democracy, with its blend of representation-via-geography with representation-via-political-tribe is inherently unappealing for the denizen of the liquid modern: for many it is not education that is required [my main prescription for the democratic malaise] but institutional change.'

I cannot help but think of Michel Maffesoli's wonderful *The Time of the Tribes* (1996) and especially his systematic theorisation of 'everyday politics' by interpreting emergent

forms of participation as what he terms 'neo-tribes'. The tribal metaphor of 'new tribes' or 'post-tribal politics' resonates with much of what Gillan seems to be arguing, and Maffesoli's focus on forms of *political power* (what he terms '*puissance*' or 'intrinsic' power) and *political legitimacy* (what he terms 'underground centrality' or 'bottom-up' legitimacy) provides a fresh and innovative way of interpreting both 'alternative' and 'mainstream' forms of engagement. But then, the shadow of individualism emerges once more in Gillan's reflection:

> But outside of mainstream political channels the activist autodidacts have already recognised that the "young and poor" are hardly a homogenous group, even if they share the objective conditions of precarity. Perhaps they also recognise that even if there were an effective party of the precarious, the very one-dimensionality that would make it appealing to the young and the poor, would be the feature that made it problematic in relation to a whole gamut of other policy domains.

Which brings us to Gillan's focus on the internet as a way not of *overcoming* individualism or issue-based politics but of *embracing* them and turning the deliberation they encourage to the service of the (inherently collective) polity. And he is certainly correct that in *Defending Politics* (Oxford University Press, 2010) I did dismiss 'digital democracy' with great polemical force. While I rage against 'echo chambers' and 'cyber-citizens', Gillan draws on Jeffrey Juris and Manuel Castells to paint a quite different account of the internet, revealing shared interests and common bonds. Online movements have, from this position, 'begun to *re-imagine* different ways of living, to *re-connect* with those around them and to *re-define* how they make democracy work.' In essence, Gillan believes that critical social movements are forging new forms of online mass mobilisation with the capacity to transform democratic politics.

So where does the conversation go from here? How would I respond to a former student's elegant essay? Where are the points of overlap and contestation, and why might they matter?

Put very simply, I think a large intellectual and normative gap exists between Kevin Gillan and myself that might in some ways reflect the gap that seems to have emerged between the governors and the governed. This is a gap I am happy to try and close or bridge through further conversations and possibly collaborations, but there is something of 'the politics of pessimism' that lurks beneath the words and between the sentences of his reflections. My thoughts on this topic remain embryonic, but they seem to revolve around the themes of individuality, pace and people. *Individuality* in the sense that Gillan's analysis appears to accept individualism as, irrespective of its intellectual roots, inevitable, whereas I believe that there is a shared collective sense of being human, a natural desire for social bonds beyond the immediate family and an innate amount of empathy that cuts across social classes, countries and religions. The inevitability of fragmentation within Gillan's proposition is underlined by his

comments on the 'activist autodidactics' who recognise that the young and the poor are by no means a homogenous group. Their shared objective conditions of precarity – the lack of permanent employment, low wages, constant re-skilling, frequent relocation, etc – might form the basis of a new political party, 'the Precarious Party', but for some reason 'the one-dimensionality that made it appealing to the young and the poor' would also be the feature that made it 'problematic in relation to a whole gamut of other policy domains.' But why? Gillan defends the individualised issue-based activist on the basis that this does not mean they fail to take account of the way that their focus overlaps with a range of broader issues, so why would the Precarious Party not achieve a similar balance of breadth and depth?

In relation to *pace* Gillan agrees with my original statement that 'our institutions and processes of democracy seem to evolve and change at a glacial pace while the world around it seems to move at an ever increasing pace', but then makes an argument that

promotes the hyper-fast low-cost capacities of networked communications: 'It is precisely the networked nature of movements that have sprung up across the world since 2011 that mean individuals can recognise … the commonality of their bonds.' But then this 'politics of optimism' is dashed on the Procrustean reality of life as he notes, 'These movements remain relatively marginal in liberal democracies and have had limited impact on mainstream political thinking.' Pace … pace … pace … democratic politics may well be 'the strong and slow boring of hard boards', but surely something has to pick up the pace when it comes to democratic change, which brings me to 'the people', social interaction and the internet. Gillan suggests that 'for a very large number of (especially young) people in the advanced liberal democracies the online and the offline are now so thoroughly inter-twined that pretty much the whole human experience is reflected in, and partially lived through, online networks.' That may well be true (I am not so sure), but that doesn't make it a 'good thing'. Or, more precisely, it appears that the blurring

Gillan refers to manifests itself in the adoption of a set of expectations that are derived from online behaviour but are increasingly projected into offline relationships. News in 140 characters, immediate location-based dating, real-time live gambling, virtual reality and lives lived through avatars. Technology-mediated citizenship does little to fire my political imagination.

On reflection

When this was written in January 2016 no one would have predicted the tumultuous events that would take place later in the year. Indeed, the problems with democracy were suddenly brought into sharp focus in ways that have created a set of fundamental questions about the capacity of politics to control or respond to a pressing set of social challenges. In the US the wealth gap is bigger than at any time since the Great Depression; in the UK the wealth of the richest 10% of the population has increased through the vaunted 'age of austerity'; and across the world levels of wealth inequality are growing and seem to underpin democratic inequality, health inequalities, equality of opportunity, etc. A deep anti-establishment strand of public sentiment has therefore dovetailed with quite a different frustration with a global economic elite that seem unrestrained by democratic expectations in terms of accountability, reciprocity or control. Amazon, Starbucks and Google have all provoked outrage for avoiding tax, and the Panama papers have exposed the use of offshore companies to shield the super-rich from the tax demands of nation states. The threat to democracy in the future, however, is the flip-side of super-rich – the emergence of a large precariat class that lives in an almost stateless position of insecurity. This is the socioeconomic phenomenon that poses the biggest problem for democracy. As the size of the precariat increases, so will pressure for a democracy that can offer a true counterweight to the power of markets. My prediction is not a positive one. It is bound up in notions of crises. We are entering the age of living dangerously – but that is a topic for a later post.

12

Do we have too much democracy?

It's finally happened! After years of watching and (hopeful) waiting, tomorrow is the day that I finally step into the TEDx arena alongside an amazing array of speakers to give a short talk about 'an idea worth spreading'. The theme is 'Representation and Democracy', but what can I say that has not already been said? How can I tackle a big issue in just a few minutes? How do I even try and match up to the other speakers when they include people like the pro-democracy campaigner and Nobel Peace Prize winner Aung San Suu Kyi? Dare I suggest the problem is 'too much' democracy rather than 'too little'?

The 'three-minute thesis test' is a relatively new form of professional training in which PhD students need to provide a clear and succinct account of their thesis and why it matters in just 180 seconds. The aim is to not only make the students think and focus on the core intellectual 'hook' of their research, but also to hone their communication skills so they can talk to multiple audiences in multiple ways about their research. This is all jolly good and to be encouraged. TEDx talks, however, represent something of the 'über-three-minute thesis test' in the sense that

not only must you tackle a big issue, but you must also do so in a way that is sophisticated yet accessible, entertaining but serious, and thought-provoking but not ridiculous. You get eight minutes to do this, not three, but you only get one shot at giving the talk in front of a large live audience and an even larger online audience of many millions. This is reputational poker. Here is the essence of my pitch.

The title of my talk is 'The Problem with Democracy'. However, the problem with even talking about 'the problem with democracy' is that it is a loaded statement. Loaded in the sense that it suggests that (1) there is a single 'problem' when it might be argued a discussion of 'the problems' (plural) with democracy offers a more rounded and sophisticated set of answers; and (2) loaded in the sense that it accepts that 'a problem' exists. I want to take on and challenge each of these assumptions in turn, but before this I want to make the rather unfashionable – even heretical – suggestion (and this is my 'hook') that one of the problems with contemporary democracy might be that in some parts of the world we have too much democracy rather than too little. Let's call this problem 'hyper-democracy'.

Something seems to have gone wrong in the relationship between the governors and the governed. Recent elections at all levels display not only low turnouts but also a shift towards more extreme populist parties that offer a general message of anti-politics and a mantra of 'If only we could get rid of all the terrible politicians, then everything would be fine!' The problem is that you cannot have democracy without politics, and you cannot have politics without politicians.

For all sorts of reasons, politics is increasingly viewed as little more than a spectator sport or a retail activity. Yet democratic politics is not a 'click-and-collect' online shopping channel where you make your choice and expect your goods to arrive. And if you don't get what you want, it has become too easy to heckle – or should I say, to tweet or blog – from the sidelines. Could it be that we have too much of the wrong kind of democracy and too little of the right kind of democracy? Democracy is about compromise and a sense of proportion. We don't always get what we want, as individuals or specific groups, in a democracy, but that's just the price we pay for living in a free society as opposed to a fear society (this might be a good time to remind you that, as the research of Freedom House illustrates, most of the world's population do not live in democratic regimes).

We may have hit a point where our political system has become too sensitive to the public's opinions and anxieties. Just think about the second half of the 20th century, the growth in the number and range of 'sleaze busters', watchdogs and audit bodies, the increasing role of the courts and the judicialisation of politics, not to mention the role of the internet and an increasingly aggressive media in holding political processes and politicians to account. This is all good. It's democratic progress. It's part of John Keane's wonderful book *The Life and Death of Democracy* (2010),[1] and he calls this stage of far greater popular controls over politicians 'monitory democracy'. But you could call this 'hyper-democracy' because the 24/7 news cycle creates a perpetual storm of scandal and intrigue.

Could it be that we need to give those politicians we elect just a little more leeway and 'space' in order to allow them to focus on delivering their promises? Could it be that politicians have become too sensitive to the immediate demands of the loudest sectional groups or the latest focus group or what's trending on Twitter? The reason I dare to ask this question is for the simple reason that 'hyper-democracy' does not seem to be producing contented democrats but disaffected democrats. It seems to be fuelling increasing mistrust and mass misrepresentation by the media.

However, on the one hand I am criticising the public for not getting involved themselves and viewing politics as a spectator sport, but on the other hand I am emphasising that politicians need a little breathing space. How do I square this circle in a manner that offers a solution to the problem of democracy? I do it like this: the problem with hyper-democracy is too much of a shallow, disengaged and generally aggressive form of individualised market democracy and too little of a deeper and more socially embedded model based on active and engaged citizenship. We need less shouting and more listening, less pessimism and more optimism, but most of all, we need more people – from a broader range of backgrounds – to step into the arena in order to demonstrate just why democratic politics matters.

On reflection

The concept of 'hyper-democracy' was never going to roll off the tongue or be adopted in public discourse. It was, however, intended to capture the explosion of democratic tools and processes, especially those linked to digital information technology. The capacity of the political system to cope with these new channels of political expression as well as the need to retain some sense of governing balance or proportionality was therefore seen as critical. Moreover, the response of politicians to systemic demands they could not cope with led to the emergence of hyper-depoliticisation as a way of almost counter-balancing populist pressures. This was the extent of the debate back in July 2014 when this was written, but what the debate overlooked – and what has become incredibly clear over recent years – was the role of emotions. The growth of nationalist populism, the election of Donald Trump, and all the other manifestations of late-stage democracy share one thing: emotional resonance. What has emerged is a state of emotional hyper-democracy around the world that risks ensuring that the ultimate failure of democracy is almost guaranteed. There is a craving among large sections of the public, notably among the precarious über-class gig generation and the long-time rudderless traditional white working classes – for a strong leader to offer them hope and certainty. Indeed, a June 2016 survey by the Public Religion Research Institute and the Brookings Institution found that a majority of Americans showed authoritarian (as opposed to autonomous) leanings, and 49% of those surveyed agreed that 'because things have gotten so far off track in this country, we need a leader who is willing to break some rules if that's what it takes to set things right.' Why is it that Andrew Sullivan's recent warning that 'democracies end ... when they are too democratic' comes to mind?

13

Calming the storm: Bernard Crick, defending politics and the importance of citizenship

Democracy is perhaps the most promiscuous word in the world of public affairs…. She is everybody's mistress and yet somehow retains her magic even when a lover sees that her favors are being, in his light, illicitly shared by many another…. Indeed, even amid our pain at being denied her exclusive fidelity, we are proud of her adaptability to all sorts of circumstances, to all sorts of company. (Bernard Crick, *In Defence of Politics*, 1962)

Bernard Crick argued that democratic politics was not perfect, it could not 'make every sad heart glad', it was often messy, cumbersome, and inevitably produced what economists might call 'sub-optimal' decisions. This, however, represented *not the failure of politics but the beauty of politics* in the sense that it could, through a process of negotiation and compromise, produce collective decisions out of diverse and often contradictory social demands. Fifty years later, however, it is possible to question whether democracy 'retains her magic', and to suggest that the concept's malleability – its 'adaptability to all sorts of circumstances' – may have been exhausted. Even the most cursory glance along the spines of the books on the library shelves reveals a set of post-millennium titles that hardly engender confidence that all is well (*Disaffected Democracies, Democratic Challenges, Democratic Choices, Political Disaffection in Contemporary Democracies, Hatred of Democracy, Why We Hate Politics, Democratic Deficit, Vanishing Voters, Democracy in Retreat, Democracy in Crisis, Uncontrollable Societies and Disaffected Individuals, Don't Vote! It Just Encourages the Bastards*, etc).

So what has happened? What has apparently gone so badly wrong? Is politics failing? Why is defending politics such an unfashionable and yet important task? How does citizenship education fit within this broader parameters of debates concerning political decline (and renewal)? To engage with such matters at any serious level in the course of this short article is, of course, impossible, and so my aim here is more modest and revolves around looking at three interlinked themes or issues:

▶ The changing nature of political rule in the 21st century.
▶ The politics and management of public expectations.
▶ The importance of citizenship education in the context of 'disaffected democrats'.

My arguments in relation to each of these points are essentially that:

▶ The nature of politics has changed to make the business of politics more difficult, more aggressive, more immediate and more complex.

▶ The demands of the public have increased at a time when the resources with which to fulfil those demands are shrinking (no politician has the capacity to satisfy a world of ever increasing demands).
▶ Citizenship education matters because it provides a way of setting out exactly how societies seek to govern and make difficult decisions without resorting to violence or oppression.

In the rest of this article I want to develop these arguments and explain my position in a little more detail.

The changing nature of political rule

How, then, has the nature of political rule altered over the last 50 years, and do these changes undermine or strengthen Crick's arguments concerning the value, importance and achievements of democratic politics? Let me answer this question (very briefly) by highlighting ten ways in which the nature of political rule has undoubtedly shifted. The first and most basic change in the nature of

political rule concerns levels of public trust and confidence in politics. Public commitment to the concept of 'democracy' remains high, whereas faith in the day-to-day operation of politics has fallen dramatically. Although understanding the causes of political disaffection is difficult, mapping out the evidence for political disaffection is relatively straightforward.

▶ Between 1970 and 2010, average turnout for elections in established democracies fell by around 10%, and the level of decline appears to be increasing.
▶ In the 1960s the combined membership of the British Labour and Conservative Parties stood at around 3.5 million, whereas today [2014] the figure is around 300,000.
▶ The 2013 British Social Attitudes Survey reported that 54% of those surveyed say they 'almost never' trust politicians to tell the truth, while 75% believe that political parties are only interested in votes (rather than principles) and 71% believe that it actually doesn't matter which party is in

power, so voting doesn't make that much of a difference.

The paradox of our current situation is that despite the fact that democracy has flourished in large parts of the world in recent decades (Eastern Europe, Southern Europe and large parts of South America), the extent of public apathy, anger and frustration with the operation of democratic politics seems to have gone beyond healthy scepticism and into the sphere of corrosive cynicism, even fatalism, about democratic politics' capacity to resolve major social challenges. This anti-political climate has fuelled a second change in the nature of politics – a shift towards the depoliticisation of public policy, as more and more functions (availability of drugs in the NHS, governance of monetary policy, decisions on the care of the elderly, regulation of new technologies, etc) are removed from the direct control of elected politicians and placed in the hands of scientists, technocrats, judges, accountants or ethicists on the basis that 'taking politics out of policy-making' will somehow produce 'better'

decisions. This rather ironic trend towards the depoliticisation of politics brings with it three unwanted side effects: first, as Alasdair Roberts' devastating critique of the *The Logic of Discipline* (2010) reveals, transferring functions away from elected politicians is no guarantee against corrupt or self-interested behaviour; second, in terms of democratic accountability, transferring functions away from elected politicians to non-elected and largely unaccountable independent bodies carries with it a certain 'out of the frying pan and into the fire' unease for those who want to revitalise democratic politics; and finally, the infolding or narrowing of the sphere of visible democratic politics that depoliticisation creates makes it very hard for members of the public to understand what their elected politicians actually do or why they should bother voting.

Other changes have affected the nature of politics in recent decades. The development of new forms of information communication technology such as the internet, Twitter, blogs, etc have increased the reach and

speed of communication while reducing the costs. Patterns of ownership, distribution and editorial policy have changed within the media with a distinct shift towards 'infotainment' and sensationalism over public service broadcasting. Scientific advances concerning – among other things – stem cell technology, human embryology, cloning and xenotransplantation have created new social opportunities while at exactly the same time arguably raising the public's expectations about exactly what democratic politics (and therefore politicians) can provide. These scientific advances also raise issues about trans-border cooperation and control, about the regulation of risks and the law of unintended consequences, and about whom to blame when things go wrong. This blurring of the boundary between science and democracy is just one element of why the institutional architecture of politics has become increasingly complex and blurred (a transition encapsulated in the shift in emphasis from govern*ment* to govern*ance*). The paradox is, however, that at exactly the time when politicians are expected to wield greater and more direct policy capacities, their ability to act has actually shrunk due to the existence of these complex delivery chains and labyrinthine bureaucratic structures.

But if the governing capacity of national politicians has, to some extent, eroded, this cannot be said for the public's expectations regarding their personal behaviour. Standards of conduct and behaviour are now exposed to the light of public and media scrutiny by the emphasis on transparency and also through the growth of a regulatory industry of complaints processes, sleaze busters and political watchdogs (a development that John Keane captures in his notion of 'monitory democracy'). At the same time, and as already mentioned, the public's expectations of politics, in terms of the behaviour of politicians and the standard of services delivered by the state, are increasing in a period in which not only the resources to satisfy these demands (public support, financial capacity, etc) appear in short supply, but the challenges faced by politicians have also arguably become more demanding. These 'new' or

'manufactured' risks, as scholars including Anthony Giddens and Ulrich Beck call them, arise from the unintended consequences of human progress to produce ever more intricate and thorny challenges like nuclear security, resource depletion, global warming and over-population. The final major change in the nature of politics in recent decades involves a well-charted shift in the role and influence of *ideology*. Simply stated, 50 years ago politicians might also have lacked resources, but they did at least arguably have a clearer and more stable ideological foundation. As Zygmunt Bauman's influential book *In Search of Politics* (1999) and his more recent focus on the notion of 'liquidity' has sought to emphasise, the politics of the left or the right provided a form of moral compass or anchorage through which politicians could rationalise their responses to social challenges and offer a relatively coherent governing narrative.

What do these ten changes add up to in terms of the changing nature of political rule? My answer would be that they combine

to create a political context that is louder and more abrasive, that is shallower and more demanding, and in which the storm is constantly raging. Calming the storm is therefore the metaphor that matters, and in this regard the future of citizenship education is vital. However, in order to understand exactly why this is the case, it is necessary to take a short intellectual detour into the politics and management of public expectations.

The politics and management of public expectations

Crick wrote that 'the disillusionment of unreal ideals is an occupational hazard of free politics', and from this sought to craft a very honest account of the limits of politics. Politics was (and *is*) a worldly art based on compromise, negotiation and adjustment that could not deliver simple solutions to complex problems; and it was, to some degree, as Gerry Stoker argues in his *Why Politics Matters* (2006), 'inevitably destined to disappoint because it is about the tough process of squeezing collective decisions out of multiple and competing interests and opinions.' Max Weber's metaphor of 'strong and slow boring of hard boards' springs to mind, and helps orientate Crick's simple point that if the public feel that democratic politics is failing them, then it may be that the public are expecting too much, rather than that politics is delivering too little.

Lying beneath a focus on the changing nature of political rule is therefore a deeper and more basic question concerning the nature of public expectations *vis-à-vis* democratic politics. My argument here is both bold and sweeping: the politics and management of the public's expectations (regarding lifestyle, healthcare, education, pensions, travel, food, water, finances, the environment, etc) will define the 21st century. My argument is straightforward: the increasing evidence of political disaffection stems from the existence of an ever-increasing 'expectations gap' between what is promised/expected and what can realistically be achieved/delivered by politicians and democratic states.

This argument can be placed within the contours of well-known debates concerning political behaviour. Anthony Downs' *An Economic Theory of Democracy* (1957) provides the foundation for exploring these debates. In this book he sought to understand politics with reference to economic exchanges within society. Downs argued that political parties and politicians (as suppliers) and voters (as consumers) can be assumed to be rational and self-interested 'utility-maximisers' who engage in market-like transactions and relationships. Consequently political actors seek to maximise their chances of (re-)election by promising to deliver better services, but at a lower cost than the competitors (other political parties). This creates a bidding war in which the process of political competition artificially increases public expectations, only for these expectations to be dashed as the elected party either seeks to renege on certain pre-election commitments or fails to achieve them. An economic theory of politics therefore seeks to provide an explanation for the frequent discrepancy between pre-

election political rhetoric and subsequent post-election performance. It also allows us to understand the oft-quoted observation of Mario Cuomo on political campaigning:

> You campaign in poetry. But when we're elected, we're forced to govern in prose. And when we govern – as distinguished from when we campaign – we come to understand the difference between a speech and a statute. It's here that the noble aspirations, neat promises and slogans of a campaign get bent out of recognition or even break as you try to nail them down to the Procrustean bed of reality. (Chubb Fellowship Lecture, Yale University, February 1985)

The analysis of public expectations regarding public services and the capacity of politicians appears to represent something of a *terra incognita* for political science. Mass data banks and survey results provide rich data about the state of public attitudes, but provide far less in terms of *why* the public hold such views or exactly *how* their expectations have been shaped, let alone the theories and methods through which political science can generate more sophisticated insights. My argument here is not in line with the advice of Bernard Baruch about 'voting for the man who promises the least as he'll be least disappointing', but it does begin to open fresh questions about whether democracy really is failing or if society is simply expecting too much. 'If we understood politics rather better', Colin Hay argues in his award-winning *Why We Hate Politics* (2007), 'we would expect less of it. Consequently, we would be surprised and dismayed rather less often by its repeated failures to live up to our over-inflated and unrealistic expectations.' The simple argument at the heart of this section is the suggestion that democratic politics would not be interpreted as failing so frequently, and people would not 'hate' it as much as they do if it was judged against a more realistic set of expectations – or, more precisely, *understandings* – about what it was intended to deliver. This, in turn, underlines the importance of citizenship education.

Citizenship education and disaffected democrats

The vast majority of the public do not 'hate' politics (or politicians). Surveys repeatedly reveal that the public are more interested in politics than ever, and are also increasingly involved in new forms of political engagement that may not be picked up in traditional surveys or questionnaires. The focus on 'endism' and apathy therefore risks over-shadowing a far more positive picture of democratic renewal and re-engagement. The great range of democratic innovations – from the Australian Citizens' Parliament, to the democratic development and citizen engagement project in Bolivia, through to the 'What You Know Is What You Get' project in the Philippines and the participatory budgeting experiments in Brazil – can all be reviewed on the Participedia website in a way that reveals a rich and simmering seam of social activity. The challenge is how to nurture and channel that energy in a positive manner, and this is why citizenship education matters. If we understood politics slightly better, then

we may well, as Colin Hay suggests, not only think better of it but also be more willing to engage ourselves. Citizenship education therefore provides a way of avoiding the onset of disaffection by forging a more mature and realistic account of the limits of politics. It should also emphasise – as Crick did in his *In Defence* – that citizenship brings with it both rights *and responsibilities*.

This is an important point that allows me to bring this article to a close by comparing two baseline models or interpretations of citizenship in a way that reveals the role and purpose of citizenship education. The first model – let us call it *individualised citizenship* – is reflected in what I call 'the Amazonian' nature of contemporary politics. This has little to do with South America and everything to do with a Balkanised and shallow consumer-based model of democracy that arguably knows the price of everything but the value of nothing. The 'Amazon' in this metaphor therefore relates not to the place (or to the specific company), but to a market-based model of politics in which you cast your vote and then wait for the post-election goodies to arrive the next day (like a DVD, book or pizza ordered online). The simple fact is that democratic politics was never intended, designed or resourced to react in such a direct and immediate manner. Democratic politics is, by its very nature, infused with a commitment to a different model – a *social citizenship* – that places 'us' and 'them' (ie, the collective) before 'you' or 'me'.

My argument is therefore that citizenship education facilitates the creation of a rich form of social glue, or what most academics would call 'social capital', by empowering young people with a rich sense of how the society around them operates, an understanding of the channels and processes through which resources are both collected and distributed, and why – at a very basic level – politics matters. Would I be going too far to suggest that some people have become 'democratically decadent' in the sense that they no longer appreciate the great benefits of living in a democratic polity, and lack any real awareness of the poverty,

disease and brutality that still exists in large parts of the world? Taking this argument forward, maybe what I really mean is that citizenship education should provide a sense of perspective and balance in a world where such things are often in short supply. There are clearly issues about *how* citizenship education is delivered and *what* is included in the curriculum. I also have major concerns about the nature and hidden values that seem to be driving the post-2014 approach to citizenship education. The current plans arguably offer an eviscerated model that removes the emphasis on the engaged – even radical – citizen that Crick originally envisaged. It risks becoming too narrow, arguably little more than a selective politics course or even a reversion to civics.

This is not to say that some element of reform is not necessary, but that the direction of reform should be towards not a narrowly constructed individualised model but, quite the contrary, towards a richer, thicker and deeper model of citizenship education. More specifically, this should embrace an active

learning model whereby young people are required to engage not in big 'P' politics but in small 'p' political activities like community schemes, volunteering projects, mentoring or shadowing opportunities, advocacy work, etc as a way of learning how to become good citizens. The great beauty of such activities is that they are driven by value rather than price, they complement classroom-based lessons about the challenges of governing, and they create safe spaces – they calm the storm – thereby allowing young people to consider their place in the world and what really matters.

▬▬▬▬

On reflection

There is little doubt that the storm of political anger and frustration has raged with increasing fervour and ferocity since this plea for calm was posted back in 2014. The nature of political rule has altered in ways that were almost unthinkable just a year or two ago. Central within this change has been the rise of nationalism, populism, anti-establishment

anger and a widening of the gap between the governors and the governed. If the public's expectations have shifted, it would have to be towards a further loss of confidence in the capacity of democratic politics to regulate and control big business and economic flows. But it is in the growth of political incivility where the real shift has occurred. The language of politics is increasingly brash, aggressive and uncompromising. The thick background of social norms and rules has disintegrated in favour of a situation in which people feel able to say and sometimes do whatever they want. People seem unable to engage respectfully across their political differences, and the rhetoric of politicians across all sides of the spectrum is increasingly isolationist, definitive and regressive. Put very simply, if the classroom is supposed to be responsible for preparing students to be good citizens, then the events of 2016 suggest that it is failing.

14

Look beneath the vote

Hands up if you've heard of National Voter Registration Day.[1] And in the somewhat unlikely event that you have, did you realise that it took place last month?

If this momentous milestone passed you by, you're not alone. Whatever 5 February means to the people of the UK, it's safe to assume that electoral participation doesn't figure prominently. This is not a surprise; it reflects a deep-seated public disengagement[2] from politics, as indicated by the fact that only two-thirds of eligible voters in the 2010 General Election actually voted. Throughout the 20th century, general election turnouts almost always exceeded 70%, but that's a level of participation that has not been seen since 1997. Incidentally, the highest turnout since 1900 was 86.8% in January 1910, although only rate-paying men over the age of 21 could vote.

Low voter turnout is clearly a problem, but arguably a much greater worry is the growing *inequality* of that turnout. As a recent report from the Institute for Public Policy Research (IPPR) makes clear, the UK is very much a 'divided democracy', with electoral participation among the young and the poor declining dramatically. In the 1987 General Election, for example, the turnout rate for the poorest income group was 4% lower than for the wealthiest. By 2010 the gap had grown to a staggering 23 points. A similar pattern is observable in relation to age groups. In 1970 there was an 18-point gap in turnout rates between 18- to 24-year-olds and those aged over 65; by 2005 this gap had more than doubled to over 40 points, before narrowing slightly to 32 points in 2010. 'If we focus on participation within these age groups,' the IPPR report concludes, 'we can see that at the 2010 general election the turnout rate for a typical 70-year-old was 36 percentage points higher than that of a typical 20-year-old.'

If this isn't bad enough there is little evidence that young people will simply start voting as they get older. On the contrary, IPPR's research suggests that, 'younger people today are less likely than previous generations to develop the habit of voting as they move into middle age.' These trends mean that politicians tend to address themselves to the older and richer sections of society – the people, in other words, who are most likely to vote. This, in turn, reinforces the views of the young and the poor that politicians don't care about them. And that, naturally, leads to even greater political estrangement.

So what's the solution? How do we re-establish a connection between ordinary people and politicians? In particular, how do we persuade the young and the poor that the political system really does have something to offer them?

The answers lie not in quick fixes or technological solutions – such as the introduction of compulsory voting, changing the ballot paper or promoting 'digital democracy' – but in adopting a fundamentally deeper, richer and more creative approach to democratic engagement. People will only

vote – be they young or old, rich or poor – when they understand why democratic politics matters and what it can deliver. Therefore, to increase electoral participation we must focus on promoting the public understanding of politics from all perspectives (conservative, traditional, radical, etc) in a way that demonstrates that *individual* responses to *collective* social challenges are rarely likely to be effective. It's this deeper understanding, this notion of *political literacy* promoted by Sir Bernard Crick[3] and defined as 'a compound of knowledge, skills and attitudes' that citizens can use to navigate the complex social and political choices that face us all. Political literacy can be seen as a basic social requirement that empowers people to become politically aware, effective and engaged while also being respectful of differences of opinion or belief.

In this regard, the message from survey after survey is a dismal one. Large sections of the British public appear to know very little about the political system. Even relatively basic questions such as 'What do MPs do?' or

'What's the difference between Parliament and the Executive?' tend to elicit a mixture of mild embarrassment and complete bafflement.

Given that levels of political literacy are so low, it's little surprise that many people choose not to vote. They're unaware of the very real benefits the political system delivers for them (clean water, social protection, healthcare, education, etc), and they no longer believe that they can become the engine of real social change. And yet they can. Worse, by opting out of elections they risk diminishing their representation as politicians focus their messages on the groups that do vote. Young people are constantly reminded that to be 'uneducated' – let alone innumerate or illiterate – is to risk deprivation and vulnerability, but in many ways to be politically illiterate brings with it exactly the same risks. Moreover, the impact of declining political literacy isn't only felt at the individual level. With so many people in society alienated from politics, democracy itself is weakened.

Such arguments are by no means abstract concerns. On 7 May 2015, a general election will be held on the basis of individual voter registration rather than the previous system of household voter registration. Research suggests that although this transition is likely to increase electoral security, it may also result in a considerable decline in levels of electoral participation among – yes, you've guessed it – the young and the poor. This is not a reason to turn back from individual registration, but it is a reason to step back and acknowledge that if we're really serious about healing a divided democracy, we need to focus on promoting engaged citizenship through different channels and processes. We need to take some risks and stir things up, but most of all, we need a long-term plan for fostering political literacy.

On reflection

Turnout in the 2015 General Election in the UK stayed relatively constant, at 66.1% compared to 65.1% in 2010. There was evidence of an 'election bounce' among the electorate in the sense of survey evidence suggesting a greater interest in politics, but this was combined with increasing evidence of low levels of political literacy and a growth in the social class gap in relation to electoral participation. This was clearly reflected in the European Union referendum where areas with higher populations of older people registered higher levels of turnout (and generally voted to leave), and working-class areas were less likely to vote at all. The good news was that younger people (aged 18-24) did vote in far higher numbers than originally expected (around 64%), but this was still way behind the 90% of over-65s who made it to the ballot box.

15

Democracy is about more than a vote: Politics and brand management

With a General Election rapidly approaching in the UK, it's easy to get locked into a set of perennial debates concerning electoral registration, voter turnout and candidate selection. In the contemporary climate these are clearly important issues given the shift to individual voter registration, evidence of high levels of electoral disengagement and the general decline in party memberships (a trend bucked by UKIP, the Greens and the Scottish National Party in recent months).

My concern, however, is that democracy has to be about far more than a vote. It's not *just* about elections; it's certainly not just about political parties; and the risk of the 2015 General Election is that without being embedded within a range of more creative and engaging forms of political participation it's just … another election.

Politics therefore has an important challenge in terms of 'brand management'. Not of the vacuous form of 'Russell Brand management', but of the challenge of re-imaging, redefining and reconnecting with a public that is changing rapidly; a mass social frenzy around the general election risks creating a situation of boom-and-bust in terms of the public's expectations and the subsequent results regarding governmental performance in an increasingly complex world.

I can't help wondering if democratic politics even has the capacity any more to produce those social highs of yesteryear – the 'Obama effect' or 'Blair effect' – where there was a real sense that positive reform was both possible and on the horizon. Could it be that democratic boom-and-bust (a largely inevitable element of democratic life) has been replaced by the dull thud of bust-and-bust politics?

The general election risks becoming part of the traditional life cycle of politics that seems to be turning an increasingly large slice of the public away from 'conventional' politics. But then again, does UKIP in the UK – or Podemos in Spain, the Five Star Movement (Movimento 5 Stelle) in Italy, the National Front in France or Syriza in Greece – really offer a rejuvenated model of democracy or (and this is the critical point) simply a thinner and more dangerous form of exclusionary politics? Is the boom-and-bust of populism not potentially louder and more destructive? In many ways the populist parties are a legitimate 'challenger brand', but they offer democracy a potentially dangerous dilemma.

In an excellent recent essay on democratic discontent, Claudia Chwalisz[1] highlighted that two decades have passed since Arend Lijphart famously identified unequal participation as 'democracy's unresolved dilemma', and this dilemma has intensified rather than diminished in the intervening years. Why? Because the correlation between voting and policy-making has eroded to the extent that the public now question whether voting actually matters. To some extent this is an issue of perception as much as reality – a perception reinforced by the 'Russell' approach to brand management. It is also, to some extent, an inevitable element of democratic politics that as the demands of the populus become more complex and varied, the compromise-orientated element of that worldly art called politics will reflect this fact and become increasingly opaque. But there is something else going on here in the sense of a dominant economic elite that appears almost insulated from democratic control or scrutiny. Votes don't seem to affect the cosmopolitan business elite and, as a result, capital in the 21st century is eroding democratic politics.

My message? Don't expect too much from the 2015 (or 2020) General Election for the simple reason that democracy is about far more than a vote. It is about everyday life, it is about community engagement, it is about personal confidence and beliefs, it is about daring to stand up and be counted, and it's about the art of life and living together in the 21st century. The problem is that democratic politics has become a toxic brand, and it needs to re-brand itself by offering a new and fresh account of both the challenges and opportunities that undoubtedly lay ahead. This is a model of democracy that is deeper and richer, creative and honest, formal and informal, amateur and professional, agile and responsive, as responsibility-based as rights-based and as innovative as it is international. The problem is that at the moment 'democracy' appears almost synonymous with 'elections', and this robs it of its potential.

Democracy is about more than a vote.

On reflection
Democracy is and always has been about more than just voting. It would be a pretty sad society if our civic obligations (or possibly opportunities) were restricted to the placing of a scribbled 'X' in a box every few years. Voting decisions themselves do not suddenly occur within the ballot booth, but are instead shaped by a vast range of conversations that

may take place on the bus, in the gym or while fell running with friends. In many ways voting represents – or should represent – the tip of the iceberg in a truly democratic polity. I would not want to take Nigel Farage's claim that 'every pub is a parliament', but he does at least capture a sense of how formal political processes are informed through informal dialogue and forms of expression. But what is arguably more important – and that has become more obvious since this post was written in 2015 – is that voting is actually an incredibly primitive procedure. There is a reason why populist parties tend to favour referendums, and that is because it generally gives them a chance to whip up the public to support a simple 'black' or 'white' decision when politics in the real world is all about shades of grey. This is not an argument against elections – although this argument is being made with growing force – but it is an argument against populism and for informed public engagement. Without this, elections risk becoming part of the problem, not part of the cure.

16

Beastly Eastleigh and the 'None-of-the-Above' Party

I'd never even heard of Eastleigh,[1] let alone been there, until a couple of weeks ago. When I did go there I wished that I hadn't. A collection of railway sidings, the headquarters of a major DIY chain, the former home of Mr Kipling's bakery and, to be honest, not much else. The fact that I am told that the 'notable residents' of Eastleigh include Benny Hill[2] and Stephen Gough[3] (the 'naked rambler' no less) did little to quell the stench of good-times-past that hung in the air. But in the by-election last week the people of Eastleigh spoke – in record numbers – and their message was clear: 'sod off'.

Eastleigh was beastly not because the Liberal Democrats haemorrhaged support, or because the Tories came third, or because UKIP[4] came through with a surge like the Flying Scotsman in full steam, but because the election signalled a growing sense of anti-politics and anti-government. The eightfold increase in UKIP's vote cannot be written off as a mid-term blip or a sign of disillusionment with any one party. In reality both the Liberal Democrats and the Tories lost around a third of their vote since the 2010 General Election.

This was the election that UKIP campaigned under the banner of 'sod the lot' and a call for a new form of politics, and in many ways UKIP is emerging not as a mainstream political party, but as a repository for protest votes.

From Rotherham to Corby and from Middlesbrough to Eastleigh, UKIP are becoming the 'None-of-the-Above' Party through which the public seek to express their disillusionment and confusion. Nigel Farage may have been right when he described UKIP's jump from 3.6% of the vote in 2010 to 27.8% last week when he said the public were 'sticking two fingers up to the establishment'. But he was wrong when he argued that 'people didn't just vote UKIP because they dislike the three main parties; they voted UKIP on policy.' Evidence for this seems scant, as survey after survey reveals that European issues rank towards the bottom of most voters' main concerns (and well below jobs, taxes and increases in the cost of living). Immigration was a key concern among Hampshire voters last week, but it was in 2010 when UKIP won just 4%. The fuel driving UKIP's success was anti-political populism[5] – a heady mix of anti-Europeanism and the promotion of populist libertarianism.

Take one anti-political context, add a sleaze-related by-election, sprinkle in a 'sex scandal saga', blame Europe for everything in a recession-hit town, and is it any surprise the 'None-of-the-Above' Party did so well? The 'sod off' mentality was captured succinctly (and with slightly more force) when the Labour candidate, John O'Farrell, blogged that 'there are doorbells telling us to "F**k Off"'. To some degree this public response was understandable – this was an election without politics. It was a circus. Blame games and sound bites triumphed, and democratic politics was left looking shallow, self-interested and self-serving: nobody campaigned in poetry.

What, then, does the Eastleigh by-election suggest – if anything – about the relationship between the governors and the governed?

First and foremost, governing in hard times is never easy, and the public can be a selfish master to serve. And yet there does appear to be an appetite for a *different* type of politics. That is, a politics – and therefore politicians – willing to engage in public conversations about the values that underpin our society and the limits of the state. These conversations will have to accept that there are no simple solutions to complex problems, and that difficult decisions will have to be taken by whoever is in power, irrespective of their party. Democratic politics, as Bernard Crick argued in his *In Defence of Politics* 50 years ago, 'cannot make every sad heart glad' but it can and generally does deliver far more than most people seem to realise. The barb in my argument is therefore designed to prick not politicians but the public.

The public in the sense that they can't simply opt out of politics: 'none-of-the-above' is not an option on our polling cards for a reason. You can't accept the rights of democratic citizenship but not fulfil your responsibilities. As Thomas Paine argued towards the end of the 18th century, 'Those who expect to reap the blessings of freedom must undergo the fatigue of supporting it.' From here my mind wants to leap a long way from Eastleigh and the River Itchen to Adam Curtis' award-winning 2007 documentary series 'The Trap: What Happened to Our Dream of Freedom', with its graphic deconstruction of how a simplistic model of human beings as self-seeking, almost robotic, creatures led to a vision of freedom that left us knowing the price of everything but the value of nothing. I'm sure there's a link – somewhere, somehow – between the broader sociopolitical concerns that Curtis sought to highlight in 'The Trap' and the notion of a 'None-of-the-Above' Party, but I just can't put my finger on it. I do, however, remember that the first episode was called 'F**k You Buddy'....

On reflection

It's pretty tough to go from a small town in Hampshire to the global rise in anti-politics, but to some extent the central argument of this post about the rise of populist 'insurgent' parties led by individuals who claimed not to be politicians is the story of politics in the years since this was written. Brexit, Trump, the rise of populist parties across Western Europe – even the election of Jeremy Corbyn in the UK – were all, in some senses, part of a 'F**k You Buddy' message that large parts of the public wanted to send to members of 'the establishment'. In this regard two recent developments appear to develop the argument made here. The first is that public opinion data on Hillary Clinton and Donald Trump in the run-up to the 2016 presidential elections revealed that 60% of the public did not hold positive views on either candidate. A significant number of voters were therefore primarily voting *against* one candidate rather than voting *for* another. This led to a debate about the need to expand the practice of the Silver State (Nevada), whereby voters are offered a non-binding 'none-of-the-above' (NOTA) option on their ballot card. (In 1976 the good people of Nevada gave more of their votes to NOTA than to any of the actual candidates.) In May 2016 a group of donors and disgruntled democrats did hatch a plan in the hope of scuttling the presidential elections by launching a campaign to have a NOTA option included in those states where neither Trump nor Clinton were likely to do well. The aim was to deny both candidates the chance to secure the 270 electoral votes needed to win the presidency, which would have meant that the House of Representatives could have chosen the next president. The last time that happened was in 1825, when John Quincy Adams was elected President. The second recent development is that NOTA parties and campaigns are emerging in exactly those countries where political disillusionment seems highest. NOTA parties exist in Serbia, the UK and Canada, while polls show growing public interest in a range of countries.

17

Where next? New politics, kinder politics and the myth of anti-politics

For many commentators, the 2015 General Election was the first genuinely 'anti-political' election, but at the same time, it was one in which the existence of a major debate about the nature of British democracy served to politicise huge sections of society. The surge in party membership for the Scottish National Party (SNP), for example, with over 100,000 members at the time of the election (ie, far more members than soldiers in the whole British Army) deserves some explanation in a context dominated by the rhetoric of disenchantment and decline. The subsequent election of Jeremy Corbyn as Leader of the Labour Party, with over a quarter of a million votes (59.5% of those cast), raises further questions about 'anti-politics being all the rage'.

The simple fact is that 'anti-politics' is a myth. It is also a dangerous myth due to the manner in which it seeks to perpetuate cynicism when the evidence is arguably far more positive. The truth is that the results of the 2015 General Election and the Labour leadership contest were actually more anti-establishment than anti-political. Take, for example, the influential writing and public interventions of Owen Jones (*The Establishment: And How They Get Away With It*, 2014) or Russell Brand's raw anti-elite, anti-establishment, anti-elections nihilism that was captured in his book *Revolution* (2014). I'm not for one moment suggesting that Jones or Brand were (or are) personally responsible for the dramatic shifts in the nature of British democracy, but I am saying that they – like Jeremy Corbyn – were able to somehow codify the moral sentiment of the age.

But that sentiment is not anti-political. It is tied to a search for a different form of politics, a 'new' politics.

It was this sense of a desire for difference that forged a deep fault line through the 2015 General Election as 'insurgent' parties such

Taken from a display of posters at Dismaland, Weston-super-Mare

18

What a mess! The politics and governance of the British constitution

Do we have a constitution?[1] What is the British constitution? Does anyone actually care? At one level the answers to these questions are relatively simple and straightforward. 'Yes' – we do have a constitution, but its constituent elements are scattered among a range of documents and within the tacit understandings of a number of parliamentary conventions; the British constitution is – through accident and design – a mess that has evolved in a muddled manner, betraying the existence of a latent form of 'club government'; 'No', nobody cares because this is how it has always been, and we don't trust politicians, and they're all the same.

The problem with these answers is that although they may have shaped the dominant view of the British constitution in the 20th century, they appear unable to capture and reflect the changing social and political situation in the 21st. When they are reframed as being concerned with the future governance of the UK, then people clearly do care about the constitution. More specifically, they care when Scotland nearly votes to leave the Union, when the Brexit vote reveals major social cleavages, and when judges appear to thwart the capacity of elected politicians. My sense from talking and (more importantly) listening to people as I travel around the UK is not that they don't care about British politics and its constitutional arrangements, but that they simply don't understand where power lies or why.

This takes us back to the second question and the evolution of the British constitution. David Marquand once characterised New Labour's approach to constitutional reform as being: 'a revolution of sleepwalkers who don't quite know where they are going or why.' The introduction of a great raft of constitutional measures without any clear statement of what (in the long run) the government was seeking to achieve, any idea of how reform in one sphere of the constitution would have obvious and far-reaching consequences for other elements of the constitutional equilibrium, or any detailed analysis of the nature or model of democracy that existed towards the end of the 20th century, therefore formed central components of the 'Blair paradox'. As such, the public's confusion about the distribution of powers – not to mention the existence of complex blame games and credit claims – reflects a deeper situation of democratic drift. Jack Straw may have argued with me publicly that my diagnosis is wrong and that New Labour's reforms were underpinned by a set of underlying principles, but such theoretical back-filling remains unconvincing. The UK is suffering from *constitutional anomie*[1] in the sense that reforms have been implemented – before and after New Labour – in a manner that is bereft of any underlying logic. Constitutional anomie is therefore an ailment of both mental and physical health *vis-à-vis* the body politic. Social and political anxiety, confusion and frustration emerge with the result that reforms that were designed to

enhance levels of public trust and confidence in politics, politicians and political institutions can actually have the opposite effect.

If the phrase 'constitutional anomie' risks over-complicating what is, in reality, a simple issue, then let us call it what it is: a constitutional mess.

It is in exactly this context that today's report, *Do We Need a Constitutional Convention for the UK?*,[2] by the House of Commons' Political and Constitutional Reform Committee, makes the case for a more thorough and explicit review of our constitutional framework. Although questions may revolve around the specific structure or nature of this review, what cannot be questioned is the urgent need to look across the constitutional landscape in order to assess what exists and why, and to look to the future in terms of what we want the UK to look like in 10 or 20 years time. The impending 2014 referendum on independence for Scotland makes a thorough consideration of the future of the UK and all its component nations all the more pressing.

I am well aware that in supporting the need for a review, commission or convention of some kind to take stock of the past, present and future of our constitutional framework, I am being terribly un-British in approach – for many the thought of adopting a set of explicit constitutional principles is almost heretical – but the malleability of the British constitution has arguably been exhausted, the relationship between its constituent parts confused, and the mess that now undoubtedly exists demands urgent review and reform.

On reflection

The simple argument of this post was that the British constitution was in a mess and that a rather grandly titled pathology of 'constitutional anomie' could be identified. I'm very glad to say that in the years that have passed since this piece was written in 2013, the British constitutional framework has been clarified, and that there are absolutely no muddles or messes left to form the focus of future exam questions. I am, of

course, joking. The warning of this post was not heeded, and the constitutional chaos surrounding British politics has intensified to a level where to talk of crisis and collapse would not be over-dramatic. 'What a mess!' can really be the only response to anyone who dares to try and understand how the various actors and institutions are supposed to engage with each other. A Supreme Court that is not supreme, reform of the House of Lords that remains unfinished, an electoral system that artificially locks in a two-party system that no longer exists, plans for English regional devolution that are dissolving into chaos, the failure to use basic thresholds in a constitutional referendum on Europe that has left the outcome incredibly divisive in all sorts of ways … and on and on and on…. And yet, possibly one of the most interesting elements of recent years is the existence of successive governments that refuse to sanction a constitutional convention that would begin to engage with these issues at a deeper level. The British constitution remains tucked away in the 'too difficult' drawer, but whether this is a viable strategy for much longer, especially in light of the Brexit decision, remains to be seen.

▬▬

19

The Dis-United Kingdom?

Is the UK really in danger of dis-uniting? The answer is 'no'. But the more interesting answer is that the independence referendum is, to some extent, a red herring. The nationalists may well lose the referendum but they have already won the bigger political battle over power and money. All the main political parties in the UK have agreed to give Scotland more powers and more financial competencies – or what is called 'devo-max' – irrespective of what happens on 18 September.

Viewed from the other side of the world the Scottish independence referendum forms part of a colonial narrative that underpins a great deal of Australian life. Some commentators take great pleasure in forecasting 'the death' of the United Kingdom and the demise of the English. Michael Sexton's headline in *The Australian*, 'Scotland chips away at the English empire', is high on hyperbole and, dare I say, even colonial gloating. It sadly lacks any real understanding of British constitutional history and how it has consistently managed territorial tensions. The UK has long been a 'union state' rather than a unitary state. Each nation joined the union for different reasons and maintained distinctive institutions or cultural legacies.

The relationships among and between the countries in the UK have changed many times. Like tectonic plates, the countries rub and grate against each other, but through processes of conciliation and compromise (and the dominance of England), volcanic eruptions have been rare. In the late 1990s devolutionary pressures were channelled through the delegation of powers to the Northern Ireland Assembly, the National Assembly for Wales and the Scottish Parliament. Different competencies reflected the extent of popular pressure within each country, and since the millennium, with the exception of Northern Ireland, it is possible to trace the gradual devolution of more powers. Wales wants a parliament, Scotland wants a stronger parliament – but few people want independence from a Union that has arguably served them well.

But has the Union really served the Scots so well? It is true that the UK as a whole and not just Scotland has benefited from the North Sea oil revenues. 'It's Scotland's oil!' might have been the Scottish National Party's (SNP) slogan in the 1970s, but it captures a sentiment that underpins today's debates. It also overlooks the manner in which Scotland receives a generous slice of the financial pie when public funds are allocated. Fees and charges for many public services that exist in England, Wales and Northern Ireland are absent north of the border. The nationalists argue that public services could be increased if Scotland had more control over North Sea oil, but they play down the fact that many analysts believe that the pool of black gold is nearly empty, and that an independent country would have to take its share of the UK's national debt. Depending on how the debt cake is cut, this would be a figure of around £150 billion.

The UK government claims Scots would be £1,400 better off if they stayed in the Union, the Scottish government claims that they would be £1,000 better off with independence, but the simple fact is that independence is a risky game to play for a small state – the political equivalent of Russian roulette in an increasingly competitive and globalised world. There are lots of questions, but few answers. On independence would Scotland remain in the European Union? How would an independent Scotland defend itself? What currency would they use? What kind of international role and influence would an independent Scotland have? Would a 'yes' vote be good for business? What happens in relation to immigration and border controls? What would independence mean for energy markets? The simple fact is that there are no clear answers to these basic questions. The nationalists understandably define many of these questions as little more than 'scare tactics', but independence must come with a price.

Nationalists (such a tired and simplistic term in a world of multiple and overlapping loyalties) may argue that independence is about culture and identity, heart and soul – not bureaucracies and budgets – and I would not disagree. The problem is that when stood in the voting booth the Scottish public is likely to vote according to their head (and their wallet) and not their heart. The twist in the tail is that support for Scottish independence has at times been higher among the English (54 million people compared to just 5 million in Scotland) than the Scottish. Therefore if the referendum on Scottish independence was open to the whole of the UK, as many have argued it should be, Scotland may well have been cast adrift by its English neighbours.

And yet the strangest element of this whole Scottish independence debate is that the model of independence on offer has always been strangely lacking in terms of … how can I put it … independence. What's on offer is a strange quasi-independence where the Scottish government wants to share the pound sterling and the Bank of England, it wants to share the British army and other military forces, and what this amounts to is a rather odd half-way house that is more like greater devolution *within* the Union rather than true independence as a self-standing nation state. The risks are therefore high but the benefits uncertain, and this explains why the Scottish public remains to be convinced that the gamble is worth it. The latest polling figures find 57% against and 43% in support of a 'yes' vote, but a shift to the 'no' camp can be expected as the referendum draws closer and the public becomes more risk-averse.

But does this really matter? A 'yes' vote was always incredibly unlikely. Mass public support has never existed, and the referendum is really part of a deeper power game to lever more power from London to Scotland, and to this extent, the game is already over. Devo-max has already been granted. The 2012 Scotland Act has already been passed and boosts the power of the Scottish Parliament by giving it a new ability to tax and borrow along with a number of new policy powers. (The most important

new measure – giving the Parliament partial control over setting income tax rates in Scotland – will come into force in 2015.) Since this legislation was passed, the three main political parties in Westminster have all agreed to devolve even more powers, specifically in relation to tax and welfare.

Mark Twain famously remarked that 'reports of my death have been greatly exaggerated', and I cannot help but feel the same is true in relation to those who like to trumpet the death of the United Kingdom. The Scottish independence referendum is highly unlikely to amount to a Dis-United Kingdom or the 'unravelling' of the Union. It may amount to a 'looser' union, but the relationship between Edinburgh and Westminster has always been one of partnership rather than domination. My sense is that what we are witnessing is not 'the end', as some commentators would like to see it, but the beginning of a new stage in a historical journey that has already lasted over 300 years.

On reflection

Reports of the death of the United Kingdom or the 'Dis-United Kingdom' remain premature, but in the wake of the Scottish referendum and particularly the UK's Brexit decision, tensions and divisions that have always existed have certainly been exacerbated. Moreover, the title of Iain Macwhirter's book on the Scottish independence referendum – *Disunited Kingdom: How Westminster Won a Referendum But Lost Scotland* (2014) – conveys a very real sense of the manner in which underpinning linkages are eroding. The success of the Scottish National Party in the 2015 General Election also suggests that certain forces have been unleashed, forces that also came to the fore in the 2016 Brexit referendum. And yet, there is arguably a specific element of the Scottish independence referendum that has so far been under-played despite the manner in which it dovetails with contemporary concerns regarding the emergence of 'post-truth' or 'post-fact' politics. As books such as Pat Anderson's *Fear and Smear* (2016) and Joe Pike's *Project Fear* (2015) illustrate, the 'Better Together'

campaign against Scottish independence adopted a very specific political strategy that played on negative campaigning and the manufacture of fears rather than on a rational review of the facts or evidence.

20

A new and fair constitutional settlement? Beware of constitutional hyper-activism

The Flower of Scotland may well be blooming, but a number of thorny issues face the Prime Minister and the leaders of the main parties in the UK. The Prime Minister's commitment to a 'new and fair constitutional settlement', not just for Scotland, but also for the whole of the United Kingdom, may well reflect the need to think in a joined-up manner about constitutional reform and the devolution of power but the simple rhetoric cannot veil the complexity of the challenges ahead.

Instead of waking up as the Prime Minister who dis-united the UK, David Cameron has suddenly emerged as the great reforming Prime Minister. Democracy could not be ducked, hard choices had to be made, democratic pressures vented, and now Scotland had clearly spoken in favour of staying in the Union.

But what next?

The status quo is not an option. Rushed commitments were made by all the main parties in the last two weeks, commitment in relation to tax, spending and welfare, and must now be delivered, diluted or derailed. "We have a chance – a great opportunity – to change the way the British people are governed," the Prime Minister declared, with a relieved and somewhat shell-shocked look on his face. "Just as the people of Scotland will have more power over their affairs, so it follows that the people of England, Wales and Northern Ireland must have a bigger say over theirs."

But what does this mean?

Two constitutional entrepreneurs have been tasked with answering this question. Lord

Smith of Kelvin will lead on the delivery of those commitments that have been made to Scotland, while Richmond MP William Hague becomes (in essence) a new Secretary of State for the Isles with the job of dealing with the English question, the West Lothian question and the ratchet-like demands for more powers for Wales and Northern Ireland.

The scale of this challenge is massive, but the coalition government risks running straight into a constitutional minefield. The Prime Minister said that the question of 'English votes for English laws' now required a 'decisive answer', and promised a detailed plan by January. But the idea that English MPs should vote 'separately' on issues of tax, spending and welfare overlooks the interrelated nature of the British constitution.

As things stand, if Labour wins the next general election in May 2015, they may not have a majority of English MPs to enact the policies in their manifesto. Accusations of Tory gerrymandering and a 'constitutional land grab' therefore point to a deeper issue

in the sense that greater independence for Scotland may well permanently shift the centre of politics in England towards the right. Ed Miliband spoke just hours after David Cameron's 'Downing Street Declaration' on the future of the constitution, but his argument that 'change begins today' sounded more like a whimper than the roar of a potential leader who has a vision of a new and revitalised British democracy.

But what are we trying to achieve?

This is the million-dollar question to which answers are sparse. The political historian and writer David Marquand once accused New Labour of overseeing a very British constitutional revolution. It was 'a revolution of sleepwalkers who don't know quite where they are going or quite why, but muddle and mess are often the midwives of change', noted Marquand, who was MP for the Nottinghamshire seat of Ashfield from 1966 to 1977 before becoming chief adviser to his mentor Roy Jenkins who had been appointed President of the European Commission.

This may well be true, but I cannot help but think that Cameron now risks unleashing a constitutional revolution forged on ridiculously rapid hyper-activism. The timescales set out will bring tears to the eyes of even the driest constitutional anorak – constitutional agreements decided and mapped out by November with draft legislation published by January 2015. Such speed brings risks and little time for any public engagement beyond the shallowest tokenism. Breathing new life into politics is not just about institutional reform, the devolution of powers and the creation of new political processes.

As the 'Yes' campaign in Scotland illustrated, politics is about belief and passion and a political culture that is united by a set of shared beliefs and values. These values form the glue that binds society together and prevents a gap emerging between the governors and the governed. The coalition's constitutional engineers – a ghastly phrase that encapsulates the government's approach – therefore need to recognise the need for bottom-up reform and engagement that is rooted in communities, families and civil society as a prerequisite to the successful design and implementation of any new settlement. (Of course, there will be no real 'settlement', only a temporary resting place.)

What should be done?

Scotland has spoken and the rest of the UK has listened. Democracy has triumphed, but now is not the time for constitutional hyper-activism. At the very least there is a case for delivering what has been promised to Scotland, then pausing to draw breath before considering the spillover effects for the rest of the UK. My message to the three main party leaders is therefore clear: a new constitutional settlement cannot be rushed.

has certainly been rapid – just not quite in the direction that David Cameron might have envisaged. The simple fact is that the Brexit vote has plunged the UK into a state of complete constitutional uncertainty, and this is the central paradox: a vote that was supposed to strengthen the UK, to make it 'great again', to return sovereignty to Parliament, to make all bread light and fluffy, etc has actually had the opposite effect. More precisely, the Brexit vote has created a constitutional clash between popular sovereignty and parliamentary sovereignty that has drawn the judiciary into the political sphere as those who must decide ultimately where power resides. The current constitutional settlement is far from settled.

▬▬▬▬▬▬▬

On reflection

So what has happened to deliver David Cameron's post-referendum promise of 'a new and fair constitutional settlement'? Since this was posted back in 2014, the pace of reform

21

Looking beyond the Scottish referendum

In British constitutional history, 2014 will undoubtedly be remembered for one thing and one thing only – the Scottish independence referendum. 'Should Scotland be an independent country?' was the deceptively simple question that veiled a far more complex reality. This complexity was revealed in the pre-election build-up as the three main parties offered concession upon concession in order to head off a 'yes' vote. As such, 'no' did not mean 'no' but a preference for 'devo-max' and a model of devolution that was 'as close to a federal state as you can be in a country where one nation is 85% of the population', as Gordon Brown put it. But what did the Scottish independence referendum really expose about the changing nature of politics?

This week's recommendations by the Smith Commission on Scottish devolution (full control over income tax rates and bands, devolution of some element of VAT plus Air Passenger Duty, devolution of responsibility for some welfare benefits, etc) represents the latest but not the final stage in the post-referendum politics of devolution in the UK. Indeed, just hours after the Smith Commission had published its recommendations, more than 100 English councils demanded more powers – 'It's England's turn now' – and David Cameron committed the coalition government to publish an English votes plan by Christmas. English votes for English laws are not quite the same as the devolution of powers that is demanded by local authorities from Cornwall to Cumbria, but it does suggest a need to stop – to step back – and reflect on the broader implications of the Scottish independence referendum. I've attempted to answer five questions below to help tease out some of the broader issues.

What did we learn?

We learned a huge amount about democratic energy and participatory zeal. Doom and gloom about democratic apathy and public disengagement from politics was replaced with a vitality and verve that was almost tangible as every school hall, pub and youth club was filled with debates about the pros and cons of independence. The lesson for the political parties and politicians is that the public will engage in politics when they feel they have been given a meaningful role, a real choice and a say in matters such as their country's fiscal policy.[1] The statistics speak for themselves: 4,283,392 people voted (85% turnout) and, as Robert Crawford[2] hoped, Scotland has emerged as a stronger country with an intensified (and globally admired) sense of itself as a democratic place.

What is the key challenge?

The Scottish independence referendum breathed new life into politics, and the question for all the main political parties is how to sustain and channel that dramatic energy[3] in other ways and across the UK. This won't be easy as the Scottish referendum tapped into a number of very deep historical and cultural issues in order to generate its energy, but there must be some way to harness and replicate the civic energy and engagement that Scotland displayed with such pride. Put slightly differently, if the main political parties cannot offer some of the hopes and beliefs that energised the referendum campaign on both sides, then the more extreme populist parties will feast on the political frustrations that currently exist.

Where does this leave us now?

Confused and divided. *Confused* in the sense of lacking any real understanding of what the United Kingdom is any more, both constitutionally and politically; *divided* in the sense that there is no shared agreement among the main parties about what is to be done. To some extent – and as James Mitchell[4] highlighted – this is not a new situation for the UK, but I would argue that the situation is now more extreme. It's increasingly a unitary state in the very loosest sense of the term, but the parties are divided on the best way to deliver a new sense of equilibrium within the system. More devolution to Scotland unleashes similar demands from other parts of the UK, but the culture of Westminster and Whitehall lacks the capacity to deal with the constitution in a 'joined-up' manner. The current situation is therefore one of classically British ad hoc, unprincipled muddling through – with the recent devolution agreement between the Chancellor of the Exchequer and the leaders of the Greater Manchester Combined Authority being a case in point.

Is the post-referendum UK experiencing a 'constitutional moment'?

Yes, it probably is, but this is the problem. The Scottish independence referendum was a '*democratic* moment' in the sense that there was a bottom-up pressure for change that was accommodated by the democratic process. The post-referendum discussions and debates have, however, been undertaken at an elite level, and the most telling evidence of this comes not in the form of the Smith Commission but in the work of William

Hague's committee on 'a fair settlement that applies to all parts of the UK'. When announcing this committee, Prime Minister David Cameron announced that 'it is also important we have wider civic engagement about how to improve governance in our United Kingdom … we will say more about this in the coming days.' But so far, these plans for 'wider civic engagement' have remained undisclosed. The idea of a national citizens' assembly has been rejected, and as a result the UK is experiencing an elite-driven top-down 'constitutional moment', but certainly not a 'bottom-up public-led' democratic moment.

What is the big issue that no one is talking about?

One of the most positive elements of the Scottish independence referendum had nothing to do with the quality of the debate, the inclusion of a cross-section of society or the level of turnout. It had everything to do with the simple fact that two countries were able to decide on their mutual futures through peaceful and democratic means. This was an independence referendum that was not driven by war, crisis or disaster; nor did it demand battle or bloodshed; and the results were peacefully accepted with grace and goodwill on both sides. In a world that too often seems bloodied and bowed by territorial politics, maybe this is the 'big issue' that we should be talking about and learning from.

On reflection

Looking beyond the Scottish referendum is now an exercise that can only be undertaken through a Brexit-tainted lens. The First Minister of Scotland, Nicola Sturgeon, initially used the results of the Brexit referendum (where a majority of Scottish voters voted 'remain') to launch strong calls for a second Scottish referendum on independence. Draft legislation on a second referendum was published by the Scottish government in October 2016, but no timetable on further progress has been offered, and this may reflect public opinion polls that suggest little increased evidence for a desire for independence among the Scottish electorate. What has emerged in place of an emphasis on independence is a statecraft based on using the break-up of the Union almost as an existential threat to lever a better deal for Scotland within the European Union withdrawal negotiations. This was clear in January 2017 when the First Minister offered to take independence off the table for the immediate future in return for an improved devolution settlement for Scotland and continued access to the free market. This is, to some extent, an exercise in brinkmanship, as the Prime Minister's emphasis on 'hard Brexit' – rather than the Scottish government's preference for 'soft Brexit' – would automatically strengthen the Scottish National Party's case for a second vote. Looking beyond the Scottish referendum therefore remains as uncertain as it did in the immediate aftermath of the vote.

22

The culture of nastiness and the paradox of civility

Headlines are by their very nature designed to catch the eye, but Teddy Wayne's 'The culture of nastiness' (*New York Times*, 18 February 2017) certainly caught my attention. Why? Because more survey evidence and datasets have identified growing social concerns about declining levels of civility. In the US, for example, a recent poll found that 75% of those members of the public surveyed believe that incivility has risen to crisis levels, and 60% expect civility to get worse in the next few years. Politics, it would seem, has become raw, rude, direct, divisive … and don't just think Trump … the rise of nationalist populism across the globe seems to have shifted the civic culture in ways that we really don't understand or know how to deal with. The problem is that no one seems to know whom to blame. There are lots of culprits in the firing line for public condemnation (politicians, activists, bloggers, tweeters, journalists, shock jocks, etc) but I cannot help but think that the challenge goes beyond the 'usual suspects' and raises far deeper issues of social interaction, social learning and social capital.

In terms of understanding the emergence of this 'culture of nastiness' or, more specifically, the perception that levels of civility have or are being eroded, this might begin from three positions, the first emphasising 'the vortex', the second 'the vacuum' and the third 'the twist'.

'The vortex' is rather obvious and highlights the manner in which being rude to an individual, organisation or community generally provokes similarly bad-mannered responses that set in train a sequence of increasingly unfriendly and discourteous interactions. Can you think of an occasion when being rude actually served a positive end? It's possible that comedy and satire can use insolence and vulgarity to good effect, but this is the exception rather then the rule. Meryl Streep was therefore on to something when she used her Golden Globes speech to suggest that 'disrespect invites disrespect'. The problem is, however, that without someone brave enough or diplomatic enough (or ideally both) to break this self-sustaining negative dynamic, all we end up with is yah-boo playground politics.

'The vacuum' focuses on how hard it is to break out of incivility exactly because it demands a politician or party with the energy and ambition to recalibrate politics. This is a critical point. If the political system were a computer you'd probably switch it off at the wall and re-boot, or you might even download some new software or anti-virus protection. The problem is that constitutional re-engineering is more difficult because those with the capacity to 're-boot' have little incentive to push the button. There is no clear alternative model of civil politics to transfer to, and all the risks rest with those who dare to adopt a different style of politics. What's more, the whole nature of the 'culture of nastiness' rests on the destruction and havoc it casts on those souls who do attempt to compromise, listen, accommodate, etc. These

are the core values of democratic politics – the oil that stops the system grinding to a halt – and yet for 'nasty people' these traits are defined and dismissed as a weakness. One of the saddest things about the murder of the British politician Jo Cox in June 2016 was the manner in which the initial period of open social reflection about the emergence of a culture of nastiness was so short-lived. After briefly doffing their caps, the media and main political parties quickly reverted to politics as normal.

And then there is 'the twist' ('hook' or 'barb'). The contemporary analysis of the problem with democracy seems increasingly focused on the unintended consequences of what is often termed 'political correctness' ('PC'). The 'paradox of civility' is therefore the manner in which the emergence of a culture shift that explicitly embraced social civility and understanding is now blamed for fuelling a culture of nastiness. Let me put this slightly differently – a set of social mores that became popularly embedded around 20 years ago in an attempt to avoid words, terms or

behaviour that might exclude or offend certain sections of society has now been highlighted as a cause of the increase in behaviour that is explicitly designed to discriminate. To some extent this is not as novel – or as twisty – as you might have thought. Right-wingers have attacked the 'PC brigade' for decades, but the contemporary situation is quite different; it has, to some extent, been legitimised by the electoral success of those candidates and parties that claim to express the longstanding frustrations of the politically disillusioned and disenfranchised. There is a certain repressive Freudian logic at play: individuals must be free to vent their emotional beliefs, no matter how irrational or hurtful they may be, in order to ensure a healthy open discussion of a full range of social concerns. Indeed, so the logic goes, the problem with the liberal elite that populists seek to displace is that they put political correctness above common sense. Large sections of the public could not voice their concerns about immigration, crime or equality for fear of being immediately labelled as racist or bigoted ... populist nationalism therefore provided exactly the lightning rod that allowed such frustrations to be vented. And vented they have been and continue to be … we are trapped in a vortex … in a spiral of cynicism that, without the emergence of a new politics of civility, risks making political failure and further disillusionment almost inevitable.

23

Learning to love democracy: A note to William Hague

British politics is currently located in the eye of a constitutional storm. The Scottish independence referendum shook the political system, and William Hague has been tasked with somehow reconnecting the pieces of a constitutional jigsaw that – if we are honest

– have not fitted together for some time. I have written an open letter, encouraging the Leader of the House to think the unthinkable and to put 'the demos' back into democracy when thinking about how to breathe new life into politics.

Dear William (if I may),

I do hope the Prime Minister gave you at least a few minutes warning before announcing that you would be chairing a committee on the future constitutional settlement of the UK. Could you have ever hoped for a more exciting little project to sort out before you leave Parliament next May? Complex problems rarely have simple answers and this is why so many previous politicians have failed to deal with a whole set of questions concerning the distribution of powers and the respective roles of various sub-sets of both politicians and 'publics'. The

timetable you have been set is – how can I put it – demanding, and those naughty people in the Labour Party have taken their bat and ball home and are refusing to play the constitutional game.

I'm sure you know how to sort all of this out, but I just thought you might like to know that among all the critics and naysayers who claim the British constitution is in crisis, I actually think that a crisis might be just what we need. Not a crisis in terms of burning cars and riots in the streets, but a crisis in terms of 'creative destruction' and the chance for a new way of looking at perennial problems. What's more – as the Scottish referendum revealed – there is a huge amount of latent democratic energy among the public. From Penzance to Perth and from Cardigan to Cromer, the public is not apathetic or disinterested about politics, but they feel disconnected from a London-based system that is remote in a number of ways.

The reasons for this sense of disconnection are numerous and complex, but as a constitutional historian you will know better than most people that British democracy has evolved throughout the centuries with a deep animosity to public engagement. The (in)famous 'Westminster Model' that we imposed on countries around the world was explicitly elitist, centralised and to a great extent insulated from public pressure. These features and values – as Scotland revealed – are now crumbling under the weight of popular pressure that will not accept their legitimacy in the 21st century. But as I said, this should be interpreted as a positive opportunity for re-imagining, for reconnecting and for breathing new life into the system.

The question is how to deliver on this potential for positive change in a way that takes the people with you?

Now I'm no Vernon Bogdanor or Peter Hennessy, and so writing notes to members of the Cabinet is not a common task, but could I just offer three little ideas that might help

smooth the path you have been asked to map out?

First and foremost, please ignore Russell Brand.

Second, make sure all your officials are also ignoring Russell Brand.

Finally, the trick to moving forward is thinking about constitutional reform not as being like moving pieces on a chessboard or as a zero-sum game in which a 'win' for one side means a 'loss' for the other. This traditional way of thinking about constitutional politics has served us badly, and the aim has to be to turn the problem upside down and inside out in a way that creates new opportunities. This means starting with the people – with the demos – and viewing the constitutional puzzle not like a board game but as a multi-level game that suddenly focuses attention on the existence of connections or bonds.

The real challenge is not a lack of political interest among the public (indeed, the appetite for meaningful engagement is huge), but a lack

of ways of drawing on the upsurges of bottom-up civic energy that keep exploding in various forms – from the offline Occupy Movement to the online growth of 'clicktivism' – but to which the 'traditional' political institutions seem to offer no answers. Put slightly differently, the public no longer believes that traditional forms of political engagement are actually meaningful. In this context the promises of populist movements suddenly become attractive, and Mr Farage gorges on a feast of anti-politics. The focus of your committee on a new constitutional settlement might therefore adopt a quite different approach to all those committees, commissions and inquiries that have gone before you by focusing on what I term 'nexus politics'. That is, on the institutions and processes that can reconnect the spontaneous and the local and the single issue with the pre-existing institutional framework in a way that positively channels, absorbs and welcomes civic energy and activism. In short, British politics must learn to love democracy in a manner that is quite different to the one-night stand of five-yearly elections.

The problem is that despite the Prime Minister's pledge on 19 September to ensure 'wider civic engagement … we will say more about this in the coming days', the days have ticked by but the plans for public engagement remain unclear. What we are experiencing is best characterised as a (classically British top-down) 'constitutional moment' in which the existing elite decide what they think is best for the public. However, it has not yet evolved into a truly 'democratic moment' in which the public decide for themselves. My note – to bring things to a close – is therefore a simple plea for the creation of a citizens' assembly on constitutional reform that takes party politics out of discussions about the future and puts power in the hands of the people. What a radical thought….

Yours truly,

Matt

P.S. Did I mention avoiding Russell Brand at all costs?

On reflection

It gives me great pleasure to announce that William Hague did take my advice and completely ignored Russell Brand in the 'gluing-back-the-pieces' exercise he had been given by the Prime Minister. That's the good news. The bad news is that his approach to addressing the consequences of the Scottish independence vote and also the plans to devolve more powers to the Scottish Parliament was very narrow. It focused on the West Lothian question and answered it with a new system of 'English Votes for English Laws' (EVEL), which, contrary to the expectations of many critics, has avoided many of the problems that were expected. There was not, however, any broader attempt to cultivate a public conversation about the changing nature of British democracy. The Labour Party largely refused to engage in discussions about EVEL in preference for plans for a much broader constitutional review, possibly involving a national citizens' assembly on the constitution, after the 2015 General Election. The political story since this point is one that has been written several times, and it is sufficient to note that many people appear unable to love democracy.

24

Let the people speak! Devolution, decentralisation, deliberation

Democratic pressure is building, cracks and fault lines are emerging, and at some point the British political elite will have to let the people speak about where power should lie and how they should be governed. 'Speak' in this sense doesn't relate to the casting of votes – the general election will not vent the pressure – but to a deeper form of democracy that facilitates both 'democratic voice' and 'democratic listening'.

In the wake of the Scottish referendum on independence the UK is undergoing a rapid period of constitutional reflection and reform. The Smith Commission has set out a raft of new powers for the Scottish Parliament, the Chancellor of the Exchequer has signed a new devolution agreement with Greater Manchester Combined Authority, the Deputy Prime Minister has signed an agreement with Sheffield City Council, and the Cabinet Committee on Devolved Powers has reported on options for change in Westminster. One critical component of this frenetic period of reform has been the absence of any explicit or managed process for civic engagement, even though the Prime Minister's statement on 19 September 2014 emphasised that 'It is also important we have wider civic engagement about how to improve governance in our United Kingdom, including how to empower our great cities. And we will say more about this in the coming days.'

The days and months have passed, but no plan for civic engagement has been announced.

In the meantime, calls for a citizen-led constitutional convention have been made with ever increasing regularity and volume. Petitions have been submitted, letters to the press have been published, a huge number of citizen groups have come together around the idea, and all of the main political parties – apart from the Conservatives –

have committed themselves to establishing a constitution convention should they form or be part of the government after 7 May 2015. But even in relation to the Conservative Party – conservative by name, conservative by nature – the pressure to let the people speak is gradually being acknowledged. The government's 'command paper' on English devolution, published on 16 December 2014, made reference to a constitutional convention as a means of civic engagement (although it fell short of a full commitment).

Such instruments of deliberative democracy may be distinctly 'foreign' and at odds with the elitist British political tradition, with the culture and rituals of a traditional power-hoarding democracy and with the predilection for 'muddling through' that defined British politics in the 20th century. But we are no longer in the 20th century. 'Muddling through' is no longer good enough. The traditional power-hoarding model of British democracy has been hollowed out and, as a result, new relationships between the governors and the governed must be put

in place. The recently published *Future of England Survey 2014* provides evidence for this argument with its conclusion that people in England see a 'democratic deficit' in the way they are governed ('devo-anxiety'), and that one dimension of that deficit is a desire for civic engagement. This conclusion focuses attention on the notion of 'nexus politics' in which the traditional institutions and processes of democratic politics must somehow engage with, channel and respond to an increasing array of more dynamic bottom-up explosions of democratic energy.

In facing new democratic challenges the UK is by no means unique, and arguments in favour of deliberative democracy have been made by scholars including Robert Goodin,[1] John Dryzek[2] and Tina Nabatchi[3] for decades.

But the recent flurry of devolutionary deals has fuelled democratic discontent in those parts of the UK that seem untouched, unloved and misunderstood by the main political parties. The sudden appearance of Cabinet and Shadow Cabinet members seeking to

ingratiate themselves with the 'Northern powerhouses' of Manchester, Sheffield and Leeds has been a sight to behold. But now the time has come to 'let the people speak'. The issue of holding a constitutional convention has shifted from the periphery of constitutional debates in the UK to the very core. Meanwhile, the likelihood of a hung parliament after 7 May and the inter-party deals that will be required to form a coalition, plus the existence of unresolved and urgent constitutional questions which require resolution, provides the necessary political backdrop for the establishment of a constitutional convention. How the convention might operate, where it would be based, how convention members would be selected, the use of the final report or recommendations are all second-order issues where experiments in other countries and test cases in the UK can offer answers. The main question is whether the political elite is really willing to embrace change, take a few risks and let the people speak.

On reflection

In many ways the people have spoken in a very dramatic manner since this post was originally written in February 2015. But what does 'speaking' actually mean in a political context? It is often used as a synonym for the holding of an election or vote, but speaking is about far more than using a stubby pencil to scrawl a cross in a box. As previous posts have emphasised, democracy is more than a vote. The arguments in favour of a constitutional convention in the run-up to the 2015 General Election were therefore aimed towards creating a deeper and more sophisticated way of understanding the position of the public on the evolution of British democracy. In theory a constitutional convention would allow for a slower, deeper and more considered public statement to emerge. The success of the only party that was not publicly committed to establishing a constitutional convention – the Conservative Party – effectively ended the hopes of those who wanted to 'let the people speak' in the short term. However, the Brexit referendum result and questions about public engagement in the withdrawal negotiations has led to further interest in establishing a citizens' assembly that would inevitably have to explore a set of broader questions about the constitutional architecture.

25

Raw politics: Devolution, democracy and deliberation

As a long-time student of politics I have often found myself assessing various kinds of attempts to create new democratic processes or arenas. From citizens' juries to mini-publics and from area panels to lottery-based procedures, the scope of these experiments with 'new' ways of doing politics has taken me from the local ward level right up to the international level. In undertaking these studies the work of leading scholars, such as John Dryzek,[1] Frank Fischer[2] and John Parkinson[3] – all, I should note, Oxford University Press authors – has been invaluable in terms of helping me understand the challenges and complexity of engaging with multiple publics in multiple ways.

And yet my knowledge had always been remote, garnered as it was through books and articles rather than being forged in the heat of running a deliberative process myself. I had, of course, observed the odd event and had even acted as an academic adviser to one or two 'experiments', but my role was always somehow peripheral and distant. Put slightly differently, as an academic I had never stepped into the political arena myself to lead and manage a deliberative event around a specific political challenge. Why soil my hands in the rough-and-tumble of real politics when so many others appear to relish the challenge?

But academic life is changing. Academics are increasingly expected to put their heads above the parapet in terms of engaging with public debates and media controversies. They are also expected to demonstrate the basic value and role of social and political sciences in increasingly visible and demonstrable ways. The point I am rambling myself (and therefore the reader) towards is that last weekend I actually did it!

I actually did it!

With a fabulous group of colleagues and researchers from the University of Sheffield, University of Southampton, University of Westminster, University College London and the Electoral Reform Society I actually helped to design, manage and deliver a large citizens' assembly. Its focus was the government's current plans for 'devo deals', 'metro mayors' and all that sort of thing, but the learning process was far more complex and enriching.

This was raw politics in the sense that 45 members of the public gave up their whole weekend to learn about, discuss and deliberate the pros and cons of various forms of localism and devolution. It was 'raw' in all sorts of ways, but not least because the citizens were new to the process, a good cross-section of society had been selected and – most of all – because it was up to the project team to look after and support these good men and women of South Yorkshire not just over the next two days, but also for the whole six-week assembly process with its constituent phases.

So what did I learn, not about devolution or localism in England, but about the politics and management of deliberative projects?

The first and most basic insight was that the planning of the event is critical in the sense that many of the participants are understandably nervous, this is a new experience for them, and therefore a smiling face and lots of help with the simple issues of finding rooms, leaving bags, registering and knowing where food and drink is available is crucial to the success of the initiative. In many ways all this underpinning work should take place in an efficient manner 'off stage', so that the participants feel valued and supported, and can therefore focus on contributing to the assembly.

The second insight became really clear to me as the weekend progressed – we were not simply facilitating an assembly in order to fulfil a very clear academic methodology (although we were doing that); we were creating a new community. This is critical because what became more and more evident as the sessions and stages progressed was that a form of social capital was emerging between the assembly members. This took the form of mutual understanding, trust, shared values, an emphasis on listening as well as talking … right through to body language and the sound of laughter as well as speech. What was fascinating to me as a political scientist was that it was possible to almost sense or smell the assembly maturing and developing together as time went on. I'm not saying that there were not challenges or that the project team got everything right all of the time, but there was something quite inspirational about bringing a group of people together, who had previously never met each other and who came from a broad geographical landscape, to explore a specific political issue. As the bonds created within the assembly grew and tightened, so the role of the project team slipped back to a more supporting function. The assembly had almost developed a personality and life of its own.

The third and final insight was more personal and revolved around my own academic experience. Indeed, it would not be over-egging the pudding to suggest that I learned more about the nature of politics in that one weekend than I had as an academic during the previous two decades. There was a raw energy, a passion and a social learning element that is simply impossible to perceive from the pages of a book. I should, however, note that running a deliberative assembly can be stressful, tiring, demanding, etc, but in this case I was very lucky to be part of a large and well-organised team. So maybe the experience was not quite as 'raw' as I'd like to think, but it certainly opened my eyes to the difference between 'the theory of politics' and 'the practice of politics' in ways that I will never forget.

▪▪▪▪▪▪▪▪▪▪▪▪▪

On reflection

Eighteen months after the end of the citizens' assemblies project it is amazing how fresh everything still feels in my mind. The assemblies model has been replicated, adapted, rolled out, applied in different policy areas, and the members of the original assemblies remain active and in contact. The whole aim of this project was to test the capacity of the public to engage in complex constitutional debates, and in this regard the two models of assembly – one 'pure', the other 'mixed' – revealed a huge amount about designing for democracy. These findings dovetailed with a broader set of parliamentary and think tank reports that highlighted the need for greater public engagement within the plans that were emerging to devolve power through new 'devo deals'. With the first elections for 'metro mayors' due to take place in the summer of 2017, the lack of public engagement about regional devolution or understanding of what the new mayors will do risks undermining the credibility and legitimacy of a reform that offers the potential to rebalance the governance of a country that by international standards remains highly centralised.

▪▪▪▪▪▪▪▪▪

Donald Trump and Theresa May's handshake, Gloucester Road, Bristol

26

Vote Jeremy Clarkson on 7 May! Celebrity politics and political reality

The news this week that Jeremy Clarkson's contract with the BBC will not be renewed might be bad news for 'Top Gear' fans but could it be good news for politics? Probably not....

I wonder what Jeremy Clarkson is up to as you read this blog. Could he be casting his eye over the jobs pages in the newspapers, possibly signing up to some online employment agencies, or simply staring at his mobile phone in the hope that it will ring with the message that says 'The BBC has changed its mind! All is forgiven'? The answer is 'probably not', but let's run with the idea for a moment and think of what a slightly grumpy Jeremy with time on his hands might do for his next big project.

I must, at this point, admit that the testosterone-soaked, 'man-fun' focus of 'Top Gear' has never quite rung my bell, but as a political scientist (yawn, yawn, yawn) I can't help but think that there is something going on. 'Top Gear' seems to be spreading as some form of international cultural craze. Indeed, its global reach appears unstoppable

and so far includes over 60 countries from Argentina to Australia and Israel to Ireland. At the same time a quite different cultural craze that was popular in recent decades (that is, democracy) appears to be in something of a retreat. This is reflected in a massive body of evidence and data that reveals increasing levels of public disenchantment with traditional politics.

Take the UK as an example. With just weeks before the 2015 General Election, the latest 'Audit of Political Engagement' from the Hansard Society suggests that just 49% of the public say they are certain to vote. In relation to 18- to 24-year-olds the picture of democratic desire is bleaker, with just 16% saying they are certain to vote, but nearly twice as many saying that they definitely will not be voting. Just 30% claim to be strong supporters of a political party, and the general picture is one of decline.

The number who believe themselves to be registered to vote? In decline. Those who feel they have some influence over local issues? In decline. Satisfaction with the overall system? In decline. A petition to reinstate Jeremy Clarkson? Surpasses one million voters.

Hold on a minute! Have I spotted something? Politics and politicians appear to be in big trouble; Clarkson appears to be surfing a wave of popular support that most politicians could never dream of. Add the fact that Jezza has a bit of unexpected free time on his hands and 'hey presto' – Jeremy Clarkson MP.

Such simple and outlandish (or should that be 'out-laddish?') calculations would be funny if it were not for the fact that Jeremy Clarkson has already threatened to stand for election to Parliament. In September 2013 he used the internet to tell his followers, 'I'm thinking I might stand in the next election as

an independent for Doncaster North, which is where I'm from. Thoughts?' he wrote.

A cruel twist of fate and a lack of hot food in a northern hotel now makes this question all the more interesting.

What are my thoughts?

This is, of course, all hypothetical, but there is a devil in me that would quite like to see Clarkson stand, and there is little doubt that he could give Ed Miliband a run for his money in a town where my family is also from. But would this really be good for democracy? Would it make or break Jeremy? The answer is that we will never know, but there is a broader question about celebrity politics and the power of populism.

With comedians like Al Murray, Russell Brand and others increasingly entering the political arena and posing as joke candidates, making 'mockumentaries' or attempting to make some sort of political intervention, our political reality seems to be becoming somewhat warped

or distorted: politics as a farcical parody of itself. Let's remember that the celebrities are themselves, whether they admit it or not, a form of social elite. Swapping one elite for another doesn't sound like a way to cure the political disengagement that appears so pronounced. So, Jeremy, just jump in your car and keep on driving….

On reflection

Jeremy Clarkson did not stand for Parliament. He was far too busy with his 'Grand Tour' to take on this role, and the traffic around Whitehall and Westminster is far too congested. Enough said.

27

After the storm: Failure, fallout and Farage

The earthquake has happened, the tremors have been felt, party leaders are dealing with the aftershocks and a number of fault lines in contemporary British and European politics have been exposed. Or have they? Were last month's European elections really as momentous as many social and political commentators seem to believe?

'Failure' is a glib and glum word. Its association with all things 'political' has become the dominant narrative of recent decades. Indeed, possibly the only surprising element of the success of the anti-European Union and protest parties last month was that they had not achieved success earlier. The share of the anti-EU and protest parties increased from 164 to 229 seats in the European Parliament (21.4% to 30.5%), and there is no doubt that European politics is set to become more fragile and unpredictable as a result. But surely this phenomenon represents not the failure of politics but the success of politics in the sense that widespread public frustration and concern has led to significant change. Put slightly differently, public opinion has changed

the balance of power within the political architecture, but without the shedding of blood.

Forgive me for daring to make such an unfashionable argument, but there is a second issue relating to the subsequent post-earthquake political 'settling' – that is, that the fallout needs to remember the turnout. This is a critical point. In many ways the people have not spoken as most of them stayed at home or simply had more interesting things to do with their time. Across Europe the average turnout was 43%, and in the UK this figure was down to 34.2%. The highest was Belgium, with 90% turnout with its non-enforced system of compulsory voting. Slovakia was at the bottom of the turnout charts, with just 13%, but this fact is in itself critical when placed against the danger that mainstream political parties will over-react towards the vocal minority.

To make such an argument is not in any way to undermine the need for the established political parties to listen and change. The rise of UKIP[1] in the UK, the Danish People's Party in Denmark, the Front National[2] in France, and the Freedom Party[3] in Austria – not to mention the far-left-wing parties in the form of Syriza in Greece or the Five Star Movement (Movimento 5 Stelle) in Italy – signals strong social currants that need to be channelled. The fluidity and energy of this current is reflected in Spain's new leftist party Podemos ('We Can'). This party did not even exist eight weeks ago, and yet it now has five seats in the European Parliament. Change has undoubtedly occurred, but the turnout was low, and these parties do not represent a coherent political group, ranging from parties with experience of government through to fringe groups and neo-fascists. They are generally a collection of 'None-of-the-Above' parties.

Enmity from the post-millennium global economic crisis has catapulted these 'None-of-the-Above' parties into office. The failure of the economic system created its own political fallout and the reverberations were felt in the recent European elections. If democracy works, then the mainstream groups in the European Parliament may well demonstrate that reform is possible and respond to voters; if democracy fails, then we'll be left with a terrible choice between more Europe or no Europe that populist and nationalistic parties will exploit in favour of the latter.

Such gloomy predictions lead me – almost inevitably – to a word about Nigel Farage,[4] the king of the 'None-of-the-Above' Party. My holiday reading last week (Cromer, North Norfolk, very nice due to the town being trapped in a time warp) was Sigmund Freud's *The Joke and Its Relation to the Unconscious* (1905). This is not a funny book, but when reading it I could not help but think of King Nigel. He is a joker, and for him 'every pub is a parliament', but this is both the asset and the problem. His jokes and banter are accessible to everyone and provide a sense of relief or release by opening up issues that were previously off-limits. For Freud this is the social role and deeper meaning of jokes and humour, but the problem for Farage is that he is generally regarded comically rather than seriously. He is a 'Spitting Image'[5] character that does not need a puppet.

On reflection

I sometimes feel slightly sorry for Nigel. I don't know why. He has the look of a slightly lost child who just wants to argue about anything just to get some attention, to be noticed. Nigel fears being insignificant, worthless, dismissed as a laughable fringe figure, and therefore his quest to humiliate 'the establishment' and to be the voice of 'the masses' is a strategy to prove, not just to those from whom he craves recognition, but also to himself, that he really exists. I cannot help but be reminded of Lord Owen's 'hubris syndrome', or more specifically the condition that R.D. Laing called 'ontological insecurity' in his book *The*

Divided Self (1960). He just wants to be friends with everyone (anyone) but everyone refuses to take him seriously … until now. Nigel has a new friend. His friend is called Donald. Donald will soon become the most unlikely President of the United States of America to ever hold the office. The joke suddenly appears to be on us as Nigel has the ear of the next American President while those who thought he (Donald not Nigel) was just a joke are suddenly starting to sweat. 'Nigel Farage may be the dumbest man ever to outwit the smartest politicians in his country', June Thomas suggested in June 2016, 'but that's exactly what he's done.' I'm just not sure whether this reflects 'a Farage factor' that the eponymous hero of anti-politics consciously seeks to foster, or whether it says far more about just how smart the smartest politicians really are.

28

Tony Benn was a true man of the people

The news that Tony Benn[1] has died at home at the age of 88 has stimulated intense reflection and discussion about his career. But when reading the obituaries and listening to the various television and radio discussions, I cannot help but think that too many commentators are missing the deep and enduring reason that Tony Benn really did become a national treasure. He listened, he spoke, and he connected with the public in a way that most contemporary politicians can only dream of.

It's too easy to focus on the obvious landmarks in a career that spanned well over half a century and overlook the deeper and richer features – often the personal and professional contradictions – that made Tony Benn such a remarkable man. And there is no doubt that he was remarkable. In a period when politicians are increasingly distrusted, reviled – even hated – he was regularly voted the most popular politician in the country. The burr of his voice, the look on his face, the cheeky smile, the smell of his pipe, the glint in his eye – these were the things that made Tony Benn such a special man, a man *of* politics but increasingly not *in* politics. Tony Benn's life seems defined by an almost stubborn desire to swim against the tide. His privileged education (Westminster School followed by the University of Oxford) was rejected at a stroke with the words: 'Education – still in progress' in his *Who's Who* entry in the early 1970s. He insisted on 'Tony Benn' rather than the full name, Anthony Wedgwood Benn, he had been given at birth, and later renounced his peerage. In June 2001 he famously left the House of Commons to 'spend more time on politics' – and in a sense this decision defined both his personal values and his approach to politics.

In a period when politicians take the temperature of the nation through focus groups and online surveys, Tony Benn spent his time talking to and listening to the public in a manner that is curiously rare among today's professional politicians. Indeed, in a period when the relationship between the governors and the governed is dominated by Twitter and blogs and conducted within a fairly narrow model of a market democracy, Tony Benn could often be dismissed (even slightly ridiculed) as a political dinosaur.

But that conclusion in itself would miss the great power he had to captivate an audience, to make people think and reflect on their assumptions, to inspire a sense of capacity and a belief in change for the better. He could unite social divides and talk sense to the senseless. As he demonstrated in relation to a range of issues – not least in the Stop the War movement – he was a man who would march *with* the public and was not afraid to stand *on* the barricades.

Politics for him was not a spectator sport but a vital element of the art of life. It was also an art form that took many forms, as demonstrated by the popularity of his diaries, his poetry, his one-man show and

his appearances at events as varied as pop festivals and school assemblies.

Put simply, he possessed the rare gift of being able to connect with the public in a manner that most contemporary politicians simply cannot do.

▬▬▬▬▬▬
On reflection
Watching Barack Obama in the final days of his presidency I could not help but remember the life of Tony Benn. Not an obvious link, you might think, and you would be correct. Until, that is, you think about the gift/skill/ power of political oratory. Tony Benn's golden charm revolved around a burring voice and an oratory style that could leap from a whispered secret to a shouting proclamation in the blink of an eye. Tony Benn was a charismatic orator with an almost theatrical presence. His oratory was natural but also, to some extent, carefully considered, often prepared and rarely off-key. Think, then, of the oratory of Barack Obama and the skills that allowed him to

captivate a nation. There is a certain 'sermon-esque' pattern or style to Obama's speeches. Common ground is identified, the nature of a challenge discussed, practical illustrations are used to add weight to the abstract, the scale of the challenge emphasised only to then lift the audience up with a crescendo of self-belief *and* collective belief. As with Tony Benn, it would be a mistake to seek Obama's oratory as unscripted, but it would also be a mistake to overlook the freedom of the speech, the lack of notes, the willingness to break into song or to pause for effect. There is an eloquence of delivery, a personal warmth, and a connection with both the past and the future. But there is something else beyond the oratory that takes us into the sphere of sensory democracy. Watch Obama walk on to a stage – see the smiles, the waves, the mouthed messages to friends identified in the audience, note the handshakes, the unbuttoning of the jacket, the smile.... Tony Benn was very different, but he had his props and his techniques – the smell of his pipe, the drop of his head, his quizzical look, a glint in his eye ... the delivery of the words in terms

of tone, the lyricism, is as important as the words themselves. Time has in no way dulled Tony Benn's political legacy; if anything, the rise of a scripted, professionalised, digitally re-mastered, staccato rhetoric has made the gift for political oratory an even rarer and therefore more precious commodity.

29

Dear Russell Brand: On the politics of comedy and disengagement

Out-Paxo'ing Paxman might be one thing, but it is quite another to make the leap from comedian to serious political commentator. Russell Brand claims to derive his authority to speak out on the state of democratic politics from a source beyond 'this pre-existing paradigm' that can only really relate to his position as an (in)famous comedian. The problem with this claim is that – as many comedians have themselves admitted – in recent years political comedy and satire has derived great pleasure and huge profits from promoting corrosive cynicism rather than healthy scepticism.

Russ,

I'm writing to let you know that when people talk about you I usually feel a dull thud in my stomach and my eyes involuntarily glaze over. Your relationship with a shallow, generally brash, and often abusive contribution to the cult of modern celebrity represents a lot of what is wrong with the world. Therefore, I was expecting your guest editorship[1] of the *New Statesman* and your interview with Jeremy Paxman to be similarly inane and egotistical affairs. And yet – and I really hate to admit this – your arguments possessed a certain depth and intensity that left me strangely impressed. Have you really just been playing the fool for all this time?

To be honest poor Jeremy was not on good form. (I wonder if there is some reverse Samson-like spell at play that *weakens* his powers as he gets increasingly hirsute.) However, your opening position about not deriving your authority from 'some pre-existing paradigm' but from an alternative source of legitimacy made me wince as I reflected on the broader contemporary role of comedians and satirists *vis-à-vis* political disengagement and apathy. In recent months there has been a groundswell of opinion *against* political comedy and satire as evidence grows of its social impact and generally negative social influence (especially over the young). 'The whole comic-entertainment species is under-attack', John Walsh recently argued in *The Independent*, 'there's a groundswell of opinion that too many stand-ups are smug, over-paid, potty-mouthed enemies of the common people.' Janice Turner recently observed in *The Times* that there was 'a tang of the school bully in the satirists' barbs', and highlighted Sandy Toksvig's recent description of Michael Gove on the BBC's 'The News Quiz' as a 'foetus in a jar', before Toksvig added that Gove 'had a face that makes even the most pacifist of people reach for the shovel.'

You might think this is all just good fun and that politicians deserve everything they get. But isn't there a deeper tension at play here that makes your recent contribution somewhat at odds with the general direction of your profession? John Morreal, a leading international authority on the social impact and role of humour, has written that 'satirists have justified their trade by saying that satire corrects the shortcomings being laughed at', but what if political comedy and satire actually contributes to and reinforces the shortcomings that are being laughed at? Mick

Billig, author of *Laughter and Ridicule* (2005), also questions whether political comedy and satire are *always* a 'good' thing, especially when 'the message more readily spread is skepticism.' It is at exactly this point that comedians and writers scoff at the suggestion that anything has changed, and without fail remind me of the historical contribution of writers such as Daniel Defoe and Jonathan Swift or caricaturists such as James Gillray and Thomas Rowlandson. Yet such nostalgic reflections overlook the simple fact that the world has changed, and so has political comedy and satire. The rise of the 24/7 media machine[2] with ever more pressure on ratings combined with the rich pickings offered by mass market DVDs and large-scale arena tours has fuelled a transition best captured in David Denby's notion of the change 'from satire to snark'. The latter being snide, aggressive, personalised: 'it seizes on any vulnerability or weakness it can find – a slip of the tongue, a sentence not quite up-to-date, a bit of flab, a flash of boob, a blotch, a wrinkle, an open fly, an open mouth, a closed mouth', but all designed to reinforce the general view that politics is failing and politicians are bastards. In a recent

piece in the *Financial Times* (a paper not known for fun and jokes), John Lloyd felt forced to ask 'Has political satire gone too far?'

Satirists often say that their trade is necessary to excoriate the decisions or prick the egos of the powerful: that they are necessary to the functioning of a democratic society; that by wit they can say what commentary and news and even polemic cannot … [and yet] Satire that is polemic can turn ugly and authoritarian when it has powerful media behind it.

Just think of the changing nature of political comedy and satire in the second half of the 20th century. In 1950 the then Chairman of the BBC, Lord Simon, blocked the broadcasting of a light comedy about a fictional Labour minister and nuclear secrets on the basis that 'this is not the moment in world history to weaken respect for democracy by jokes of this kind.' The BBC, he claimed, had a duty 'to do what we can to maintain and strengthen democracy and the belief in democratic values.' Fast forward through the path-breaking satire of 'That Was

The Week That Was' in the 1960s, through to the slightly sharper 'Not The Nine O'Clock News' and 'Yes, Minister' in the 1970s and 1980s, through to 'Spitting Image' in the late 1980s and 1990s and the weekly politician-bashing of 'Have I Got News For You' from the 1990s into the noughties, and finally to programmes like 'The Thick Of It' and 'In The Loop' with their docu-entertainment style and non-stop expletives. In thinking that political comedy and satire is heading in the wrong direction, I am by no means alone. Jon Stewart, presenter of 'The Daily Show' and arguably *the* leading American satirist, has argued 'if satire's purpose was social change then we are not picking a very effective avenue.' Stewart's 'Rally to Restore Sanity' on 30 October 2010 attracted around a quarter of a million people and was designed to provide a venue for members of the public to be heard above what Stewart described as the more vocal and extreme 15-20% of the American population. Debates continue to rage as to whether this was a spoof event or an attempt to make a serious point about the state of the American media – 'the country's 24-hour politico-pundit[2] perpetual

panic "conflict-inator"' – but at the very least Stewart recognised the power of political comedy and satire to frame political debate and public attitudes.

On this side of the Atlantic, concerns have been raised by Rory Bremner, Armando Iannucci, Eddie Izzard and David Baddiel about the increasingly aggressive and destructive nature of modern humour – and this brings me back to your recent entry to the political fray. I believe in change. I want genuine alternatives. But I want to know what role political comedy and satire might play in producing this new way of organising our society and facing the common challenges we face. How can political comedy and satire help us engage with that widespread feeling of disconnection and then channel it into a new beginning? I ask these questions because – like you – I am angry, because for me politics *is* real. There was no Eton or Oxbridge in my life, and I have an acute grasp that politics is not just some peripheral thing that I turn up to, as you put it, 'once in a while to a church fete for'. Politics defined me and it defined you. It matters. My question is really whether satire

continues to play a positive social role that helps explain just why politics matters. If, as I think, your profession is generally destructive – politically concerned with 'joking *apart*' rather than pulling together – surely this undermines your claim to an 'alternative' source of authority beyond the 'pre-existing paradigm'?

One last thing, the way you stuffed Paxo was exquisite – the line about the 'lachrymose sentimentality' of his 'emotional porn' was, if anything, a little *too* good – and yet there was just one moment when you let your mask slip. Do you remember? Right at the beginning, when Paxman jabbed you about your right to edit a political magazine? The jump between your feigned ignorance of 'the typical criteria' for an editorial invitation and your leap to a comparison with Boris Johnson seemed just a touch too quick, too pre-prepared: "he has crazy hair, quite a good sense of humour, doesn't know much about politics." The problem with this comparison with the King Clown of British politics is that everyone knows that Boris may be foolish, but he is no fool. He is, in fact, a deceptively polished über-politician who uses buffoonery and comedy as a political self-preservation mechanism. You also seem to have pushed buffoonery and comedy to new limits but (unlike Boris) you have never actually dared to step into the political arena. I just wonder if it's a little too easy to heckle from the sidelines, to carp at the weaknesses and failings of others, to suggest that there are simple solutions to complex problems and to enjoy power and influence within society but without ever shouldering any direct responsibility. Apologies if I am being just a tad too serious and boring about these issues!

All the best, Matt

▪▪▪▪▪▪▪▪▪

On reflection

One of the most depressing elements of writing political posts or letters is that no one ever replies! Take this letter to Russell Brand, for example. I'd have thought that a 'bad-boy-turned-good-boy-turned-political-guru' would definitely have responded to my little note, but the postman's sack was always

(metaphorically) empty when it came to Russ. This might reflect Russ' (I'm sure that, as a pen pal of his, I am OK calling him 'Russ') volte face – or should that be 'volte farce' – when he decided to suddenly tell his squillions of young fans that they should, in fact, vote after all. The fact that he changed his mind after the deadline for electoral registration understandably disappointed quite a few people, but R (I'm sure that, as a very special pen pal of his, I am OK calling him 'R'). But it was OK because he later explained his change of mind: 'Ultimately what I feel, is that by not removing the Tories, through an unwillingness to participate in the "masquerade of democracy", I was implicitly expecting the most vulnerable people in society to pay the price on my behalf while I pondered alternatives in luxury.' *R – that's fine with me. No need to write. M*

▪▪▪▪▪▪▪▪▪

30

Foolish, but no fool: Boris Johnson and the art of politics

It would be too easy – and also quite mistaken – to define Boris Johnson as little more than the clown of British politics; more accurate to define him as a deceptively polished and calculating über-politician.

The news that receives the least attention arguably tells us the most about contemporary politics and society. Therefore, the fact a recent Court of Appeal decision – that it was in the 'public interest' for people to know Boris Johnson had fathered a child in 2009 – was met with little or no public outcry or debate pricked my attention (a poor choice of phrase, I admit). Philandering politicians are rarely popular, and in this case the British judicial system seemed intent on underlining the manner in which Boris Johnson's 'recklessness' raised serious questions about his fitness for public office. And yet there appears to be one set of rules for Boris and a completely different set for all other politicians. Social attitude surveys consistently reveal that the public expects *higher* moral standards and behaviour from its elected representatives than from any other profession. The public are, however,

far more forgiving when it comes to Boris. A poll last week found that over three-quarters of respondents disagreed that the revelation about him secretly fathering a child would make them any less inclined to vote for him in a general election.

As Paul Goodman, editor of the ConservativeHome website,[1] said, 'In modern politics unconventional politicians are judged by different rules from conventional ones. Boris is part of a small band of unconventional politicians.' However, the danger of this interpretation is that it risks adding to 'the cult of Boris' in a way that simply overlooks the carefully manufactured foppishness. The head scratching dufferishness, slightly confused – even deranged – look of a person who doesn't seem to know where they have been, where they are, or where they are going is little more than an act. An act, more importantly, that veils the existence of an incredibly sharp, astute and calculating politician.

The public may therefore be entertained by Boris Johnson's antics, and he certainly adds a dash of colour to an increasingly grey and soulless profession, but there is value in looking a little deeper at someone who covets the very highest office. I'm not actually bothered if 'ping pong is coming home' or if he 'mildly sandpapered something somebody said' (and was sacked from *The Times* as a result), or about any of the other misdemeanours and indiscretions that form part of his personal or political history. I am, however, interested in understanding his capacity for political survival and isolating what distinguishes Boris from his contemporaries. The answer lies in a combination of charisma and guile.

Charisma is, as Max Weber[2] famously argued, a critical element of political leadership despite the fact that it is almost impossible to measure, define or quantify. The simple fact is that – like him or loathe him – Boris Johnson is charismatic. I remember watching him address a large public audience in Bromley during the summer of 2010 as part of the Mayor of London's 'Outreach' initiative. What was immediately striking was the manner in which he captivated the audience. They were entranced to the extent that strident political opponents seemed disarmed by his rhetoric, energy and emotion. He knew how to play the audience like a conductor on a podium, and play them he did. Yet charisma on its own is not enough, and just as Machiavelli argued that a true leader needed the strength of a lion and the cunning of a fox, so, too, must charisma be matched by guile.

One central element of Boris Johnson's political arsenal rests in answering every question not with an answer but with a joke or an anecdote – guile in the form of distraction. The hot gymnasium in a large Bromley secondary school therefore provided a master-class in political oratory and theatre but little in terms of 'Questions and Answers with the Mayor of London'. The critical point, however, was that nobody in the audience seemed to care. They had come – from all walks of life and from all parts of the political spectrum – to see 'the Boris Show', and that's what they got. As I loitered by the exit to the gym at the end of the event I asked one or two questioners how they felt about the manner in which Boris had dealt with their questions (obliquely in one case, not at all in the other): the responses – "Isn't he lovely!" and "I don't care – it was good fun!" – left me strangely puzzled and downcast. The point I am trying to make is that Boris Johnson is no fool. He may often be foolish in terms of how he behaves or what he says, but he is no fool. His buffoonery provides a rather odd but strangely effective political self-preservation mechanism that often distracts opponents or inquisitors from the more important issues of the day.

Defining Boris Johnson's statecraft[3] as little more than *politics as the art of distraction* may be unfair; suggesting that the public is unable to see beyond the japes of an old Etonian may be equally unfair. But as more and more people comment on Boris' Teflon-like ability to shrug off personal, political and sexual controversies, I thought it might be useful to try to make something stick.

On reflection

Can there ever have been a post that demanded updating! Boris is no fool, and the bluffery bluster is little more than a distraction machine but I – like many others – always thought it had limits in the sense that at some point he would come 'a serious cropper', as we say 'up North'. The great Brexit text mess underlines both the calculating approach and ambition of Boris. After weeks of flip-flopping about whether he was pro 'leave' or 'remain', he made a desperate pitch to become prime minister when David Cameron announced his resignation in June 2016, only to be foiled by Michael Gove who told the world that he did not think Boris was up to the job (and then announced that he would therefore be standing). Even in politics, such open treachery is rare, and 'doing a Gove' has entered the political lexicon for stabbing someone in the back (Gove has now apologised and asked for forgiveness). Boris withdrew from the competition to lead the Conservative Party, David Cameron allegedly sent a barbed text saying 'You should have stuck with me, mate' (according to Tim Shipman's aptly titled book *All Out War*) and Michael Gove was sacked by Theresa May within hours of her becoming Prime Minister. But not even the most proficient professor of the art of politics could have predicted 'the Boris bounce' as May astounded observers by appointing him Foreign Secretary. It may well be, however, that May herself is playing the joker in the sense that the Foreign Office is not the mighty office of state it once was, Brexit negotiations will fall to the new Brexit Department, and there is a basic logic for keeping a popular 'big beast' within government rather than causing trouble on the backbenches. With foreign commitments, lots of luncheons and spotted dicks to delight even the most boring dinners, Boris will be close, but not *too* close. This is also his chance to prove he can be a serious statesman and not just a joker in the pack. Only time will tell who ends up looking the fool.

31

Remembering Margaret Thatcher

Can it really be almost a quarter of a century since one of the most defining moments of my own personal political history? I can still remember the day as if it were yesterday. An A-level Politics seminar on the fifth floor of Swindon College, 28 November 1990, a bright and clear day, and suddenly the door bursts open and someone screams,

"She's gone! It's over! She's gone!" Exactly *who* had gone and what was *over* were not immediately obvious to me, but in a strange way they didn't need to be because at a deeper level, what was obvious from the reactions of everybody around me was that a distinct chapter in British political history had ended. Two decades on, and as a Professor of Politics I clearly have a much sharper awareness of exactly *who* Mrs Thatcher was, and what was thought to be *over* (or *not over*, as the case proved to be) in terms of a distinct approach to governing. But the announcement of her death takes me back to that seminar room and to that strange feeling that a distinct chapter in British political history had – once again – ended.

But what can I say that has not already been said about this grocer's daughter? What can I write that will separate this obituary from

the countless others that are at this moment being written (or – more accurately – rapidly retrieved from pre-prepared files)? The answer to these questions lies not in outlining the contours of Mrs Thatcher's political career (an already well-furrowed literary terrain), but in teasing out exactly why her approach to politics provoked such strong reactions, and how she managed to cast such a long shadow over the past, present and future of British politics. Approached in this manner at least three interlinked issues deserve brief comment – her ideology, her style and her vulnerability.

First and possibly foremost, Margaret Thatcher forged a new relationship between the state and the market. Having witnessed the trials and tribulations of the Heath government in the mid-1970s and then the 'Winter of Discontent' in 1978/79, Mrs

Thatcher was adamant that the relationship between the state and the market had to change. From reforming the state to reducing the power of the trade unions, from privatisation to economic reform, and from European affairs to selling off council houses, Mrs Thatcher undoubtedly shifted the political economy of Britain in ways that subsequent prime ministers have sought to modify or amend but not significantly alter. Indeed, it is possible to argue that a post-Thatcherite consensus appears to exist in a thread that runs through Major, Blair, Brown and Cameron. Whether this is viewed as a 'good' or 'bad' thing is, for the moment, secondary to the fact that Mrs Thatcher's legacy has cast a shadow both far and wide. If her policies were distinctive, then so, too, was her uncompromising political style. The 'Iron Lady' was a conviction politician in the sense that she believed in the capacity of her political philosophy and economic convictions to deliver positive social change. There was no middle way; you were either with her or against her. From her 'The lady's not for turning' speech to the Conservative Party in October 1980 through to her European Union rebate negotiations, Mrs Thatcher was in many ways the original 'Ronseal politician' – to steal a coalition phrase – in the sense that her rhetoric was generally backed up by subsequent political reality.

There is, however, a need to dig a little deeper. An obituary should expose the essence of a person and not simply repeat their achievements (or failures). To highlight Mrs Thatcher's ideology or style – even to dissect the various subsequent forms of Thatcherism – are hardly new additions to a congested historical canvas. The twist or barb in the tail of this obituary is therefore not a focus on Mrs Thatcher the politician, but on Mrs Thatcher the person *qua* politics. Framed in this manner what one achieves is a unique perspective on a quite remarkable but possibly isolated and vulnerable woman. To describe the 'Iron Lady' as vulnerable might appear to some readers as an almost ridiculous statement, but even the mighty Achilles had a weak heel. Indeed, if – as I will argue – Mrs Thatcher exhibited three potential vulnerabilities in her life, then it is possible to use these to further underline her remarkable career and achievements.

Mrs Thatcher was a woman who succeeded in a man's world. She became an MP in 1959, the first woman to lead a major British political party in 1975, and the first female Prime Minister in 1979. There is little doubt that in some ways being a women brought advantages when faced with a political party that had overwhelmingly been educated in single-sex public schools and was therefore ill-prepared to deal with a powerful woman. But it also brought with it a sense of exceptionalism and difference. A second source of vulnerability stemmed from the fact that Mrs Thatcher was not 'one of them'. Born the daughter of a grocery shop owner – indeed, being brought up in the flat above the shop – she was not born into the 'great and the good' British political establishment. Resting between the lines of almost every political biography of Mrs Thatcher is a sense that she was always *in* the Conservative Party but never quite *part* of the Conservative

Party, never quite accepted or respected by Tory grandees or elements of the political establishment. This is a critical issue as her *outsider-within* status arguably helps explain her style of governing and her almost clinical approach to defining friends and enemies. The final element of vulnerability has, I would argue, become clearest since her departure from frontline politics. Since leaving the House of Commons at the 1992 General Election – saying that this would allow her more freedom to speak her mind – what has been most striking is the manner in which she generally refrained from heckling from the political sidelines. Her illness may have played some role in this, but I sense there was also a degree of social and political isolation, a sense that she no longer fitted in, a frustration that her 'there is no such thing as society' speech was always taken out of context and used against her, or a fear that no one would want to hear what she had to say. I could be wrong, but deep down I can't help but think that maybe the 'Iron Lady' was a little softer than many of us understood.

On reflection

Margaret Thatcher died of a stroke in London on 8 April 2013 at the age of 87. She was staying at the Ritz Hotel at the time in order to recover from surgery, and to some extent such a grand hotel was a fitting place for such a grand lady of British politics to pass away. I had no time for Thatcher's political views, but that doesn't stop me acknowledging the achievements of a woman who redefined what was (and to some extent still remains) a man's world. It is therefore somewhat fitting that in 2017 the *Dictionary of National Biography* added her to this authoritative reference work with more space than anybody else apart from Shakespeare and Elizabeth I. Eclipsing records for Queen Victoria, Winston Churchill and Henry VIII, historian David Cannadine's biography of Britain's first female Prime Minister is the third longest of the 60,000-plus entries in the 72m-word work. Editors wait four years after the death of a notable figure in order to assess whether their legacy makes them worthy of a place in what is, in effect, the canon of British public life. Cannadine provides a commanding review of Thatcher's life that also captures the subtle side of her personality and politics that is often overlooked. There is, of course, no way of avoiding the combative side of her political impact, and Cannadine concludes, 'There are times when nations may need rough treatment. For good and for ill, Thatcher gave Britain plenty of it.'

32

Trump that: The failure and farce of American politics

There is something very odd and bizarrely impressive about Donald Trump's approach to democratic politics: it is quite obviously undemocratic. Indeed, if anything, his campaign is fuelled by anti-political sentiment and populist slogans. It's strong stuff. So

strong that it deserves to be recognised in the form of a new and eponymous political ideology: 'Trump-ism'. I've tried *so* hard not to write a piece about 'you know who' Trump. I really have! It's just too obvious and to some extent just too easy, but as his popularity in the US appears to grow, so does my concern about who might actually hold the most powerful political office on the planet.

But in many ways my concern has nothing to do with partisanship, less to do with politics and everything to do with democracy.

I don't care what party Mr Trump belongs to; I know that politics is a worldly art, but it strikes me that Donald is not a democrat.

Indeed, so far 'democrat Donald' appears distinctly undemocratic and strangely anti-political (in his approach to securing the very

highest elected political office in the world). You might respond with the common refrain 'only in America', but the rise of anti-political populist politicians and parties seems a far more widespread phenomenon. And yet there is something stunningly brutish about 'Trump-ism' (every good politician wants to be associated with an eponymous ideology, so let's just make him happy).

Let us compare the concept of democracy with the ideology of Trump-ism.

Democracy is an institutionalised form of conflict resolution: nothing more, nothing less. We all agree to have limits placed on some freedoms and to contribute some of our money to the common pot in return for the freedom to live in a society in which certain basic standards and expectations are upheld. Put slightly differently, democratic politics is about the art of compromise. We all give a bit, some people might get a little bit, but overall the great beauty of democracy is that it provides a way for increasingly diverse and interdependent societies to live together. It is not perfect, it is messy, and failure and disappointment are, to some extent, inevitable because no system can please all of the people all of the time.

Trump-ism, as far as I can understand it, appears almost the opposite of democracy. It seems to deny the existence of basic limits, it seems set on antagonism rather than resolution, it seems to philosophise with the subtly of a sledgehammer. More worryingly, it seems to rejoice in the identification of 'others' who are to blame for the ills of modern America, it promotes a politics of fear and a politics of pessimism, and it promises simple and pain-free solutions to complex problems (when there are no simple solutions). Deal-making and compromise is the grease and the oil that allows democratic politics to work, and yet Trump-ism seems

to reject such mechanisms as signs of weakness.

And yet, the politician who refuses to compromise is not a democrat. He or she is an authoritarian, the antithesis of a democrat. (Question of the Week to the Reader: 'Trump-ism is little more than authoritarianism dressed in a thin veneer of democratic politics.' Discuss at leisure.) But as David Brooks suggested recently in *The New York Times*,[1] there is something deeper, possibly more dangerous, at play. In recent weeks the Trump campaign has in several cities promoted a strong public response, especially by sections of society that feel potentially isolated or threatened by Trump-ism. The response of 'democrat Donald' (as opposed to, say, 'Comrade Corbyn' in the UK) when a protestor interrupted him mid-speech in Nevada – "I'd like to punch him in the face" – suggests a bludgeoning approach to politics or a heady mix of hubris syndrome and schoolboy bully that combines to create Trump-ism.

The real problem with Trump-ism as a model of democracy rests not with the man, but with the public that cannot see the dangerous game they are unwittingly playing. Psychologists have for several decades revealed the manner in which normally calm and rational individuals can be caught up in the emotions of a crowd or a mob to the extent that they lose their sense of perspective. In Nevada the crowd roared in approval and so – never one to disappoint – Trump told them, "You know what they used to do to guys like that when they were in a place like this? They'd be carried out on a stretcher, folks."

Punching and stretchers are exactly what democracy is intended to avoid, but Trump-ism seems bound to a masculine and testosterone-fuelled politics that appeals to a very specific type of individual. In this regard the research of the political scientist Matthew MacWilliams[2] possibly tells us more about the principles and values of Trump-ism than Trump himself – the only single statistically significant variable that predicts whether a voter supports Trump is not race, income or education, but authoritarianism. 'That's right, Trump's electoral strength – and his staying power – have been buoyed, above all, by Americans with authoritarian inclinations', MacWilliams concludes, 'and because of the prevalence of authoritarians in the American electorate, among Democrats as well as Republicans, it's very possible that Trump's fan base will continue to grow.'

This really is the failure and farce of American politics. Trump that!

On reflection

It's hard to believe that since this post was originally penned in April 2016 Trump has actually been elected President of the United States of America. To some extent this sense of disbelief – a sentiment that I am by no means alone in feeling – is about the man himself, his personality, his politics. But it is arguably more about the nature of a society that is willing to elect an individual that in many ways appears totally unaware of the nature of democratic politics. Bellicose pronouncements about Muslims and Mexicans form just one element of a dangerous tendency to demonise 'the other' as the default response to any social challenge. Clinicians and observers have already analysed his speeches and behaviour, and raised fears of narcissistic personality disorder. "I am your voice", Trump told his supporters at the Republican National Convention before outlining a number of problems facing America. "I alone can fix it", he proceeds to proclaim. But what does the election of this man suggest about the psychological state of the American public?

33

Mad politics

If you are reading this blog, then you've obviously survived 'Blue Monday'. That is, the day in the third week of January when suicide levels tend to peak and demands for counselling rocket as a result of post-Christmas debt, dashed New Year resolutions and the inevitable sense that this year is actually unlikely to be much different than the last. The recent publication by the coalition government, *Priorities for Essential Change*

in Mental Health, underlines the fact that mental health is likely to become the defining problem of the 21st century. But what does the politics of mental health – and particularly the mental health of our politicians – tell us about the state of our society?

It is estimated that approximately 450 million people worldwide have a mental health problem. Nearly 60 million Americans suffer from some form of mental illness and, in the UK, the Office for National Statistics estimates that one in four British adults experiences at least one diagnosable mental health problem in any one year. This might range from anxiety and depression to more extreme forms of psychosis or schizophrenia, but whatever the condition, mental illness is scary, painful and exhausting. It's also woefully under-funded. 'There is a substantial gap', the opening line of the latest version of the

World Health Organization's *Mental Health Atlas* states, 'between the burden caused by mental disorders and the resources available to prevent and treat them.' Even today, only one penny is spent on mental health for every pound spent by the NHS, and mental health services seem to have borne the brunt of the 'age of austerity'.

What makes the experience of mental health arguably far worse is the social stigma and almost ridicule that often accompanies even the merest hint of a mental health condition. Those lucky enough to have supportive friends and family will generally find that recovery is not only possible, but that the whole experience may also have unexpected positive side effects in the sense that experiencing the lows of life can add new vitality, colour and understanding to even the simplest things. *Sunbathing in the Rain* by

Gwyneth Lewis (2002) is undoubtedly one of the best books I've ever read. But those who lack supportive families, friends or lots of money frequently find themselves shunted between a bewildering range of services and the decline into unemployment, homelessness or worse can be rapid.

But what about those individuals whose roles in society are seemingly *designed* to undermine their mental health? The work–life variables associated with mental breakdown are relatively clear from the rich seam of literature in the field of organisational psychology – high stress and unrealistic expectations, divided and incompatible loyalties, a high-blame low-trust work environment, living away from home, long hours, an adversarial atmosphere, unpredictable hours, precarious employment, low levels of public regard, etc – and in many ways the role of a modern politician ticks every one of these boxes. Therefore, it is not surprising that stress levels among politicians tend to be incredibly high. The life of an MP is frequently associated with poor decision-making, ruined health, family break-up and the occasional bizarre walk on Clapham Common. For those MPs with young children, ministerial duties and constituencies many miles from London, the pressure can be intense – even brutal.

And yet, how MPs manage their mental wellbeing and cope with the pressures of their profession remains a largely hidden topic. This is reflected in the manner in which periods of poor mental health are generally admitted only in the past tense in memoirs and autobiographies. John Biffen, a Cabinet minister under Margaret Thatcher, suffered from debilitating depression for most of his career, but this fact was only recently revealed six years after his death in his posthumous autobiography, *Semi-Detached* (2013). More recently, Jack Straw, former Foreign Secretary, has written of his secret battle with depression but – as Alastair Campbell has explained – it remains incredibly difficult for a British politician to stand up and admit to being human.

But it's not only the adversarial culture of Westminster and Whitehall that explains this reluctance to speak out; the public understanding of mental health issues remains very poor and the dominant narrative, perpetuated by the media, is that 'mad = bad'.

The 14 June 2012 is therefore likely to go down as a significant moment in parliamentary history as a number of MPs used a debate on mental health in the House of Commons to discuss their own psychological problems. Charles Walker MP described himself as a 'practising fruitcake' while outlining a battle he has been fighting with obsessive compulsive disorder for more than three decades, Kevan Jones MP admitted to having suffered from bouts of depression, and two female MPs (Sarah Woolaston and Andrea Leadsom) also discussed their experience of post-natal depression. If we add Jack Straw and the Labour MP John Woodcock, who last December admitted to suffering from depression, this makes a grand total of six out of 650 MPs who have acknowledged their own mental health challenges.

In reality, the available data on mental health, in stressful occupations in particular, would suggest that a far higher number of MPs will actually have experienced (or be experiencing) some form of mental disorder. Obviously it is up to the individual to decide on the boundaries between their private life and public duty – but what's really interesting is that we actually know very little about the mental health of our politicians. David Owen has written about the 'hubris syndrome' and the poor decisions made by those intoxicated with power, but for most politicians politics is – if we are honest – generally quite dull. It is often just the 'slow boring of hard boards'.

There are, however, signs of progress. In 2007, Section 141 of the Mental Health Act – whereby MPs who were incapacitated through mental illness could be automatically removed from the House of Commons after six months – was considered and then *retained* by Parliament. This example of

institutionalised intolerance and inequality was repealed in February last year with the passing of the 2013 Mental Health (Discrimination) Act. More recently still, a small budget has been agreed within the Palace of Westminster to cover the costs of counselling for MPs who are understandably reluctant to seek help within their constituency.

Even so, the stigma surrounding mental health remains acute in Parliament. The hook, twist or barb in this argument is that recent surveys suggest that significant sections of the public would not vote for a political candidate who admitted to previously suffering from mental health problems. And yet, at the very same time, the public constantly demand that they want MPs to be 'normal' people – an adjective generally followed by the phrase 'like you and me' – but normal people suffer from mental health problems. The tension is obvious, and as a result, the secrecy and stigma surrounding mental health continues. It's mad politics at its worst.

On reflection

The previous 'On reflection' concluded by asking 'what does the election of this man suggest about the psychological state of the American public?', and in many ways this provides a link to the focus of this post on the mental wellbeing of politicians. I am sure there is a strong link between the psychological health of a society and the health of democracy. The relationship between these two elements is unlikely to be direct, linear or easy to see, but I am confident an as yet under-examined relationship exists. Think about what's happened in the world since this post was written in February 2014 – the rise of nationalist populism, the UK's decision to leave the European Union, the election of Donald Trump plus a more insidious general decline in social civility and mutual respect. Might there not be some relationship with the rising levels of mental ill health across exactly those countries where these political phenomena have surfaced? There is almost certainly a 'chicken-and-egg' sort of process in existence whereby declining mental health creates a political context in which the claims

and promises of populists achieve more traction. Take the US as an example. Since the 1980s all the main mental health indicators have been pointing in the wrong direction. The use of anti-depressants and anti-anxiety drugs has increased massively which, to some extent, reflects increased feelings of loneliness and isolation among large sections of the public, particularly among older generations. While younger people are displaying increasing levels of depression and anxiety, they are also displaying the continuing rise of attention deficit hyperactivity disorder.[1] These disorders (and in some cases, the drugs prescribed to treat them) may also contribute to the continuing rise of chronic health problems such as obesity.[2] 'Mental health issues such as unhappiness and anger can often lead to scapegoating, sexism, racism, xenophobia and many of the behaviours seen during the election season', Bruce Lee has argued, '[But] In the long run, blaming others does not solve anything and just make things worse.' This focus on social psychology and individual psychology flows into broader debates about the psychological impact of being part of the increasingly large 'precariat' in a world of short-term, self-employed, unprotected, mobile working, etc, and its likely long-term impact on mental health. It's mad politics.

▬▬▬▬

Banksy's 'Mild Mild West', Gloucester Road, Bristol

34

Shake your chains: Politics, poetry and protest

This year, 21 March marks not just the beginning of the Political Studies Association's 2016 Annual Conference in Brighton, but also World Poetry Day. Formally ratified by UNESCO in 1999, but with antecedents that date back to the middle of the 20th century, World Poetry Day's aim is to promote the reading, writing, publishing and teaching of poetry throughout the world and, as the UNESCO session declaring the Day says, to 'give fresh recognition and impetus to national, regional and international poetry movements.' But is there a link between poetry and politics that deserves fresh recognition?

One of Sir Bernard Crick's last pieces of published scholarship was a chapter in the *Oxford Handbook of British Politics* entitled 'Politics and the Novel'. The argument was simple and clear: novels provide a powerful mode of political expression due to the manner in which they allow writers to re-imagine a different world, to suggest alternative ways of living or highlight the risks of taking democracy for granted. But what arguments might a similar chapter on 'Politics

and Poetry' take? How would a scholar even begin to unravel, let alone prove, the existence of relationships and influences that trespass across traditional disciplinary and professional boundaries? (Why do I persist in setting myself such challenging questions?)

The only thought that comes to my mind as a starting point for engaging with these questions is Mario Cuomo's powerful slogan that all politicians 'campaign in poetry, but govern in prose', and I can understand the contrast between the emotive and free-floating nature of speechmaking compared to the Procrustean reality of actually trying to govern and 'the slow boring through hard boards' that Weber emphasised with almost poetical form. But I'm scratching the surface of something far deeper … and then I see the link that allows me to drill down into not only the 'poetry/prose' distinction that Cuomo highlights, but also in relation to Crick's work on the power of the novel. This drilling down releases two veins of thought. The first can only be explained through the use of a section of David Orr's wonderful essay 'The Politics of Poetry' (2008) in which he writes,

> Shortly before Ohio's Democratic primary, Tom Buffenbarger, the head of the machinists' union and a supporter of Hillary Clinton, took to the stage at a Clinton rally in Youngstown to lay the wood to Barack Obama. "Give me a break!" snarled Buffenbarger, "I've got news for all the latte-drinking, Prius-driving, Birkenstock-wearing, trust fund babies crowding in to hear him speak! This guy won't last a round against the Republican attack machine." And then the union rep delivered his *coup de grace*: "He's a poet, not a fighter!"

Ouch.

The implication was Cuomo-esque in the sense that Obama was being framed as someone who could play the game of winning votes but did not have the mettle for the worldly art of politics. Of course, he did win, and he has demonstrated an impressive capacity for 'playing the game' while maintaining a relatively clear moral position and vision. In many ways, the great skill of Obama rests not just with his clarity of thought but with his oratory skills: he connects with large sections of 'the public' within and beyond the US. But does this connection have anything to do with poetry?

I think it does ... but not in the sense of 'being a poet' in the big 'P' sense of the term (learned, professional, somewhat aloof, etc) but in a small 'p' sense that is actually far easier to comprehend in relation to the role and skills of professional politicians. 'The Presidency is not merely an administrative office. That's the least of it', Franklin D. Roosevelt once argued. 'It is more than an engineering job, efficient or inefficient. It is pre-eminently a place of moral leadership. All our great presidents were leaders of thought at times when certain historic ideas in the life of the nation had to be clarified.' Roosevelt captures not only the sense of political leaders acting as lightning rods for public frustration, or figureheads to rally around in times of crisis; but someone who claims to offer direction, a set of imagined relationships and certainty in an era of increasing risk. Roosevelt therefore points towards a deeper emotive bond between the politician and the public. And it was exactly this emotive, affecting relationship that Percy Bysshe Shelley pinpointed when he wrote,

> Poets are the hierophants of an unapprehended inspiration; the mirrors of the gigantic shadows which futurity casts upon the present; the words which express what they understand not.... Poets are the unacknowledged legislators of the world.

But if poetry can act as a form of expression in the relationship between the governors and the governed, then it must also act as a tool for the masses and not just the elites. And it does, and has and continues to fulfil this role. Poetry as a mechanism of protest, as a call to arms, has a distinguished history that has in recent years evolved and exploded into a rich repertoire of online and offline forms that broaden into the realm of the spoken word, hip-hop, rap and protest music. Three reference points provide just the historical hop-skip-and-jump that we need to provide a sense of that evolution. The first brings us back to Shelley, a radical in his poetry and his political and social views, whose 'The Masque of Anarchy' (1819) – 'Shake your chains to earth like dew / Which in sleep had fallen on you / Ye are many – they are few' – provides just a taste of the thrust and power of his verse.

If Shelley provides the 'hop', then Gil Scott-Heron provides the 'skip' with his muscular and powerful approach to political poetry as both an *interpretation of* and *call to* protest. His satirical spoken word poetry, 'The Revolution Will Not Be Televised' (1970), took its title from a popular slogan among the 1960s Black Power movements in the US, and its lyrics either mention or allude to several television series, advertising slogans and icons of entertainment and news coverage that serve as examples of what 'the revolution will not' be or do:

You will not be able to stay home, brother
You will not be able to plug in, turn on and cop out
You will not be able to lose yourself on skag
And skip out for beer during commercials
Because the revolution will not be televised.

Jumping forward to today, the work of Scroobius Pip continues this critique of ephemera and commercialisation in works such as 'Thou Shalt Always Kill' (recorded with dan le sac, 2007). The central message, as with Gil Scott-Heron's work, is that young people should always think for themselves rather than getting caught up in the shallow market-led trends of modern culture:

Thou shalt not judge a book by its cover.
Thou shalt not judge Lethal Weapon by Danny Glover.
Thou shalt not buy Coca-Cola products.
Thou shalt not buy Nestlé products….Thou shalt not put musicians and recording artists on ridiculous pedestals no matter how great they are or were.

The style and pace may be far removed from traditional poetical forms and, as such, sits within the broader 'spoken word' genre of political expression, but the emotive power and the political argument remain clear. It is a protest. It is a call to arms. It is not, however, a call to violence. 'Thou shalt think for yourselves. And thou shalt always…. Thou shalt always kill!' may provide the final lines of the verse, but 'killing' in this sense refers to vernacular street slang for 'excellence'.

'To kill' in the modern vernacular sense provides us with a valuable lens on the link between poetry, politics and protest that this article has attempted to tentatively explore. To challenge convention; to think for yourself; to dig deep; to refuse to follow the crowd; to think the thoughts that society does not allow. The poetry itself, in the sense of specific written prose, is also arguably less important than the sociopolitical context in which individuals are free to write, which is why poetry, and literature in all its genres, often has most impact in those authoritarian regimes that seek to repress not just movement but thought. Taking this further – and I must now warn the reader that I am writing well beyond my intellectual comfort zone – one might argue that the role of a political leader is not just about the use of language and oratory or being a small 'p' poet as a form of statecraft, but of actually daring to facilitate an environment in which poetry can flourish. Speaking at Amherst College in 1963, John F. Kennedy made an incredibly perceptive statement, 'Society must set the artist free … to follow his vision wherever it takes him.' James Joyce uses his literary alter ego to make a similar point in *A Portrait of an Artist as a Young Man* (1916), 'When the soul of a man is born there are nets flung at it to hold it back from flight. You talk of nationality, language, religion. I shall try to fly by those nets.'

It is for exactly this reason that politicians have often felt threatened by poetry and why dominant political orthodoxies have often insisted that art should remain subservient to politics. Fly by those nets, shake your chains.

On reflection

If there was ever a man who was willing to shake his chains, then Bob Dylan would be an obvious candidate. He was never, however, an obvious candidate for the Nobel Prize for Literature, and therefore the announcement in October 2016 that he had been awarded the prize created a major debate. The politics of this decision was multi-layered, but at the broadest level underlined the argument in this post about the link between the arts and politics. With over three decades of touring and a recording catalogue dating back 55 years, Bob Dylan was hardly the new author or struggling poet that the prize has often been used to promote. And yet, in his song writing and approach to music, Dylan has consistently adopted a political position with which generations of people could relate to, even draw inspiration from. His 1963 album, 'The Times They Are A-Changin', for example, anticipated the mass social protests ahead in the decade, whereas his 'North Country Blues' offers the lament of a woman living in a mining town that has lost its mine, and provides something of an emotional anthem for millions of Americans across the post-industrial Rust Belt. In response to whether songwriting was a form of literature, the Swedish literary critic Horace Engdahl, who formally presented the award, defended the decision by noting that when Dylan's songs were heard first in the 1960s, 'All of a sudden, much of the bookish poetry in our world felt anemic', and that the Prize Committee's decision 'seemed daring only beforehand and already seems obvious.' I can't help but think that contemporary democratic politics often feels a little anemic, and that a little more daring might be needed.

35

DIY democracy: Festivals, parks and fun

Wimbledon has started, the barbeques have been dusted off, the sun is shining, and all our newly elected MPs will soon be leaving Westminster for the summer recess. Domestic politics, to some extent, winds down for July and August, but the nation never seems to collapse. Indeed, the summer months offer a quite different focus on, for example, a frenzy of festivals and picnics in the park. But could this more relaxed approach to life teach us something about how we 'do' politics? Is politics really taking place at festivals and in the parks? Can politics really be fun?

The recent suggestion that the Glastonbury Festival[1] provides a model for policy reform took many academics and commentators by surprise. 'If you want to know how to achieve those things the politicians promise but never quite deliver – a "dynamic economy", a "strong society", "better quality of life" – stop looking at those worthy think-tank reports about the latest childcare scheme from Denmark or pro-enterprise initiative from Texas', Steve Hilton, former Director of Strategy for David Cameron, argued in *The Spectator* in June this year, 'just head down to Worthy Farm in Somerset … it's got so much to teach us.' Personally, I've never been 'a festival person' (and yes, there is such a type), and images of the festival each year only convince me that I should never go.

But the notion of festivals as the source of a new politics, of a new way of organising society, and for delivering and protecting collective goods without the 'hard' elements of the modern state (ie, police, laws, prisons, etc) keeps nagging at my mind. After studying political science for nearly two decades, maybe I can no longer see the wood for the trees (please note the nice use of the park-based metaphor). Have I become so fixated on the formal institutions and procedures of representative democracy that I no longer recognise the emergence of 'insurgent' patterns of engagement? Are festivals the source of new forms of 'civic-ness' and arenas for debate?

Steve Hilton's comments were not, in fact, that new. At a pre-election debate at the University of Sheffield in April, the former Home Secretary David Blunkett and *The Times* columnist Matthew Parris both reflected on the growth and role of arts and culture festivals in terms of promoting public engagement in politics. Parris suggested that "festivals are the new political arenas", adding that "conventional politics is out of favour and festivals have emerged to fill an important social function." There are limits to this argument. Indeed, it is only a short intellectual hop, skip and jump before one takes this logic and ends up with Nigel Farage and his cliché that 'every pub is a parliament', but there is something about the ethos and culture of festivals, especially the smaller and less professional music, literary or arts events, that does resonate with the broader anti-political climate. Put slightly differently, in a climate dominated by 'disaffected democrats', is there something about how festivals do

everyday politics that MPs might reflect on during summer recess?

I think there is, but I am not sure exactly what 'it' is.

What does the existing academic research tell us about the politics and political implications of festivals? Very little, if anything at all. The existing research has been captured by an economic lens that generally attempts to measure the financial value of festivals to a town, village or community – in this regard, it tells us a lot about the price of everything, but absolutely nothing about the broader social value.

So what might the 'it' be that makes festivals potentially important in democratic terms?

In reality it is unlikely to be just one issue and it is equally unlikely to be able to tangibly define, bottle or transfer this quality or essence to other forums, but one crucial element seems to be letting the people govern.

"Let the people govern?" I hear our MPs cry in fear – as they pack their flip flops, sun cream and their already well-thumbed copy of Bernard Crick's *In Defence of Politics* – but there is something about stepping back, trusting the public and seeing what happens.

Steve Hilton gives the example of the Dutch town of Oudehaske where all traffic lights, road markings, speed limits and traffic signs were removed so that road-users would be forced to interact with each other and consciously navigate the streets. "When you treat people like idiots, they'll behave like idiots," the project's leader, traffic engineer Hans Monderman, said. "Who has the right of way? I don't care. People here have to find their own way, negotiate for themselves, use their own brains." By removing external controls imposed by bureaucrats, the transport system was made more human. And everything improved: fewer accidents, better traffic flow.

In the UK the thousands of people who can be seen doing the ParkRun[2] every Saturday morning provide a wonderful example of the power of one person to make a big difference. In 2004 Paul Sinton-Hewitt had the idea of people in local communities coming together for a regular run in their local parks. You could try and win if you wanted, but most of all it was for fun and personal challenge. Since then the ParkRun initiative has emerged into a social movement. Run by volunteers on a rota basis there is no fee to take part, the internet and bar codes make registering easy and social media provides easy access to results and 'nudges' to come again. Over 40,000 people have volunteered to marshal races and over a million people participate each year. In 2009 Sinton-Hewitt was presented with the *Runner's World*[3] 'Heroes of Running' award for philanthropy for his work with ParkRun, and in 2014 became a CBE in the Queen's birthday honours for services to grass-roots sports participation.

You might not think that running in the park is at all political – but it is. It is a perfect example of the 'everyday politics' that has a very real and direct impact on people's lives.

It is a mass participation activity for collective community benefit that is facilitated by the internet and delivered by volunteers. There is no profit motive (what a refreshing thought). 'The implication being?' I hear you ask. Well, the implication is not some neoliberal Tea Party argument about the need to get the state and those meddling politicians out of our lives. But it is to think about the potential for unleashing similar participatory endeavours and, most of all, to think about how such projects and opportunities can be genuinely opened up to all sections of society. Possibly even do a little detailed research. But I would say that, I'm an academic.

On reflection

Where might you go to escape the stresses and strains of modern life? Where might you take your children to experience a different way of living and a range of new experiences? Where might you go if you just want a little time to … think? The answer is increasingly to one of a multitude of festivals – music,

literature, arts, theatre, dance, etc – that have mushroomed all over the world since this post was first written in the summer of 2015. Festivals encapsulate the bringing together of a specific community of individuals around a specific shared interest or set of values. They are highly political in the non-partisan sense, and especially when explicitly tied to a utopian vision of cultivating a different society. The idea being that as festival folk are transformed by the festival experience, so they will, in turn, transform the communities they form part of beyond the festival gates. This 'rippling out' effect is clearly subject to a form of societal 'pushback' in all sorts of ways, but that doesn't undermine the core essence of festivals as a potentially transformative political arena. It is in this sense that festivals have always played a role in mediating the boundary between the political and public spheres. In Western civilisation, dramatic theatrical performances in Greece were early examples of festivals, and in *The Republic*, Plato argued in favour of state-sponsored public events and performances as a way of cultivating an obedient and educated public.

In the medieval period festivals, carnivals
and fiestas were often used by local political
elites as a way of venting public frustrations.
Jesters and minstrels, comedy and dance
offered a valuable political pressure valve,
and to some extent I cannot help but think
that contemporary festivals, although rarely
state-sanctioned or enjoying royal patronage,
continue to play a similar role.

36

Participatory arts and active citizenship

What does arts and culture deliver in terms of social benefits? How can these benefits be demonstrated? What role do arts and culture play in re-engaging 'disaffected democrats'? And can this offer further proof of the social value of arts and culture? An innovative new participatory arts project in South Yorkshire is examining the 'politics of art' and the 'art of politics' from a number of new angles.

'The general value of arts and culture to society has long been assumed', a recent report from the Arts Council acknowledges, 'while the specifics have just as long been debated.' It is this focus on *the specifics* that forms the rub because in times of relative prosperity there was little pressure from either public or private funders to demonstrate the broader social impact or relevance of the arts. In times of austerity, however, the situation is very different. For example, a focus on the STEM subjects (science, technology, engineering and maths) within education policy risks eviscerating the funding for the arts and humanities (and the social sciences) unless these more creative and less tangible intellectual pursuits can demonstrate their clear social value. The vocabulary of 'social return', 'intellectual productive capacity', 'economic generation' – or what some might prefer to label 'the tyranny of impact' – may well grate against the traditional values and assumptions of the arts and culture community, but it is a shadow that cannot be ignored.

The publication of *The Impact of the Social Sciences* (Bastow, Dunleavy and Tinkler, 2014) provides more than a sophisticated analysis of the value of the social sciences across a range of economic, cultural and civic dimensions. It provides a political treatise and a strategic piece of evidence-based leverage that may play an important role in future debates over the distribution of diminishing public funds. I have no doubt that the impact of the arts and humanities is equally significant. But the problem is that the systematic creation of an evidence base remains embryonic. The belief that the arts and humanities are educationally critical, essentially humanising and therefore socially essential elements of any modern society is meaningless without demonstrable evidence to support these beliefs, presented in a language policy-makers will accept. The methodological and epistemological challenges of delivering that research base are clearly significant. It cannot only be measured in simple economic terms, social benefits rarely can be, but as the Arts Council emphasises, 'it is something that arts and culture organisations will have to do in order to secure funding from both public and private sources.' The integrity of the arts needn't be undermined by robust and in-depth exploration of its social benefits.

As a political scientist I have always been fascinated with the relationship between art and politics. Though heretical to suggest to the arts community, I have often thought that the role of the professional politician and the professional artist (indeed, with the amateur politician and the amateur artist) was more similar than was often acknowledged. Both seek to express values and visions, to inspire hope and confidence or dread and disgust, and both seek – if we are honest – to present a message. It is only the medium through which that message is presented that differs (and relationships of co-option, patronage and dependency are common *between* these professions). Similarly, the problems faced by the cultural sector and formal political institutions are by no means dissimilar. Both seek to expand and diversify their 'audiences'. Both have the potential to offer a medium of expression for all, but, fundamentally, only manage to give voice to those who are already well heard. The analogy may go further still in the potential solutions. 'Art should not be sequestered in special zones, where special people – the artists – deploy their special skills and experience,' argues Charles Leadbeater in 2010, 'art should be grounded in the common experience of everyday life.' Could the word 'art' in this statement not be easily changed for politics? Having (crudely) established a connection or relationship between art and politics (or artists and politicians), could it be that one of the true values of the arts lies not in how it responds to the needs of the economy or its importance in our education system, but in how it responds to the rise of 'disaffected democrats' and the constellation of concerns that come together in the 'why we hate politics' narrative?

François Matarasso's *Use or Ornament?* (1997) provides one of the most systematic explorations of the social benefits of participatory arts, and concluded that 'one of the most important outcomes of [the public's] involvement in the arts was finding their own voice, or perhaps, the courage to use it.' As artists and as citizens we yearn for meaningful routes to engagement that are relevant to us all, rather than token gestures from those with real decision-making power. Vromen (2003) offers us this definition of participation: 'acts … that are intrinsically concerned with shaping the society that we want to live in.' Inadvertently, Vromen offers another parallel between politics and art, but this time specifically between political participation and participatory arts. More recently the New Economics Foundation's report *Diversity and Integration* (2013) suggested that young people who participated in arts programmes were more likely to see themselves as 'holding the potential to do anything I want to do' and being 'able to influence a group of people to get things done.' Participatory arts originates in a concern for community development and a wish to promote 'better living' for all, or a concern for 'shaping the society we want to live in', and can therefore be interpreted as a form – a potentially powerful form – of political participation. But is there potential for it to be taken further? In a time of increasing social anomie and political disengagement, especially among the young and the poor, can participatory arts projects provide a way of reconnecting communities and offer a means for broader political re-engagement?

On reflection

The relationship between participatory arts and political engagement has generally been assumed rather than proven. To some extent this reflects the complexity within which participatory arts takes place and its relationship with the wider social milieu. But it also reflects a more specific failing on the part of scholars to attempt to create a clear research base on the question as to why the arts and culture matter (and how their multiple and varied impacts on society can be measured). Since this post was written back in 2014, this knowledge gap has, to some extent, been filled through the completion of the Arts and Humanities Research Council's 'Cultural Value Project' (2014-16) that explored the value of arts and culture to individuals and society through a range of projects and methodologies. What emerges from the Cultural Value Project is the imperative to reposition a focus on the individual experience of arts and culture so that it is at the core of evaluations rather than being viewed as a secondary issue of far less importance than, for example, the impact of arts and culture on the economy, cities or health. Participatory arts were found to have a significant impact in terms of promoting greater reflectiveness, empathy and imagination among those participating, and that these impacts had major social implications in terms of citizenship, social capital, community resilience, etc. The general value of arts and culture to society has now been demonstrated, but whether this will lead to a shift in educational priorities or social investment is still to be seen.

37

The body politic: Art, pain, Putin

The phrase 'scrotum artist' was never going to be easy to ignore when it appeared in a newspaper headline. It is also a phrase that has made me reflect on the nature of politics, the issue of public expectations and even the role of a university professor of politics. In a previous blog post[1] (see post 25), I reflected on the experience of running

a citizens' assembly and how the emotional demands and rewards of the experience had been quite unexpected. 'Raw politics' was the 'headline' phrase, but now I cannot help but wince with embarrassment when I think about this phrase. 'Wince' being the apposite word, given the manner in which the Russian political artist and protestor, Pyotr Pavlensky, nailed his scrotum to the cobblestones of Red Square and sat there naked until the authorities arrested him.

This, it appears, was just the latest in a series of art installations by Pavlensky in which he uses his body to symbolise not only the abuses committed by the Russian state, but also as a symbolic sign of taking back control, in light of the authorities' constant attempts to impose restrictions on personal freedom. Not surprisingly Pavlensky's mother is somewhat bewildered by her son's disturbing

artistic interventions, while others praise him for pushing the boundaries of political protest in an attempt to expose the state of oppression under Putin. The intervention with the nails and his scrotum was just the latest in a series of subversive acts. In 2012 a project entitled 'Seam' saw Pavlensky sewing his lips shut with garden twine in order to protest at the jailing of Pussy Riot. In May 2013 a project called 'Carcass' saw Pavlensky naked, wrapped in layers of barbed wire, and dumped motionless and powerless at the main entrance to the Legislative Assembly of St Petersburg. The more the confused policemen attempted to untangle and remove him, first by putting a blanket to hide the horror then attacking him with wire cutters, the more Pavlensky was gashed and cut by the self-imposed net. If this were not enough, in October 2014 he sat naked on the perimeter wall of the Serbsky Centre, a psychiatric hospital used in Soviet times to imprison dissidents, and cut off his right ear lobe with a kitchen knife, in order to protest at the political abuse of psychiatry in Russia.

"I'm perfectly sane and that's been widely proven", Pavlensky responds to anyone who questions his mental health. "To seek to dismiss me as a madman is exactly what would suit the state." And yet the power of his art to shame and harass, to expose and discredit, cannot be so easily dismissed. His performances are filmed, photographed and receive growing global attention. "Art has the power to send a message other mediums like the media have long lost", Pavlensky states. "It's my way of resisting and I have no intention at all of giving it up." Now that's what you really call raw politics!

On reflection

Although I admire his pain-defying qualities and his commitment to political activities, unlike Pyotr Pavlensky, I don't think I was ever cut out to be a 'scrotum artist'. Since this post was originally written, Pavlensky has spent seven months in a Russian jail for setting fire to the door of the Federal Security Service in Moscow (or 'damaging a cultural monument', as the authorities preferred to describe the offence). But jail is little more than a minor inconvenience for a man who has displayed such commitment in terms of nailing his political colours to the mast, and on his release he immediately pledged to continue "testing the limits of political art". In this regard Pavlensky will be joining a global network of political artists who are using a range of media to agitate and denigrate in equal measure. Unsurprisingly, the American presidential election provided the inspiration for a vast range of artistic interventions that ranged from David Gleeson and Mary Mihelic's section of wall along the US/Mexico border that was made from ropes, ladders and shoes that they found nearby; through to a song by a Swedish musical artist Ledinsky called 'DonaldTrumpMakesMeWannaSmokeCrack'; Mark Wagner's collage of Mr Trump and Mrs Clinton, made entirely of banknotes, that offers a powerful visual representation of the relationship between capitalism and democracy; Conor Collins' surrealist portrait of Mr Trump made out of the candidate's offensive statements, which makes for an uncomfortable visualisation; and at the far extreme is Sarah Levy's menstrual blood portrait of Donald Trump as a presidential candidate. Now that really is raw politics.

38

It's just a joke!

Satire is dangerous because some people just don't get it. They don't get it in the sense that they seem unable to grasp the fact that the role of a comedian or talk show host is to get laughs by launching a barrage of cheap shots at politicians. Some politicians undoubtedly deserve it, and to some extent standing for political office comes with a side-order of politically barbed jokes and insults, and the link between politics and satire goes

back centuries – Aristophanes,[1] Aristotle[2] and even Machiavelli[3] understood the advantages of incorporating humour into political commentary – but my concern is that not only has the nature of the audience changed, but so has the nature of political comedy and satire itself.

In modern comedy and comment it is possible to identify a subtle change from using wit and sarcasm as an element of constructive social criticism towards a use of comedy as an element of toxic, destructive 'attack politics', which perpetuates a shallow and misleading view of politics. In his book *Snark: It's Mean, It's Personal and It's Destroying our Conversation* (2010), David Denby[4] illustrates the emergence of a form of humour that aims to reinforce pre-existing prejudices (through a combination of personal, low, teasing, rug-pulling, finger-pointing, snide,

obvious and knowing sneering, etc) rather than developing substantive critiques. A vast body of scholarship on modern comedy and satire from Iceland to Israel charts the manner in which comedy now tends to focus on the physical flaws and personal failings of politicians rather than their achievements or long-term commitment to social causes. It reveals a focus on the trivial, rather than issues that are central to political affairs, and an approach with a high degree of negativity that frames almost all politicians as selfish, incapable and corrupt.

Moreover, where issues of substance are raised, the challenges are defined not by way of the natural complexities of modern democratic governance, but simply as a function of the absurdity and incompetence of political elites. From 'The Daily Show'[5] and 'The Colbert Report'[6] in the US, through to 'Have I Got News for You'[7] and 'Mock the Week'[8] in the UK, to 'This Hour Has 22 Minutes'[9] in Canada, the world of contemporary political comedy and satire is a generally crude portion of the public sphere in which a gutter-level version of anti-politics reigns supreme.

But the audience has also changed in important ways. The broader 'democratic malaise' in which large sections of the public have become disinterested, apathetic and disengaged from conventional party politics has created the situation in which younger people are increasingly tuning in to late-night comedy as their main source of political information. The main audience for political comedy and satire is therefore almost primed to absorb the 'bad faith model of politics' that is offered (or should I say, 'spewed out'). If this wasn't bad enough, recent research also suggests that an increasing number of television viewers cannot easily distinguish between entertainment and fictional dramatisations on the one hand, and news or current affairs programmes on the other[10]

(meaning the former significantly effects how they think about 'real' politics). Moreover, opinion polls reveal that most people trust comedians and talk show hosts far more than politicians[11] to tell the truth and accurately represent issues.

Is kicking the life out of politics and politicians really that funny, or do comedians and writers need to spend more time thinking about their social responsibilities and less time thinking about how to get cheap laughs? Jon Stewart, host of 'The Daily Show', might, with justice, respond that his programme 'is comedy, not even pretending to be information', but a lot of viewers don't seem to understand this. The aim of political comedy and satire, as I am sure Stewart understands, is to convey a point, argument or message. It has become one that almost exclusively promotes distrust and the abuse of those in politics. In March 2006 Michael Kalin used his column in the *Boston Globe* to explain 'Why Jon Stewart isn't funny'[12] in the following terms:

The ascension of Stewart and "The Daily Show" into the public eye is no laughing matter. Stewart's daily dose of political parody characterised by asinine alliteration leads to a "holier than thou" attitude towards our national leaders. People who possess the wit, intelligence, and self-awareness of viewers of "The Daily Show" would never choose to enter the political fray full of buffoons and idiots.

I can already hear the massed ranks of comedians and dramatists screaming: "That academic bore needs to get a life ... it's just a joke!" Yet my concern is that this shift from healthy scepticism to destructive cynicism is actually exerting a real-world effect of sustaining or fuelling political cynicism. Although proving this link in hard terms is incredibly difficult, persuasion models from the discipline of social psychology reveal how the constant repetition of clear messages, in contexts that reinforce the credibility of those messages, tend to change attitudes. Comedians are seen as credible, and programmes like 'The Daily Show', 'The Colbert Report' and 'Saturday Night

Live' provide softened echoes of hard news content, but usually with an anti-political barb. Jay Leno may well promote a view of comedians and writers as thermometers[13] rather than thermostats[14] of public opinion about politics by arguing that "we reinforce what people already believe", but studies suggest that comedy and satire may well have a more influential and darker edge.

To suggest that writers, comedians or satirists have real political power is by no means new. Aristophanes' powers of political ridicule were feared and acknowledged to the extent that Plato singled out his play 'The Clouds'[15] as contributing to the trial and execution of Socrates. The media (in all its forms) is a largely invisible political actor that arguably wields great power with very little responsibility. In *From Art to Politics* (1995) Murray Edelman explored the link between comedy and public attitudes. He suggested that because only a very small proportion of the public has any direct involvement in politics or with politicians, fiction supplied a substitute form of knowledge that was unchallenged by personal familiarity. 'Art is,' he argued, 'the fountainhead from which political discourse, beliefs about politics and consequent actions ultimately spring.' For many people the jokes they hear comedians telling and what they hear on the late-night talk show is their main, if not their only, source of information about politics. What this very brief foray into the sphere of political comedy and satire suggests, however, is that comedians, satirists and writers are themselves political actors. They frame and discuss certain events, so their role has very real social implications in terms of either fostering public understanding and engagement or creating a generation of 'disaffected democrats'.

Comedy and satire can be used to foster political engagement by building a sense of community among viewers and making politics more enjoyable. This is exactly what happened in October 2010 when thousands marched through Washington, DC to attend a mass rally organised by the Comedy Central team of Jon Stewart and Stephen Colbert under the banner of 'Rally to Restore Sanity'.[16] Linked rallies were also held in over 20 American cities. The aim of the event was described as allowing the mass public to express their voice in order to promote reasoned discussion and end the 'partisan hockey' (whereby the more extreme voices of American politics dominated debates and engaged in shallow forms of demonisation that alienated most of the public). Maybe hope does lie in humour after all, but there was a subtle irony in the manner in which, despite Stewart's insistence to the contrary, most news coverage across America portrayed the rally as nothing more than a 'spoof' event that was designed to mock Al Sharpton's 'Reclaim the Dream' rally that had been held a couple of months earlier.

Whatever the underlying aims of the 'Rally to Restore Sanity' were, the simple fact is that events of this kind, alongside more constructive forms of behaviour, represent very much the exception rather than the rule. As P.J. O'Rourke's painful *Don't Vote! It Just Encourages the Bastards* (2010) illustrates, politics is for most comedians and satirists little more than a punch-bag that deserves to be hit. But I can't help wondering whether the time might have come to turn the tables on the comedians who have become such masters at heckling from the sidelines (and have become very rich in the process). For those who deride democratic politics – and therefore politicians – let me leave you with Theodore Roosevelt's famous speech about 'The Man in the Arena' and his warning that "It is not the critic who counts; not the man who points out how the strong man stumbles, or where the doer of deeds could have done them better. The credit belongs to the man [or woman] who is actually in the arena."

On reflection

What can we say about the evolution of political comedy and satire since this post was written five years ago? As has already been mentioned in post no 9, to some extent the challenge for contemporary comedians and satirists is that the politics itself has almost become beyond satire in the sense that comments or suggestions that would have seemed ridiculous and unthinkable just 12 or 18 months ago may very well appear completely believable today. Politics may have punctured satire in a manner that no one expected. But there is also something more profound emerging in relation to the positioning of comedians and satirists that has so far been overlooked: the indirect co-option of satire. What I mean by this is that until recently satirists and comedians, on the one hand, and the rise of 'insurgent' populist anti-political politicians, on the other, shared a core focus for their fury in the form of 'the establishment'. Beppe Grillo provides the perfect example of the anti-establishment comedian who then steps into the arena and leads a populist revolt, but with the rise of right-wing populism, particularly of a nationalist variety, this coalition has fragmented, and very often the focus of comedians and satirists is on the 'new' wave of dangerously disruptive politicians who smuggle xenophobic sentiments into the mainstream. This has been clear in the UK with the almost non-stop satire and personalised mockumentaries about Nigel Farage. It was also obvious in relation to the US presidential elections and particularly Trump's candidacy. But with the benefit of hindsight, what appears to have happened is that the comedians and satirists have fallen into a trap of their own making that unintentionally may have assisted the focus of their barbs. First and foremost in terms of simple attention it ensured that Trump and Farage received non-stop media attention and commentary, and even when they made idiotic statements, the comedy response arguably distracted deeper attention away from the candidates' core traits. Second, in a time of increasingly fluid and post-tribal politics, the nature of satire remained powerfully partisan and ideological. It was poison-laden attack politics in another form when the public were fed up with traditional attack politics or traditional ideological positions. There is no evidence (as yet) that withering criticism from left-leaning writers, comedians and satirists radicalised and motivated Trump supporters. That is not what I am saying. What I am saying is that

left-leaning writers, comedians and satirists
inadvertently ensured that it was difficult for
other candidates to feature on the political
agenda and that – new point – they failed
to realise how easy it was for Trump, Farage
and any other alt-right 'punk-ish' populist
to dismiss them as simply part of the elite
political establishment. The positioning or
framing of comedians and satirists within the
fold of the mainstream establishment is, of
course, the world turned inside out and upside
down, but in democratic terms, it's also not
a joke. (The comedian Samantha Bee did tell
the best presidential election joke when she
noted that in relation to the election of Donald
Trump, "This was the democratic equivalent
of installing an aboveground pool," she said.
"Even if we're lucky and it doesn't seep into
our foundations, the neighbours will never
look at us the same way again.")

39

Left behind? The future of progressive politics

Centre-left social democratic parties appear to have been left behind in the last decade. 'Early in this century you could drive from Inverness in Scotland to Vilnius in Lithuania without crossing a country governed by the right,' *The Economist* highlighted just weeks ago, 'the same would have been true if you had done the trip by ferry through Scandinavia. Social democrats ran the European Commission and vied for primacy in the European Parliament.' But recently their share of the vote has plunged; they have been *left behind*.

The challenge for anyone thinking about the future of social democracy is that we no longer have *a vocabulary of politics* that resonates with the broader public sphere. Even the title of this little piece – 'Left behind?' – embraces an arguably tired and prosaic attachment to a notion of politics that remains tied to a 'left-right' spectrum. One might argue whether this 'spectrum approach' was every really capable of grasping the subtle complexities of political life – either at the personal, party, organisational or social level – let alone the innate irrationalities of political life itself with its inevitable mixture of messiness and compromise. A 'new political project' might from this perspective focus not simply on the concept of 'the centre left' but on the very nature of collective politics itself. This is the 'new approach' that offers huge potential in terms of redefining and revitalising democratic politics – a rejection of the defensive and callowed version of social democracy that currently exists in the wake of the global financial crisis.

The simple argument here is that any starting point in a discussion about revitalising politics – and therefore society – cannot be rooted in conceptions of either 'the left' or 'the right' (or 'the centre'). Such historical signposts are now too crude to grasp the social complexity that defines the 21st century. The research of Jonathan Wheatley, for example, suggests that the terms 'left' and 'right' are of little relevance to the contemporary electorate. 'Evidently, left and right are amorphous concepts that mean different things to different people at different times', Wheatley notes. 'Amongst younger, less well-educated and especially less politically interested users, items belonging to the economic scale were barely coherent at all. *For these voters, the notions of "left" and "right", at least in economic terms, are really not meaningful at all.*' The electoral basis of democracy therefore needs to be accepted not only in terms of its complexity but also in terms of the decline of monolithic class groups, the re-scaling of economic activity, combined with a shift towards single-issue or valence politics. The rise of political complexity therefore reflects a broader increase in social complexity.

If I were being provocative I might dare to suggest that, at one level, there was no such thing as 'the public' because as any politician (or impact-engaged academic) knows, there are, in fact, '*multiple publics* with whom it is necessary to engage in *multiple ways*.'

This argument may have academic roots (in this case, Michael Burawoy's work on public sociology), but in many ways it speaks to the challenges faced by those thinkers, scholars, politicians and policy-makers who aim to craft a new political project for what really are *new times*. The challenge for any of the 'mainstream' political parties – or for any of the new 'insurgent' parties – is to learn how to engage with multiple audiences in multiple ways with a message that has resonance and meaning while also being accessible. From this perspective the 'traditional' parties too often appear like dinosaurs wandering aimlessly across the political savannah like prehistoric sleepwalkers who don't really understand where they are going and why. The terrain, the savannah, has become more complex and yet the beasts remain incredibly cumbersome with their committees, conferences, headquarters and *desiderata* of an arguably earlier political age. The elements of this increased complexity are diverse, contested and interrelated (social media, increased public expectations, individualisation, migration, etc), but they

culminate in a well-known focus on 'the problem of democracy' with its 'disaffected democrats' and 'critical citizens'. (The irony for the Labour Party is that the 'Corbyn effect' was fuelled by anti-politics and populist sentiment within an established political party.)

One way of thinking about this problem – and possibly a solution – is to think of Zygmunt Bauman's work on 'liquid modernity' which, when stripped down to its core components, emphasises the decline in traditional social anchorage points (jobs for life, national identity, religion, marriage, close-knit communities, trade unions, etc). All that was once solid has apparently melted away and has been replaced with a hyper-materialism that ultimately leaves the public(s) frustrated. To make such an argument is to step back to C. Wright Mills' classic *The Sociological Imagination* (1959) and his arguments about 'the promise' and 'the trap'. We have identified a perceived trap in the form of the decline of the centre left and the dominance of market logic across and within social relationships, but where is 'the promise' in terms of a new vision possibly inspired by the insights of the social sciences that cuts across traditional partisan lines?

Politicians make promises but the public no longer perceive that these promises are ever delivered, or fail to understand exactly why – as Bernard Crick argued – democratic politics tends to be so messy. Politicians have no simple solutions to complex problems and nor do I in this short piece. And yet, as a way of generating a discussion, I would suggest that 'the promise' of social democratic politics will only be achieved when three elements are secured:

▶ *Clarity* in terms of not only a stable vision of why 'working together' through collective endeavours matters, but also in terms of how it can provide meaning, clarity, control and choice.
▶ *Confidence* in terms of a positive political narrative that inspires belief and hope, and redefines specific 'threats' as opportunities.

▶ *A clear and confident 'language of politics'* that is not defensive or defined by the past, that makes no mention of Guild Socialism, Golden Ages, Fabianism, Richard Crossman, 'lefts' and 'rights', etc.

The challenge for the Labour Party in 2020 already looks greater than it did in 2015, not least because the party too often appears engulfed in (internal) tribalism within an increasingly post-tribal world. The challenge for a future political leader is to reject and re-frame the dominant anti-political sentiment for the simple reason that it is rarely *anti*-political in nature and more accurately interpreted as frustration with the current system. Redefining 'anti-politics' as '*pro*-a-different-way-of-doing-politics' lies at the heart of any new political project that seeks not to be left behind.

On reflection

I cannot help but think about the life and work of Zygmunt Bauman when re-reading this post from June 2016. He died in January 2017 at 91 years of age after experiencing a life defined by social change and a constant search for social meaning. Zygmunt not only understood the crisis of social democracy, but he also predicted the contemporary lurch to the right and towards populism long before most others. His central intellectual idea focused on the notion of liquidity and the emergence of a social search for solidity, stability and safe anchorage. Readers of my posts will recognise the influence of his thinking on my own mind, and although there is no doubt that his work could often be bleak and unforgiving, it also shone great light on the emergence of social division and its underpinning consumption-based drivers. And, of course, the crisis of social democracy that has been discussed in such detail for so long has suddenly entered a new and arguably more dramatic phase with the rise of the alt-right. The 'crisis' is both structural and social-psychological in the sense that just a decade ago social democracy was interpreted as very much 'a good thing' – 'the guardian of a new Gilded Age', as John Keane put it. Now it is associated in the minds of the public with untrustworthy politicians, sound bite speeches, cartel parties, an intellectual vacuum and the bailing out of banks and bankers. Many social democratic theorists highlight the historical flexibility and adaptability of the concept, and suggest that it is far too soon to announce its death. Others are exploring the civic potential of online social movements in an attempt to identify a new moral purpose and institutional structure; others are focusing on inequality as the moral focus for the future; others are looking back to history in order to derive 'wish images' that might be reimagined for the future; others see the future in a red-green coalition ... but the basic question that needs to be answered is, 'what are parties on the left actually trying to achieve?' My sense is that the simplest questions are being over-looked.

40

Why Parliament matters: Waging war and restraining power

29 August 2013 will go down as a key date in British political history. Not only because of the conflict in Syria, but also due to the manner in which it reflects a shift in power and challenges certain social perceptions of Parliament.

"It is very clear to me that Parliament, reflecting the views of the British people, does not want to see British military action," the Prime Minster acknowledged, "I get that and the government will act accordingly." With this simple statement David Cameron mopped the blood from his nose and retreated to consider the political costs[1] (both domestically and internationally) of losing the vote on intervention in the Syrian conflict by just 13 votes. While commentators discuss the future of 'the special relationship' with the US, and whether President Obama will risk going into Syria alone, there is great value in stepping back a little from the heat of battle and reflecting on exactly why the vote in the House of Commons matters. In this regard, three interrelated issues deserve brief comment.

The broader political canvas on which the vote on military intervention in Syria must be painted can be summed up by what is known as the Parliamentary Decline Thesis (PDT). In its simplest manifestation the PDT suggests that the government became gradually more ascendant over Parliament during the 20th century. Texts that lamented the 'decline' or 'death' of Parliament – such as Christopher Hollis' *Can Parliament Survive?* (1949), George Keeton's *The Passing of Parliament* (1952), Anthony Sampson's *Anatomy of Britain* (1962), Bruce Lenman's *The Eclipse of Parliament* (1992), to mention just a few – have dominated both the academic study of politics and how Parliament is commonly perceived.

What the vote on Syria reveals is the manner in which the balance of power between the Executive and the legislature is far more complex than the PDT arguably allows for. There is no doubt that the Executive generally controls the business of the House, but independent-minded MPs are far more numerous, and the strength of the main parties far more constrained than is generally understood. (Richard Crossman's introduction to the 1964 reprint of Walter Bagehot's *The English Constitution* provides a wonderful account of this fact.)

Drilling down still further, this critique of the PDT can be strengthened by examining the changing constitutional arrangements for the use of armed force. The formal legal constitutional position over the use of armed force is relatively straightforward: Her Majesty's armed forces are deployed under Royal perogative, exercised in practice by the Prime Minister and the Cabinet. However, the last decade has seen increased debate and discussion about Parliament's role in approving the use of armed force overseas.

From Tam Dalyell's proposed 10-minute rule bill in 1999 that would have required 'the prior approval – by a simply majority of the House of Commons – of military action by the UK forces against Iraq' through to the vote on war in Iraq on 18 March 2003, the balance of power between the Executive and legislature in relation to waging war has clearly shifted *towards* Parliament. Prior assent in the form of a vote on a substantive motion is now required before armed force can be deployed. The problem for David Cameron is that he is the first Prime Minister to have been defeated in a vote of this nature.

Defeat for the coalition government brings us to our third and final issue: public engagement and confidence in politics (and therefore politicians). The data and survey evidence on public attitudes to political institutions, political processes and politicians is generally overwhelmingly negative, with a strong sense that MPs in particular have become disconnected from the broader society they are supposed to represent and protect. The public's perception is no doubt

related to the dominance of the PDT, but on this occasion it appears that a majority of MPs placed their responsibility to the public above party political loyalties.

With less than 22% of the public currently supporting military intervention in Syria, Parliament really has 'reflected the views of the British people'. The bottom line seems to be that the public understands that 'punitive strikes' are unlikely to have much impact on a Syrian president who has been inflicting atrocities on his people for more than 30 months. (Only in Britain could war crimes in Syria be relegated for several months beneath a media feeding frenzy about Jeremy Paxman's beard!) War is ugly, brutal and messy; promises of 'clinical' or 'surgical' strikes cannot hide this fact.

At a broader level – if there is one – what the 'war vote' on the 29 August 2013 really reveals is that politics matters and sometimes works. Parliament is not toothless, and it has the ability to play a leading role in restraining the Executive in certain situations. Could it be that maybe politics isn't quite as broken as so many 'disaffected democrats' seem to think?

On reflection

The role of Parliament in the deployment of military forces is not an issue that has received a huge amount of attention. And yet it is one that arguably deserves a lot of attention, especially given the continuing atrocities that are happening in Syria. In many ways this post framed the government's decision to abide by the general view of the House of Commons and to establish a parliamentary convention that the deployment of troops would have to be approved in a vote on the floor of the House as a 'good thing' – as an example of the legislature actually being able to exert itself over the Executive and to claim some real power. While this interpretation still holds true, it is now possible to sketch out a counterargument based on the nature of events since this post was written in September 2013. More specifically, it is possible to understand the delicate balance between representative government, where there is an emphasis on control and transparency, and responsible government, where ministers have more capacity for immediate action without prior legislative approval, with slightly more precision. The simple fact is that winning a vote on the floor of the House of Commons for military intervention anywhere in the world – irrespective of the scale or extent of the atrocities that might be stopped or prevented – is a high bar for any government to successfully surmount. David Cameron was able to secure Commons support for airstrikes into Syria in December 2015, but a strategy involving placing troops on the ground would be far more difficult to secure. This explains why Boris Johnson has been so frustrated as the UK's Foreign Secretary at not being able to respond to the crisis in Aleppo. Interestingly, the ramifications of Cameron's decision to effectively create a legislative veto over military intervention back in 2013 went far beyond the UK and effectively derailed the US' plans to use force against the Assad regime. This was admitted in January 2017 by the outgoing US Secretary of State, John Kerry, when he confirmed that once Cameron had decided to go to Parliament, that President Obama had felt compelled to secure approval from Congress. Mr Obama's decision to try to secure Congressional approval for strikes drastically slowed down what appeared to be an American willingness to flex its muscles. While negotiations were taking place on Capitol Hill, a deal was made with the Assad regime to give up its chemical weapons, and airstrikes were taken off the agenda. Analysts have since suggested that this failure to enforce a 'red line' by America shattered their credibility and emboldened both Russia (in relation to the Crimea) and Assad in relation to atrocities against opponents. Nevertheless, the British government's future freedom in relation to military intervention remains constrained by a parliamentary convention that would be almost impossible to row back from. Whether that is a 'good' or a 'bad' thing is a highly political question.

41

Rip it up and start again

London Bridge is falling down, falling down, falling down; London Bridge is falling down, my fair lady. "Oh no it's not!" I hear you all scream with oodles of post-Christmas pantomime cheer, but Parliament *is* apparently falling down. A number of restoration and renewal studies of the Palace of Westminster have provided the evidence with increasing

urgency. The cost of rebuilding the House? A mere £2 billion! If it was any other building in the world its owners would be advised to demolish and rebuild.

The Georgian Parliament Building in Kutaisi might be a rather odd place to begin this New Year blog about British politics, but the visionary architecture behind the stunning new building offers important insights for those who care about British politics.

Put very simply, the architecture and design of a building says a lot about the values, principles and priorities of those working within it. The old Parliament building in Tblisi was a stone pillared fortress that reflected the politics of the Soviet era, whereas the new Parliament is intended to offer a very public statement about a new form of politics. Its style and design may not be to everyone's

taste – a 40-metre high glass dome that looks like a cross between an alien spaceship and a frog's eye – but the use of curved glass maximises transparency and openness. It represents the antithesis of what went before it.

I'm not suggesting that the London Eye is suddenly upstaged by the creation of a new frog-eye dome on the other side of the Thames, but I am arguing in favour of a little creative destruction. Or, to make the same point slightly differently, if we are to spend £2 billion in an age of austerity – and probably far more once the whole refurbishment is complete – then surely we need to spend a little time designing for democracy. Designing for democracy is something that imbued the architecture of the new Scottish Parliament and the National Assembly of Wales; it also underpinned the light and space of the Portcullis House annex to the Palace of Westminster.

It is difficult to overstate the importance of Portcullis House in terms of providing a contrast between the intelligent design of modern buildings and the inherited design that ancient buildings inevitably possess. The underground corridor that connects the 'old' Palace of Westminster with the 'new' Portcullis House is far more than a convenient pathway: it is a time warp that takes the tired MP or the thrusting new intern back and forward between the centuries. The light, modern and spacious atmosphere of Portcullis House creates an environment in which visitors can relax, committees can operate and politicians can – dare I say – smile. The atmosphere in the Palace of Westminster is quite different. It is dark and dank. It is as if it has been designed to be off-putting and impenetrable. It is 'Hogwarts on Thames', which is great if you have been brought up in an elite public school environment, but bad if you were not. It has that smell – you know the one I mean – the

smell of private privilege, of a very male environment, of money and assumptions of 'class'. It is not 'fit for purpose' and everyone knows it. And yet we are about to spend billions of pounds rebuilding and reinforcing it.

There is, however, a deeper dimension to this plea to take designing for democracy seriously: architecture matters. The structure of Parliament, in terms of the seating and the corridors, the lack of visitor amenities, the lack of windows and the dominance of dark wood, represents the physical manifestation of that 'traditional' mode of British politics that is now so publicly derided. The structure delivers the adversarial 'yah-boo' politics that now turns so many people off.

The Palace of Westminster should be a museum, not the institutional heart of British politics.

In recent years the Speakers of both Houses of Parliament have made great strides in terms of 'opening up' Parliament, but

modernisation in any meaningful sense is fundamentally prevented by the listed status of the building. A window of opportunity for radical reform did open up when an incendiary bomb hit the chamber of the House of Commons on 11 May 1941. The issue of designing for democracy was debated by MPs with many favouring a transition to a horseshoe or semi-circular design. But in the end, and with the strong encouragement of Winston Churchill, a decision was taken to rebuild the chamber as it had been before in order to reinforce the traditional two-party system. 'We shape our buildings', Churchill argued, 'and afterwards our buildings shape us.' Maybe this is the problem.

The refurbishment of Parliament has so far escaped major public debate and engagement. And yet, if we really want to breathe new life into British democracy, then the dilapidation of the Palace of Westminster offers huge opportunities. The 2015 General Election is therefore something of a distraction from the more basic issue of how we design for democracy in the 21st century. Fewer MPs but with more resources? Less shouting and more listening? A chamber that can actually seat all of its members? Why not base Parliament outside of London and in one of the new 'Northern powerhouses' (Sheffield, Manchester, Newcastle) that politicians seem suddenly so keen on? £2 billion is a major investment in the social and political infrastructure of the country, so let's be very un-British in our approach, let's design for democracy. Let's do it! Let's rip it up and start again!

On reflection

Very rarely have my posts formed the focus of such a vigorous and at times aggressive debate, but this was one of them. There must be something very special in the psyche of many British (probably just English) men and women that seem to make them incredibly protective of the Palace of Westminster. For them it is not a building made of bricks and mortar, but a symbol of all that is good and proper about being British, and as a result, the posting of this piece did generate quite a critical postbag (both online and in more traditional envelope + stamp form). And yet this psychological attachment is also strangely apparent in relation to those elected souls who work in the Palace of Westminster. The building seems to cast a spell that suddenly makes even the most radical reformer become quite wistful and reluctant to consider even the meekest of reforms. And so we come to the planned 'Restoration and Renewal' of the Palace of Westminster that has been the subject of detailed reviews and inquiries since 2012, and is likely to cost several billion pounds. The building is in a state of advanced physical disrepair and decay – 'a crisis', according to the Joint Committee of both Houses, that not only examined the need for reforms but also concluded that the most efficient, speedy and low-risk way of undertaking the unavoidable works was for MPs and Peers to vacate the building completely for a period of up to a decade. This recommendation was made in the summer, but by early 2017 the government had still not managed to find time on the floor of the House of Commons for the debate and vote on this recommendation to take place. This might not be entirely unconnected with the beginning of a notable 'pushback' by MPs – led by Edward Leigh – that rejects the need for the building to be vacated at all. For politicians the use of billions of pounds of public money on repairs and refurbishment to an institution that still operates under the shadow of the MPs' expenses scandal is obviously a toxic issue, and one to be parked at all costs. As a result, the debate about the Restoration and Renewal of the Palace of Westminster has so far been framed very much as a heritage project, and those who wish to see some broader consideration of the opportunity such works bring for thinking about 'designing for democracy' remain sidelined.

42

Democracy Day: We need to break free

Freddie Mercury and Queen might not be the first thing that pops into your head when you think about the BBC's Democracy Day,[1] but for some reason I cannot get the Queen song 'I Want to Break Free' out of my head. Real democratic energy seems to be building up in the UK, but the existing system doesn't seem

able to vent or channel this demand for fresh thinking about how we live our lives.

Sometimes it's not the big things in politics, like violent protests or changes of government, that tell you most about where power lies or the likelihood of reform. It's the little things. Small and apparently insignificant decisions and events can tell you far more about the nature of a political system or the attitudes of its ruling class.

We had one of those small but significant events last week when the Administration Committee of the House of Commons rejected a proposal from the Political and Constitutional Reform Select Committee to project an image on to Big Ben of a vote going into a ballot box to promote National Voter Registration Day on 15 February. Why

was this recommendation rejected? The Committee did not provide an explanation.

This might seem a small issue, but given the extent of political disengagement and voter apathy, the British political system arguably needs to show a little vim and vigour in how it promotes engagement. Phrased in this manner, the projection of an image on to Big Ben (or more specifically, on to St Stephen's Tower) is hardly radical, but even this was judged a step too far.

It's not as if Big Ben hasn't formed the backdrop for significant social statements in the past. In 2009 the campaign group 'Vote for a Change' engaged in some brilliant guerrilla projection activities and beamed a huge job advert on the side of Big Ben that announced 'Part-Time Jobs: Apply Within'.[2] In 2010 the general election results were projected live on to Big Ben as they came in, and more recently an image of falling poppies was projected on to the building to celebrate the centenary of the outbreak of the First World War. And of course there was Gail Porter's naked image … but, and getting to the bottom of the issue, a significant number of MPs don't seem to realise the scale of the problem when it comes to political disengagement. They don't realise that democratic inequality in the UK *is growing* in the 21st century.

In Parliament we have an 18th or 19th-century institution – in terms of its architecture, rituals and working methods – trying to govern in the 21st century, and as a result, the gap between the governors and the governed is widening. Two things make this situation worse. The first is that the public purse is about to spend at least £2 billion – that's an eye-watering £2,000 million – on refurbishing the Palace of Westminster. Designing *for* democracy seems to have been set aside in favour of rebuilding Hogwarts-on-Thames. Yes, I know

traditionalists will criticise me for raising such inconvenient matters but, to return to my classic '80s earworm, 'we have to break free'. The second and possibly more frightening fact is that so many MPs seem unable to understand, acknowledge or react to the extent of public ill feeling. As a senior journalist said to me last week, "They just don't get it!"

But they need to 'get it' if we are to breathe new life into politics. I'm not anti-politics, anti-politician or even anti-the Palace of Westminster (I just think it would work better as a museum than as a parliament), and I spend my life trying to promote engaged citizenship. My last book was called *Defending Politics* so I am no Russell Brand when it comes to criticising politics. But if Democracy Day is going to mean anything more than National Sausage Day or National Tartan Toothpaste Day then we need our MPs to – as the Americans might say – 'wake up and smell the coffee'. Maybe this is why I keep thinking of Freddie Mercury and his song. How did it go? '…You're so self-

satisfied, I don't need you. I want to break free. God knows I want to break free….'

<hr>

On reflection

The previous post on the Restoration and Renewal of the Palace of Westminster offers a critical insight into the challenges of what political scientists would call 'path dependency' and the constraining effects of sunk costs, previous decisions, etc. 'Waking up and smelling the coffee' is therefore a process that the embedded institutional structure and culture almost militates against. This explains the role of crises within politics and the manner in which far-reaching disruptions may at least open up a political space in which previously unthinkable reforms suddenly become possible. In July 2016 a Joint Committee of both Houses concluded that a crisis existed in relation to the state of the physical fabric of the Palace of Westminster, and that, 'It would be an error for Parliament to miss this rare opportunity to deliver a more open, efficient, inclusive and outward-facing

Parliamentary building.' But over six months later, the government's lack of appetite for reform was reflected in the fact that they had still not found time for a debate or vote on the Joint Committee's recommendations to take place. In the meantime, architectural firms competed to gain publicity for ever more incredible but unrealistic proposals for temporary parliamentary accommodation. My favourite was a vast floating slug that was made of glass and would float alongside the Palace of Westminster in the middle of the Thames.

"PROPERTY IS THEFT
NOBODY OWNS
ANYTHING.
WHEN YOU DIE
IT ALL STAYS HERE."
GEORGE CARLIN
1937-2008

Graffiti in the Republic of Stokes Croft, Bristol

43

Attack ads and American presidential politics

Politics appears to have become a 'dirty' word not for the few but for the many. Across the developed world a great mass of 'disaffected democrats'[1] seems increasingly disinterested in politics and distrustful of politicians. My sense is that the public long for a balanced, informed and generally honest account of both the successes and failures of various political parties and individuals, but what they tend to get from the media, the blogosphere, most commentators and (most critically) political parties is a great tsunami of negativity, or what I call 'the bad faith model of politics'. Put slightly differently, public scepticism is a healthy element of any democracy, but surely we have slipped into an atmosphere that is awash with corrosive[2] cynicism?

The American presidential race provides arguably the most far-reaching and destructive case study of the 'bad faith model of politics'. The Republican Party plans, according to *The New York Times* (2012), to run a series of anti-Obama hard-line attack ads[3] that will plum to new depths in terms of what is generally known as 'attack politics'.

The Democrats, to be fair, will undoubtedly seek to frame Mitt Romney in ways that are hardly designed to flatter.

Politics fuelled by aggression has created a form of political competition akin to modern warfare (strategy, communication, troops, etc) in which the role of political actors is to 'attack' anyone who disagrees with them. As such the language, discourse and tactics of politics is generally focused on negative campaigning, personal slurs and a view of politics that defines any willingness to engage in serious debate, offer to negotiate or change your mind as evidence of weakness. It is bitter, short-tempered, and its ambition is to sneer and jibe mercilessly, so obsessed with winning at all costs it cannot see that a political strategy based on the use of aggression to win office can only fail in the long term.

More importantly, away from the bear pit of the legislature or television studio, political life is focused on the maintenance of a system in which ideas, conflicts and interests are openly articulated and peacefully resolved. It is rarely glamorous or easy, it is often dull and messy, and it is generally not a profession full of liars, cheats and scoundrels (every profession has its bad apples, and politics is no different). It is, however, an increasingly hard and brutal business. It is not for the faint-hearted, and although this has always been the case, there has been a step-change in recent years in relation to the intensity of the pressures, the brutality of the criticisms, the personalised nature of the attacks and the arbitrary targeting by the media and political opponents. The storm that to some extent inevitably encircles democratic politics has for a range of reasons become more intense and toxic. My concern is that we are hollowing out the incentives that need to exist to attract the best people from all walks of life to get involved and to stand for office. A process of demonisation[4] has occurred that can only end in a situation where 'normal'

people feel inclined to walk away, leaving only the manically ambitious, socially privileged or simply weird in their stead. In a sense we risk creating a self-fulfilling prophecy that politicians are 'all the same' exactly because of the climate we have created.

This narrowing of the talent pool from which politicians are drawn is directly attributable to the sheer force of the storm that is constantly breaking upon the shores of politics. Politicians must operate with an almost perpetual swirl of scandal and intrigue breaking around their heads. Many good people currently brave the storm in the hope of making a positive difference to their community, city or country. But someone with a life, a family, interests beyond politics and the ability to do other things can feel deeply inclined to stick to them and leave the political storm to itself. We need to calm the storm. Attack politics in general and attack ads in particular benefit only the sellers of expensive advertising space, and certainly not the public.

On reflection

On 16 June 2016, Labour MP Jo Cox was stabbed in the street as she left her constituency office. Four hours later the police announced that she had died from her injuries and a period of informal national mourning was initiated. Jo Cox was a much-loved and respected young woman with two children, and her murder by a man with far-right sympathies was interpreted as reflecting a broader shift in the nature of politics. That is, a shift towards a stage beyond the simple 'attack politics' discussed in this post from 2012, and that will accept apparently any lie, falsehood, fairy tale or verbal act of aggression in order to scare the electorate into supporting a specific cause, candidate or position. This is the dimension of contemporary politics that many commentators have overlooked. The emergence of 'post-truth' or 'post-fact' politics has a very dark and dangerous underbelly. Whereas traditional attack politics (see Emmett Buell and Lee Sigelman's *Attack Politics: Negativity in Presidential Campaigns since 1960* [2008]) is hardly a recent phenomenon, it is generally crude

and its latest incarnation tends to be more insidious and invisible. It works through the planting of seeds, the creation of fears, the identification of 'others', the exploitation of frailty or weakness and – most of all – it thrives on incivility. There is a link – albeit embryonic in my thinking – here with the alt-right movement. On the one hand, it projects a traditional image of aggressive attack-attack-attack … the victim is secondary to the attention secured through controversy and condemnation; but on the other hand, there is also the promotion of an existential threat in the sense that if you dare to challenge the movement's righteousness, to suggest their use of the collective 'us, the people' might not include 'you', then you risk becoming defined as the enemy in a vulgar political culture that can only comprehend politics as a battleground. Everything about campaigns revolves around feeding the crowds with grand narratives – meaningless emotive phrases – that depict a world of stark and simple choices. The result is known as 'peak polarisation' in the sense of social fragmentation and inter-community distrust

– the world that Jo Cox dedicated her life to avoiding.

44

Dante and the spin doctors

First it was football, now it is politics. The transfer window seems to have opened and all the main political parties have recruited hard-hitting spin doctors – or should I say, 'election gurus' – in the hope of transforming their performance in the 2015 General Election. While some bemoan the influence of foreign hands on British politics and others ask why we aren't producing our own world-class spin doctors, I can't help but feel that the future of British politics looks bleak. The future is likely to be dominated by too much shouting and not enough listening.

Dante is a 15-year old African American with a big Afro hairstyle. He looks into the camera and with a timid voice tells the viewer, "Bill de Blasio will be a mayor for every New Yorker, no matter where they live or what they look like – and I'd say that even if he weren't my dad." This was the advert[1] that transformed Bill de Blasio from a long shot into a hot shot, and ultimately propelled him into office as the 109th and current Mayor of New York. De Blasio also benefited from a well-timed sexting scandal and an electorate ready for change, but there can be no doubting that the advert in which his son, Dante de Blasio, featured was a game changer. *Time Magazine* described it as 'The Ad That Won the New York Mayor's Race', the *Washington Post* named it 'Political Advert of 2013' – 'No single ad had a bigger impact on a race than this one.'

Such evidence of 'poll propulsion', 'soft power' and 'data optimisation' has not gone without notice on this side of the Atlantic, and a whole new wave of election gurus have been recruited to help each of the main three political parties (Nigel Farage, of course, would never recruit such blatant overseas talent, ahem). The Liberal Democrats have recruited Ryan Coetzee who played a leading role significantly increasing the Democratic Alliance's share of the vote in South Africa. The Conservatives have appointed the Australian Lynton Crosby with his forensic focus on 'touchstone issues', while last month the Labour Party revealed they had hired one of President Obama's key strategists, David Axelrod, to craft a sharp political message and to re-brand Ed Miliband.

It was David Axelrod's former Chicago firm – AKPD Message and Media – that had made the Dante advert for Bill de Blasio.

Of course, such spin doctors, advisers and consultants have always and will always exist in politics. The existence of new forms of offline and online communication demands that political parties constantly explore new techniques and opportunities to improve their standing, but I cannot help but feel that with the recruitment of such powerful electoral strategists we risk losing touch with what politics is really about. We risk widening the worrying gap that already exists between the governors and the governed. 'Resilience', it would appear, seems to be the buzzword of modern party politics as a general election approaches. It is about who can promote a powerful narrative and deliver an aggressive onslaught; it is about a form of 'attack politics' in which a willingness to listen or compromise

is derided as weakness, and weakness cannot be tolerated; it is a form of politics in which family and friends become political tools to be deployed in shrewd, cunning and carefully crafted ways.

But does turning to the masters of machine politics from Australia and America bring with it the risk that the campaign will become too polished, too professional, too perfect?

David Axelrod's role in relation to Ed Miliband provides a case in point. Apparently opinion polls suggest that poor Ed is viewed as too 'nerdy' and more than a little bit 'weird'. The strategists suggest that this 'image problem' is a weakness that must be addressed through a process of re-branding. The danger, of course, is that by knocking off all Ed's quirks and peculiarities you actually end up with just another production-line professional politician. Personally, I quite like politicians who are a bit different, even weird. Isn't that why people find Boris Johnson and Nigel Farage so annoyingly refreshing?

A really smart election strategist might dare to think a little differently, to turn the political world upside down by focusing not on who can shout the loudest for the longest, but on *the art of listening*. As Andrew Dobson's brilliant book, *Listening for Democracy* (2014),[2] underlines, the art of good listening has become almost completely ignored in modern politics despite being prized in daily conversation. Were any of the foreign election gurus employed for their listening skills? No. And that's the problem. That's why the future feels so bleak.

▮▮▮▮▮▮▮▮

On reflection

If asked to write this post again, it would have to be entitled 'Cameron and the spin doctors' for the simple reason that the Brexit vote highlighted hyper-spin on one side and what might be termed hypo-spin on the other. Therefore, while the pro-Brexit campaign launched a thunderously aggressive and often untruthful campaign, the 'Remain' campaign never really offered a coherent

communications strategy of any kind. The former was loud, proud and deafening; the latter was meek, mild and spoke in whispers. This is reflected in Craig Oliver's *Unleashing Demons: The Inside Story of Brexit* (2016) that provides an incredibly flat and dull account of a flat and dull campaign. The fact that Craig Oliver was Cameron's Director of Communications for five years suggests that he should know a thing or two about both spinning and what happened within the No 10 machine. But if anything, what the book reveals is a complete failure to unleash any demons that might have undermined some of the Brexit campaign's simple narratives. 'We struggled to communicate a complex truth', Oliver admits, 'in the face of simple lies.' And yet, in the midst of chaos, the golden light of humour shines through. When David Cameron comes down from his flat the morning after the night before to discuss his future with his closest aides, what is the first thing he says to them? 'Well, that didn't go to plan!' But with the benefit of hindsight, that was the problem – there had never been any real plan.

The 'Remain' campaign had been out-spun and out-manoeuvred.

▬▬▬▬▬▬▬▬▬

45

Democratic realism

Politics is messy. Period. It revolves around squeezing collective decisions out of a multitude of competing interests, demands and opinions. In this regard democratic politics is, as Gerry Stoker has argued, 'almost destined to disappoint.' And yet, instead of simply defining Obamacare[1] as a good illustration of what is wrong with democracy in the US, it's possible to reject 'the politics of pessimism' that seems to surround contemporary politics, and instead see the splendour and triumph of what Obama has achieved.

Such an interpretation would take us back not to the ancient history of Pericles,[2] but to the modern political history and writing of Sir Bernard Crick, and notably his *In Defence of Politics* (1962). For Crick the fact that democratic politics was imperfect, that it tended to grind rather than flow, and that it often produced sub-optimal decisions was not a failing of politics but its beauty. Democratic politics was a civilising activity that allowed an increasingly wide and diverse array of social groups to live together without resorting to violence or intimidation. I'm not for one moment arguing that democratic politics is perfect or that all politicians are angels, but I am suggesting that to define the complex outcomes of political deliberations in such pejorative terms risks spreading the cynicism and misunderstanding that weighs so heavily on those who have at least 'stepped into the arena' (to paraphrase Theodore Roosevelt's famous speech).

The creation of an alternative arena in the vein of a 'government-by-lot', as Pericles may well suggest, will do little to address the underlying paradoxes, tensions and frustrations of democratic politics. Pericles was no god; he was a manipulative demagogue and a hawkish populist who ruled through a faux democracy in which the majority had no stake. I'll take no lessons from Pericles, but instead bring the debate full circle and back to a focus not on democracy per se, but on American democracy as it currently exists.

Politics in America has mutated into a shallow and ultimately unsatisfying form of market democracy. Citizens have therefore become customers, political parties little more than companies, and everything is available at a price. The problem, however, is that 'democracy.com' can never be like 'amazon.com'. You don't vote for your candidate and wait for the goods you have chosen to arrive like a book, DVD or pizza. Democratic politics is about 'we' and 'us', not 'me' and 'I'. Could it be that 'disaffected democrats' who appear to inhabit the US in such numbers have become so dazzled by materialism that they are failing to see what really matters? Could it be that the public actually gets the politicians it deserves?

I'm actually quite glad that Obama turned out not to be Superman, as too many people expect politicians to be able to deliver simple solutions to complex social problems without contributing to the solutions themselves. There are no simple answers to complex questions, no easy wins, no magic bullets or technological fixes to the challenges that will define the 21st century (climate change, over-population, resource depletion, etc). The public should be wary of the man or woman – or ancient Greek statesman – who suggests otherwise. Now what would Pericles say to that?

▬▬▬▬▬▬▬

On reflection

Looking back on the five years since this post was written, and writing now, just hours before the inauguration of Donald Trump, there is one sentence that jumps out at me: 'I'm actually quite glad that Obama turned out not to be Superman.' But in a context of considering the notion of democratic realism there is great value in reflecting on the broad contours of the Obama presidency. In this sense, one of the biggest challenges and achievements of his term in office was coping with the global financial crisis of 2008, and it was noteworthy that as Obama gave his final farewell address in Chicago, the Labor Department released its final employment update for his administration. It was a strong report.

Unemployment stood at 4.7%, average hourly wages were 3% higher than they had been a year before, and this was the 75th consecutive month of job growth, a record for the modern era. Since 2010 nearly 16 million jobs had been created despite the fact that the challenges created by the Great Recession in the US in 2009 were larger than those at the outset of the Great Depression in 1929-30. Then there is Obamacare – the biggest effort to tackle inequality since the 19th century, and an explicit policy to make the very rich pay more to the very poor. These are, to some extent, superhuman achievements, not to mention the general day-to-day pressures of surviving the strains of being in office. But possibly the most critical element of his presidency was how someone who was elected very much as a unifying candidate and who promised to govern above the fray of partisan politics managed to become such a divisive figure. 'I serve as a blank screen on which people of vastly different political stripes project their own views,' he wrote in *The Audacity of Hope* in 2006. 'As such, I am bound to disappoint some, if not all, of them.' But could he really

have expected to have handed over to his successor – the 44th to the 45th – such a racially divided and polarised country? I doubt it, but maybe this was always the trap that a President who lifted public expectations so high was never really going to avoid. Maybe that's the sharp end of democratic realism.

46

Bang, bang – democracy's dead: Obama and the politics of gun control

…Tennessee State University, Northern Arizona University, Texas Southern University, Winston-Salem State University, Mojave High School, Lawrence Central High School, Umpqua Community College, Harrisburg High School, Sacramento City College, Savannah State University, Southwestern Classical Academy, Bethune-Cookman University, Frederick High School, Wisconsin Lutheran High School, Marysville Pilchuck High School … the list of school shootings goes on (and on). Over 12,000 people died in the US last year from gunshot wounds. Since the Sandy Hook massacre of 2012 there have been no fewer than 161 mass shootings. Does Obama's frustration suggest that democracy is part of the solution or part of the problem?

It would seem that President Obama has a new prey in his sights. It is, however, a target that he has hunted for some time but never

really managed to wound, let alone kill. The focus of Obama's attention is gun violence, and the aim is really to make American communities safer places to live. The New Year therefore brought with it an Executive Order from the President that requires all firearms sellers to seek a license and initiate background checks on purchasers. There is no doubt that this will make the process of buying a gun a slightly slower and more cautious process, but in reality it will do little to reduce the scale of gun crime. Obama knows this well, and his measures are themselves borne from a frustration that has seen Congress repeatedly block his attempts to push through more significant measures.

The killing of 20 school children in Newtown, Connecticut in December 2012 fuelled a national discussion about gun control. Mass killings by gunmen in civilian settings, children covered in blankets, screaming parents rushing to see if their child had missed the carnage … the emotive politics of gun control turned from individual liberty and protection to individual responsibility and collective freedom, but Obama's attempt to limit the availability of semi-automatic assault weapons was defeated in the Senate. Body bags and public support, it seemed, were not enough to deliver change.

And yet crises – as political science frequently tells us – generally create 'windows of opportunity' into which radical new policy shifts can occur. Not, it would seem, in the case of gun atrocities in America. The paradox of the American psyche is that Obama's call for restrictions on the sale of guns actually stimulated the biggest spike in gun sales that the country had seen for nearly two decades (1.6 million guns sold in December 2015).

So is democracy the problem or the solution?

Democracy is, as Bernard Crick sought to underline in his *In Defence*, inevitably slow and cumbersome. It is messy simply because it somehow has to squeeze simple decisions out of a vast array of competing and often intractable social demands. As a result the democratic process tends to contain multiple veto points that can stifle responsiveness; a smooth policy change is suddenly turned into a sluggish and grating process that too easily morphs into gridlock and inaction.

Could it therefore be that the problem with democracy is that it prevents the implementation of measures that look eminently sensible to the rest of the world?

To some extent this might be true, and the interesting element of Obama's recent move is that by using an Executive Order to promulgate gun control, he is, in effect, circumnavigating elements of the democratic process. But even here his weakness shines through. First, in the sense that by adopting this approach he risks setting a precedent for future presidents who have a very different approach to gun control and wish to shift the balance via Executive Order in a very different direction. And (second) the significance of the measures are so far removed from any notion of actually disarming the country that they could be interpreted as a sign of weakness rather than strength.

President Obama is clearly using some of his final 'lame duck' year freedoms to push the issue of gun control back onto the political agenda. But at the moment, the lack of political will is making gun control look too much like a 'sitting duck' for the National Rifle Association and other pro-gun groups that want to take it back off the agenda. Some opinion polls suggest that the mood of the American public is shifting away from unlimited ownership, but the pace of change appears glacial. In some ways American gun control has regressed rather than progressed in recent years, as the federal ban on military assault weapons and high-capacity magazines that existed between 1994-2004 has not been renewed by Congress. It's too easy to exaggerate the threats or to ridicule gun-toting Americans, but the reality is far more sad: most deaths occur from guns being used to commit suicide, or are found by children and toddlers who mistake them for toys, with devastating effects. When it comes to gun control and American politics, then maybe, just maybe, could there be a case for a benevolent dictator who understands that the ballot and bullets, like guns and safety, just don't mix?

…Reynolds High School, Seattle Pacific University, Kennedy High School, Georgia Gwinnet College, Paine College, South Carolina State University, Purdue University, Los Angeles Valley College, Rebound High School, Widener University, Delaware Valley School, Berrendo Middle School, Magne High School, Arapahoe High School, Brashear High School, Carver High School, Massachusetts Institute of Technology….

On reflection

The previous post's focus on democratic realism flows into this discussion of gun control in the US. Was it ever realistic for Obama to set his target on gun control in a country so wedded to the right to bear arms? Just weeks after this was written in February 2016, President Obama flew to Orlando to meet the families of victims of a nightclub shooting massacre in which 49 people had been killed. It was his tenth visit to a community affected by a mass shooting during his presidency. And yet, in June 2016, the Senate voted down four gun control measures that were intended to limit the sale of guns in the wake of the Orlando atrocity. The President responded with a tweet that veiled a deeper emotional rage, 'Gun violence requires more than moments of silence. It requires action. In failing that test, the Senate failed the American people.' But to some extent the realist in me wonders about Obama and his Sisyphean task – is it really a failure that can be laid at the door of the presidency or Congress? Or is it – if we are really honest – a failing on the part of the public to support stricter gun control? Is a clear element of 'the American problem' the absence of any mass, professionalised social movement (a counter force) to the embedded position of the gun lobby? The benefit of this question is that it creates a way of highlighting democratic alignment and success rather than dis-alignment and failure. Although willing to shed tears at specific (but generally distant) massacres, if the public does not translate these emotions into a stronger and applied commitment to gun control, it is not surprising that the political system appears unresponsive. Maybe the public gets the politics and the politicians it deserves.

47

Fig leaves and fairy tales: political promises and the Truth-O-Meter

The *Tampa Bay Times* is a very fine newspaper. One of its most insightful features – indeed, a feature that was awarded the Pulitzer Prize in 2009 – is its PolitiFact[1]

website. This is an independent online platform through which a legion of reporters and editors fact-checks every statement, promise and half-hearted mumble ever made by a politician, political candidate, political party or campaign group. In many ways this is public service journalism of the very highest standard, and what's interesting about the website is that very often – deep intake of breath before I even dare to write these words – sometimes politicians tell the truth!

Such definitive judgements are clearly difficult, and therefore a lot of political statements or promises result in a 'mostly true' or 'mostly false' conclusion that begins to tease apart the complexity of the issue being discussed. Or, put slightly differently, there are no simple answers to complex questions that anyone can offer – be they politicians, candidates, parties or advocacy

groups. But taking this to the top of the political tree in the US, what's interesting about the 'Obameter' (which is following more than 500 promises made by President Obama in the 2008 and 2012 election campaigns) is that the might of American journalism seems to conclude the following:

Promises kept – 239 (45%)
Compromises – 130 (24%)
Promises broken – 116 (22%)
Stalled – 6 (1%)
In the works – 39 (7%)
Not yet rated – 2 (0%)

Now I can already hear the mass ranks of 'disaffected democrats' stamping their feet and sharpening their pencils in light of any evidence that politics might actually – even in some small way – 'work'. I'm also sure that the statistics may well contain subtle but important nuances that rotate around the fact that some promises may well be far more significant than others. But for the time being let's just use the Truth-O-Meter as a concept that deserves further discussion, specifically in relation to how it relates to politicians, for at least three reasons.

First and foremost, the Truth-O-Meter works on the basis that politicians will always tell the truth. This is – at first glance – a fairly simple and straightforward assumption that would seem to exist (alongside motherhood, breast feeding, cuddly pets and apple pie) in the pantheon of 'good things'. Now I am not for one moment arguing against the centrality of political truth telling or the need for high levels of democratic accountability, but I do wonder if the assumption is not – how can I put it – a little simplistic. Once in power, even the most idealistic politicians will quickly realise that politics is a worldly art in terms of negotiating with rivals (within and beyond their party) and particularly when it comes to working with non-democratic regimes. Truth is and can be

a difficult concept simply because politics is a messy business.

I would, at this point, invoke the arguments of Bernard Crick and heap praise on his *In Defence of Politics* (1965),[2] but regular readers of this column know the intellectual canvas on which I write. Far better to move on to a second element of the Truth-O-Meter, the democratically dubious – that 'Promises kept' seems to be rated above 'Compromises'. The immediate logic of such a position seems obvious ... until you think about the incredible complexity and fluidity of modern politics. To be a politician is to exist in a world of ever-increasing and rarely compatible demands in a context of shrinking resources. This is the simple problem. The great beauty of democratic politics (here comes the 'Crick moment') is that it provides a way of squeezing collective decisions out of a great multitude of conflicting demands. The process might not be pretty or easy for outsiders to understand, but the central emphasis of the whole democratic structure is towards achieving consensus

and compromise. Put slightly differently, the risk of keeping promises in an over-simplistic manner in order to please the Truth-O-Meter is that it may actually lead to decisions being made that are simply irrational and 'bad', or simply undemocratic and designed to appease a vocal minority.

My aim is not to defend those devilish politicians, but simply to highlight that the Truth-O-Meter may – in some strange ways – end up valuing and measuring the wrong things. The stateswoman or statesman politician will be the one who stands up and says 'I was wrong' and reneges on a promise or commitment made in haste or under undue pressure.

This thought brings me to my third and final point, and shifts our focus across the Atlantic from the US to the UK. With just days to go before the general election, all of the main political parties are engaging in what can only be termed a 'promise orgy'. Money is being found for just about anything; you want a budget protected from future cuts – 'you got it!'; you want to pay less tax – 'you got it!'; you want to pay no tax – 'you got it!; you want to fill the rivers and streams of England with Cola – 'you got it! (This last promise was just my own personal fairy tale, but you know what I mean.) To some extent the whole game of democratic politics forces politicians to over-promise, but my concern in the UK is that the promises have become ridiculous and the public simply do not believe them. 'Where exactly will the money come from?' is the core question that has no real answer. This has been an anti-political general election.

So please can I say to the *Tampa Bay Times*, keep up the good work, but it's probably best if you don't bring the Truth-O-Meter to the UK in the near future.

On reflection

One of the benefits of looking back at posts is that they often reveal just how much a person, place or issue has changed during the intervening period. This piece about 'fig leaves and fairy tales' is a very good example. When set against the contemporary controversy surrounding the emergence of 'post-truth' politics and 'fake news', this focus on the Truth-O-Meter seems slightly quaint. That said, it seems appropriate to present President Obama's final Truth-O-Meter score, and of 596 'fact-checks' of presidential statements, 21% were found to be 'True', 27% 'Mostly True', 27% 'Half-True', 12% 'Mostly False', 12% 'False' and 2% 'Pants on Fire'. The worrying fact, however – and one that ties into previous posts that have emphasised a decline in political civility, a narrowing of space for open discussion and a more brutal, aggressive political climate, a willingness to 'defecate in the corner', as Slavoj Žižek puts it – is that Donald Trump's pre-election statements scored 4%, 11%, 15%, 19%, 33% and 18% (respectively). Look also at the popularity ratings – Trump's rating of about 40% compared with 78% for Obama in 2009 and 62% for Bush in 2001. This is a dangerous warning sign about the state of democracy. The American electorate were willing to set aside their concerns about Trump for what they perceived as the greater cause to give Washington the shake-up they thought it needed.

48

Disengaged Britain: 'Don't vote, it just encourages the b**tards'

Although Russell Brand's recent interview with Jeremy Paxman is unlikely to be remembered as a 'classic' political interview that redefined a debate or shaped the career of a specific politician, it did focus attention on the fact that large sections of the British public are becoming increasingly disengaged with politics. The 2013 British Social Attitudes Survey reveals that only a small majority of the public now turns out to vote, and fewer than ever before identify with a political party. The UK is by no means unique in terms of the relationship between the governors and the governed, and even a quick glance at the titles of recent books on this topic – *Why We Hate Politics*, *Democracy in Crisis*, *The Life and Death of Democracy*, *Don't Vote! It Just Encourages the Bastards* (yes, it does actually exist), the list is almost endless – reflects the fact that 'disaffected democrats' appear to exist in every part of the world. But what is to be done?

There are, as Bernard Crick emphasised in his classic *In Defence of Politics* (1962), no simple answers to complex questions, and in many ways the political process and capacity of politicians is defined by this simple fact. And yet, in the intervening half-century since Crick's classic book was published, public attitudes to political institutions, political processes and politicians have become increasingly negative. Today, three-quarters of the public feel the political system is not working for them, younger people are less likely to identify with a political party, less likely to believe it a civic duty to vote, and are less likely to have engaged in any conventional political activities. Recent research suggests that at the moment only around 12% of those aged 18-25 report that they will definitely vote in 2015. The other 88% appear unsure whether it is worth voting at all.

In this context Russell Brand's arguments appear slightly more sophisticated than some of his critics might have appreciated. The comedian's position was not that people should not vote, but that it was rational for people not to turn out and express their democratic right when there was, in fact, no real choice between the main parties. To do otherwise was simply to participate in a sham that actually gnawed away at the health of democratic politics. The problem, however, with this argument is that it polarises the debate around a set of rather crude and simplistic options – 'vote!' versus 'don't vote!', the 'engaged' versus 'the disengaged', 'politicians' versus 'comedians' – okay, so I made the last bit up, but you know what I mean. My point is therefore whether the arguments about voting and turnout and elections risk unnecessarily closing down options when we should, in fact, be reinvigorating the options we have while looking to create new forms of political engagement.

In terms of voting, surely the real question is how to make voting matter. For some people this might involve the introduction of compulsory voting or reform of the electoral system, and these ideas merit consideration (although in Australia, where voting is compulsory, levels of public trust in politics make the UK look positively healthy), but a simpler and more effective reform might include the addition of a 'None of the Above' option on all ballot papers. In this way citizens could make a formal and recognised contribution to the electoral results without having to demonstrate their frustration through spoiling their ballot paper or simply not bothering to vote. The danger is that, at the moment, the 'None of the Above' option might actually win quite a few elections!

A more radical option involves the introduction of time limits for MPs. Let us say – for the sake of argument – a maximum of two or three terms (ie, 10 or 15 years), after which the individual would have to leave Parliament and serve the same period 'in the real world' before being eligible to stand

for re-election. I'm always slightly nervous when I hear people asking why we can't have more 'normal' people serving as MPs, or suggestions that politicians don't exist in 'the real world', but introducing a term limit would at least end the current system – the political equivalent of 'bed blocking'. By shaking up the notion of 'safe seats', it would give more chances to more people, it would offer a balance between stability and fresh thinking, and it would help illustrate the fact that reform can occur in a way that responds to social concerns. It would also make voting a far more significant political act. Although I am no 'Mystic Meg' (is she still around?), my guess is that our current MPs will hate this idea. Protestations and all manner of reasons not to even open up a debate on this matter will inevitably pour forth, but to some extent, my interest lies not with the current generation of politicians, but with the future.

The simple fact is that the vast majority of the public do not 'hate' politics (or politicians), and it is closer to the truth to suggest that they no longer understand how politics works or what politicians actually do. Why does everything seem to take so long and never be quite right? Why does there tend to be such a gap between what is promised before elections and then delivered in office? The crux of the issue therefore lies not so much with voting, but with bridge building and promoting public understanding of politics (and therefore the political understanding of the public).

Two things flow from this. First, in terms of fostering political understanding, the importance of citizenship education cannot be over-stated. Citizenship education not in the sense of teaching what is 'wrong' or 'right', but in teaching 'how' and 'why' the political process attempts to reconcile competing social demands in a manner that is broadly fair and transparent but – most of all – guards against the brutal 'politics of fear' that still exists in large parts of the world. It is not therefore politicians or political parties that matter but the democratic process and the existence of engaged citizens. Citizenship education was introduced into

the national curriculum in 2002, following the recommendations of the advisory group chaired by Bernard Crick, and it has survived the recent curriculum review ordered by Michael Gove, but it has struggled to establish itself as a fully-fledged subject. The future of citizenship education therefore depends on the degree to which it can shift from a passive subject taught in classrooms to a more active discipline that reaches out beyond the classroom and assembly hall.

The second element of fostering political understanding therefore focuses on bridge building between political institutions and politicians, on the one hand, and the public, on the other, in such a way that the whole citizenry might be educated (politicians, officials and professors of politics included). Put slightly differently, how can we create 'safe spaces' in which the aggression and noise of contemporary politics is set aside for a more mature and considered discussion about the issues that really matter? Once again – as has already been admitted – creating such arenas will not deliver simple

solutions to complex problems because no such 'pain-free' solutions exist. But it may allow new voices to be heard, it may allow disengaged communities to reconnect, and it may allow more non-traditional forms of political engagement (offline and online) to feed into and deepen more traditional and formalised processes.

On reflection

'We aim at no less than a change in the political culture of this country both nationally and locally,' Sir Bernard Crick argued in 1998, 'for people to think of themselves as active citizens, willing, able and equipped to have an influence in public life and with the critical capacities to weigh evidence before speaking and acting.' In the two decades since Crick's assertion it is possible to argue – in the UK and beyond – that the political culture has changed, but not in the manner Crick had hoped or intended. The attitudes revealed by Gabriel Almond and Sidney Verba in *The Civic Culture* (1963) crystallised around a British

public that was deferential and respectful of their leaders, but confident of their role and capacities and the responsiveness of government. This blend of activity and passivity, for Almond and Verba, created a balanced civic culture; half a century later Gerry Stoker concluded, in his brilliant book *Why Politics Matters* (2006), that 'the civic world described by Almond and Verba has gone.' A decade later it seems that the civic culture has changed dramatically and in ways that are increasingly worrying. Crick's response – as outlined in the Crick Report of 1998 – was the introduction of citizenship education as a statutory part of the national curriculum. In 2014 Paul Whiteley's statistical analysis of the available datasets discovered that where citizenship education had been delivered consistently and by committed teachers, it had started to achieve success. These results dovetailed with a broader set of political socialisation studies that revealed how political habits and identities forged in adolescence continue to shape attitudes and behaviours into adulthood. The reverse was also true in the sense that young people who are not encouraged to consider why politics matters or to vote are unlikely to develop such characteristics later in life – a negative cohort effect with the potential to silence generations. The worrying trend – when it comes to the delivery and content of citizenship education in the UK – is that recent studies reveal a shift within the curriculum towards a market-based and individualised model of citizenship rather than the broader and more participatory model originally promoted by Sir Bernard Crick.

49

The blunders of our governments

The title of this book is taken from a series of 18th-century American essays known as *The Federalist Papers*, in which the statesman and political philosopher James Madison referred to 'the blunders of our governments.' He considered the laws and activities of the incipient republic to be 'monuments of deficient wisdom.' Not surprisingly, then, this

is a book that focuses on what might be termed the über-blunders and omni-shambles of British government, from the Poll Tax disaster in the late 1980s through to New Labour's failed attempt to introduce identity cards between 2006 and 2010 (with 10 other 'blunders' in between). This is a well-written, entertaining and enlightening book that serves to shed light on some of the generally well known pathologies of the British constitution. The problem from the position of both political science and the public understanding of politics is that this book arguably fails to engage with the challenges of governing in those decades that spanned the millennium, or, to put the same point slightly differently, it fails to set its analysis against any detailed appreciation of the changing nature of political rule.

The normative tone of the book is therefore one of critique bordering on ridicule that is evident from the first sentence, 'Our subject in this book is the numerous blunders that have been committed by British governments of all parties in recent decades. We believe there have been far too many of them and that most, perhaps all, of them could have been avoided.' Anthony King and Ivor Crewe complete the opening paragraph by noting, 'Sadly, the British system is no longer held up as a model, and we suspect one reason is that today's British governments screw up so often' (p xi). The main problem, however, is that although the authors state, 'In our view, British governments in general are blunder-prone,' they provide no clear way of assessing that claim either historically or comparatively in a manner that provides any real analytical depth. It therefore seems somewhat odd when the authors write, 'Are they more blunder-prone than they used to be? Are governments in Britain more blunder-prone than the governments of other, comparable liberal democracies? Both questions are pertinent, but, alas, we are not in a position to answer either of them' (p x). Can these two questions really be so simply sketched over when the authors are at the same time making such sweeping claims about the nature and failings of British government? The authors clearly feel they can, and proceed to argue, 'But, whatever Britain's past experience and whatever the experience of other countries, our central point remains the same: that modern governments in Britain blunder too often.'

There can be no doubting that King and Crewe provide 12 'horror stories' to support their argument, but without any meaningful reference points against which to evaluate the frequency or nature of these cases, the reader is left with little more than an entertaining list of policy failures. Put slightly differently, it is difficult to really assess whether modern governments in Britain blunder too often or

whether, when gauged against the challenges of governing in the 21st century, the real surprise might be that governments do not blunder more often. This is a critical point. This is really a polemic rather than a balanced analysis of British government. The authors may reply with reference to the second chapter's attempt to focus on 'an array of successes' (just 12 pages in length in a book of nearly 500 pages) to deny this argument, but the tone and content of the other 26 chapters leave the reader in no doubt as to the authors' core argument that modern governments in Britain blunder too often. However, without any way of scientifically underpinning this argument, could it be that this book risks adding an oversimplified layer of veneer to an already dominant anti-political culture that generally thinks that governments and politicians never do anything else but fail or blunder?

The problem with such an interpretation is that it is not actually true. The realm of fate has, to some extent, been narrowed through collective social endeavour (ie, democratic

politics, and therefore, to some extent, by politicians). In the 50 years since Bernard Crick wrote *In Defence of Politics*, there has been a 17% increase in life expectancy worldwide. 'The world is a much better place today than it was in 1990 or even in 1970.' The United Nations *Human Development Report* for 2010 concludes that 'over the past twenty years many people around the world have experienced dramatic improvements in key areas of their lives … they are healthier, more educated, wealthier and have more power to appoint and hold their leaders accountable than ever before.' This report also highlights the clear positive relationship between democratic politics and human development, but King and Crewe provide little flavour of this broader global context. This might in itself reflect the fact that it has become highly unfashionable to talk or write about politics in anything but the most negative language. As Andy Smith argued in his review of *The Blunders of Our Governments* (*The Independent*, 20 September 2013),

In our anti-politics culture it may be thought that governments never do anything else but blunder. That is not actually true: a serious academic work could be written examining the things governments got right and lessons learnt there from – but who would buy a book entitled *The Successes of Our Governments*. Change the title to *The Blunders of Our Governments* and the readers are there.

The readers certainly are there, and this is a book that deserves to be read, but there is a risk that it taps into a strong social current of negativity and despair ('the politics of pessimism') without offering a greater sense of balance or governing perspective. Even the briefest discussion of Bernard Crick's classic *In Defence of Politics* (1962, and recently republished by Bloomsbury), with his warnings about the innate messiness and fragility of democratic politics, would have brought warmth to an otherwise cold book. The insights and arguments offered by scholars including Andrew Gamble (*Politics and Fate*, 2000), Gerry Stoker (*Why Politics Matters*, 2006) and Colin Hay (*Why We Hate Politics*, 2007) would all have added tone and texture and balance in way that intensified the social relevance and reach of the book. Others who would have challenged the general narrative offered by King and Crewe – Natan Sharansky and Ron Dermer (*The Case for Democracy*, 2007), Peter Riddell (*In Defence of Politicians*, 2011), Danny Oppenheimer and Mike Edwards (*Democracy Despite Itself*, 2012), Stephen Medvic (*In Defense of Politicians*, 2012) and Wendy Whitman Cobb (*Unbroken Government*, 2013) to mention just a few – are equally absent and sorely missed. It is also true that many of the 'blunders' – but not all – will be well known to many readers, as will many of the explanations that King and Crewe offer to explain the frequency of such failings. *Failure in British Government* (David Butler, Andrew Adonis and Tony Travers) and *Groupthink in Government* (Paul 't Hart), books that deal with specific failures or explanations, were both written two decades ago, whereas Gerald Kaufman's *How to Be a Minister* (first published over three decades ago) provides a magisterial insight into the dangers of departmentalism, reshuffles and ministerial hyperactivism that King and Crewe offer as explanatory variables. More recent books like Christopher Hood's *The Blame Game* (2010) or the content of specialist journals like the *Journal of Contingencies and Crisis Management* might also have added a clearer sense of the complexities of modern governance. The theories, concepts, analytical depth and comparative analysis are absent to a great extent because this is a book that is written for a broad public audience and not a narrow band of political scientists. Such endeavours are to be applauded if they contribute to the public understanding of politics, but the risk is that without some sense of balance, they contribute to rather than address public cynicism about politics.

In many ways, and like all good books, *The Blunders of Our Governments* raises as many, if not more, questions than it answers. In many ways, it provides a rich seam of empirical material that has been expertly prepared and now demands careful mining from a range of perspectives and positions in order to tease out exactly what, if anything, the 12 cases of failure provided by King and Crewe tell us about the changing nature of British government. One provocative step along this intellectual journey might attempt to turn King and Crewe's thesis inside out and upside down by daring to suggest that the changing nature of political rule (ie, the sociopolitical context within which political decisions are now taken) actually undermines their argument about blunder frequency and blunder avoidance. Could it be that a careful analysis of the changing nature of political rule in the 21st century leads to the conclusion that blunders are actually far rarer – actually far more infrequent – than analysts might expect from the scale of challenges faced by those in the business of government? The hook, twist or barb in this argument is the manner in which it draws on Anthony King's own work on the concept of 'political overload' in the mid-1970s.

'Once upon a time, then, man looked to God to give order to the world,' King argued in *Political Studies* (1975, vol 23, p 288). 'Then he looked to the market. Now he looks to government. The differences are important.... One blames not "him" or "it," but "them"', and in the decades since King's article was first published, a massive literature on 'disaffected democrats', 'the crisis of democracy' and 'why we hate politics' underlines the simple fact that large sections of the public increasingly blame 'them' (that is, politicians and governments) for a range of social ills. The important element about King's analysis, however, was his focus on expectations and intractability (or what we might re-label capacity and demand). The former simply highlights that the range of tasks, issues and functions for which governments are now held responsible increased greatly during the quarter of a century following the Second World War; the latter adds a qualitative dimension to this fact by noting that not only had the responsibilities of governments increased, but also the nature of the challenges being faced by governments was becoming more intractable. The business of government was becoming far more difficult, and there were no simple solutions to complex problems. The crux of the issue for King in the mid-1970s was therefore that 'the reach of British government exceeds its grasp; and its grasp, according to our second proposition, is being enfeebled just at the moment when its reach is being extended' (p 288). Feed that logic through the three decades covered by *The Blunders of Our Governments* and then set it against even the most cursory appreciation of the social, technological, economic and political trends that are so beautifully captured in Zygmunt Bauman's notion of 'liquid modernity', and 'the blunders of our governments' arguably appear far less damning and our systems possibly even slightly more resilient that at first might appear.

The challenges faced by governments are more complex (the 'wicked issues' of the 20th century replaced by the 'super-wicked issues' of the 21st that demand complex and inevitably risky 'megaprojects'), and the public's expectations more immediate and unrealistic than ever before. (No government can fulfil a world of ever-greater public expectations.) If the resources of governments (physical, financial, intellectual, etc) have declined relative to the rate of demands (quantity and intractability), then is it any wonder it is possible to identify a series of blunders? Although counterintuitive, an increase in the number and visibility of government blunders is theoretically consistent with a less blunder-prone, more resilient and ever more transparent governmental structure. The problem is that we have no counterfactuals or even cases where blunders did not take place (eg, the London Olympics), even though the conditions that King and Crewe associate with blundering may have been prevalent. Could it be that blunders are, to some extent, woven into the very fabric of modern governance in a way that defies political science's way of interpreting the world? Could it be that blunders are, to some extent, and echoing Bernard Crick, little more than the price we pay for living in a democracy? Can something really be a blunder if it is a failed response to a unique problem? Could it be that this book is not really about the politics of failure but the value of hindsight? These are the questions that *The Blunders of Our Governments* points to but arguably does not answer.

On reflection

This is really a note that returns to the theme of democratic realism through the lens of what we might call 'blunder amplification'. My plea is really for a little proportionality in the sense of being alert to the pressures of democratic governance, and the fact that there is within both 'politics as theory' and 'politics as practice' a certain sense that failure is inevitable. This is not meant to be a glib or pessimistic point, but simply an acknowledgement that politics is a tough profession, things will go wrong, and that you cannot please everyone all of the time. If there is a 'failure' that needs to be highlighted, it is the failure of governments to ask quite basic questions about the impact of their policies. Did the policy work? How would policy success be defined? How much did it cost? What can we learn from this experience? This lack of analytical reflection within government is, to some extent, a product of partisan politics – there is rarely any credit to be claimed for success, whereas failure will be exploited mercilessly by opponents. Political science has also tended to focus on policy failure rather than policy success (with King and Crewe's *The Blunders of Our Governments* representing the latest in a distinguished lineage of failure-focused analyses). It is therefore with some relief that I am able to report the emergence of a new and far more (politically) sophisticated seam of policy analysis – led by scholars such as Allan McConnell – that embraces 'policy failure, policy success and the grey areas in-between.' It is, of course, this 'grey area' where most policies end up residing for reasons that take us back to the complexities and mess of democratic politics. To overlook this inevitable mess would itself be a terrible … blunder.

50

Dear Maria Miller, it really wasn't all your fault

The news that Maria Miller decided to resign as Culture Secretary[1] was not really much of a surprise. The only real surprise was the way that she had seemed to be toughing out the media feeding frenzy and the gradual, but very clear, loss of political support for so long.

And yet, beyond the sensational headlines the real – and arguably more important issues – remain unexamined.

Politics is a rough and sometimes brutal business. I'm sure that this morning Maria Miller is more aware than most of this fact, but it seems too obvious, slightly too clean and simple, to blame just one person for a political saga that has rolled on for some time. In order to learn from this affair it is necessary to step back and examine the bigger picture in order to reveal where blame really lies. Indeed, what this less personalised account reveals is a set of blame games at three levels.

At the first and most obvious level, Miller really was to blame, if not for the incorrect claiming of expenses, certainly for appearing to treat the House with contempt.[2] This is a critical point. Politicians at Westminster

– irrespective of their party – will generally tolerate many failings and indiscretions on the part of their colleagues, but standing up in the chamber and giving such a brief and curt apology was a terrible error.

And yet, Miller's general attitude to the whole investigation over her expenses seems to have been generally dismissive. The Commons Standards Committee criticised her attitude[3] during their investigation, which it ruled was a breach of the Parliamentary Code of Conduct. But why would a member of the Cabinet adopt an approach that was almost designed to ruffle feathers and prolong an investigation? Humble pie might not taste very nice, but sometimes it needs to be eaten, whether you believe you are hungry or not.

I can't help wondering what her ministerial aides and advisers – her spin doctors – were whispering into her ear as she adopted such a strident approach to the issue of her expenses.

System is broken

Although far less sensational – and therefore by modern media standards less newsworthy – the bigger issue in the 'blame game' that needs to be unravelled is not so much 'Media Maria' or her team, but the whole issue of parliamentary self-regulation.[4] The principle that MPs should make the final decision over the disciplining of their errant colleagues has been stretched to breaking point, and it seems hardly fair to blame Miller for the outcome of a self-regulatory system that has been the source of ridicule and concern for some time.

The system is to blame for much of the chaos and confusion that has surrounded the former Culture Secretary. The big question does not relate to Miller, or how £45,000 became £5,800, but to how we stop this situation happening again. Self-regulation is incredibly

tricky, for the simple reason that not only must justice be done, but it must also be seen to be done – and the public simply do not trust politicians in this sense. It really is as simple as that. And yet, the relationship between MPs and the Independent Parliamentary Standards Authority[5] remains at a simmering heat, and the idea of giving the parliamentary watchdog increased powers is unlikely to attract support within the house. "Create a new body!" I hear the readers cry, but this in itself creates new challenges over appointments, control, legitimacy and control. But something needs to be done.

So, Mrs Miller … Maria (if I may), it really wasn't all your fault. I have no idea about the advice you received from your ministerial aides and advisers, but in many ways it doesn't matter as you'll all fall from grace together. You were, however, a victim of a system that has let everyone down. Your resignation is not a triumph for democracy or a victory for the media, but yet another example of the need to drag Parliament into the 21st century.

On reflection

Question: Is this post really about Maria Miller? Answer: No. It is about two things – the concept of blame within contemporary politics, and about the concept of parliamentary self-regulation. The interesting element about Maria Miller's resignation was that it had more to do with her perceived failure to show any remorse and to treat Parliament with respect than it did with the specific questions concerning her expenses. There was, however, a major shift in terms of the governance and regulation of MPs' expenses in the wake of the scandal that engulfed Parliament in 2009. The Independent Parliamentary Standards Authority (IPSA) now regulates and administrates the *MPs' Scheme of Business Costs and Expenses* and publishes annual reports on overall costs. Such independent regulation might be seen as part of a process of 'dragging parliament into the 21st century', but whether the provision of ever more information to the public in the name of transparency has actually helped restore public confidence in political institutions and politicians is a moot point.

The annual IPSA report on MPs' spending is generally met with howls of derision by the media, with a handful of MPs generally highlighted for public naming and shaming to the extent that many politicians are reluctant to actually make *any* expense claims for fear of a media and public backlash. For many MPs the acronym 'IPSA' doesn't stand for the constitutional watchdog that controls pay and expenses, but for a phrase that captures their collective sense of being under-valued, even under attack – 'I'm Paid Sod All.'

51

Bring me a scapegoat to destroy: Babies, blame and bargains

When reading this week's coverage of the independent report into the regulation of Morecambe University Hospital Trust by the Care Quality Commission (CQC), I couldn't help but reflect on the links between this terrible episode in public sector management and Stanley Cohen's famous work on moral panics and folk devils. The public, the media, interest groups, politicians, vaunted 'experts' – just about anyone and everyone – lined up to join the 'moral barricade' to decry the failure of the CQC to intervene in Morecambe Bay. An interesting element of this social outrage was the manner in which, as Cohen's thesis would suggest, a very specific 'folk devil' was quickly identified in the form of the three senior officials (now identified as Jill Finney, Cynthia Bower and Anna Jefferson).

The three officials were accused of putting political convenience above the care of newborn babies. A process of full-blown demonisation has subsequently occurred in which the three women are now the focus of online and offline threats to the extent that they have been forced to leave their homes and go on the run. The three women have become unfavourable symbols for a set of social concerns that run far deeper than this scandal – a perceived culture of secrecy within the NHS, and healthcare demands outstripping resources. As a result, as with all folk devils, all mention of these women now revolves around their central and exclusively negative features.

My point here is not to deny that a tragedy has occurred. The Secretary of State for Health's comment that "what happened at Morecambe Bay is above all a terrible personal tragedy for all the families involved" fails to capture the raw pain, the complete physical and psychological numbness, felt by a parent at the loss of a child. My point revolves around the manner in which we, as a society, have dealt with this tragedy. Is it simply too easy to create and then destroy a folk devil? Could it be that the tragedy actually points to the existence of a set of issues that no one is willing to take on? Indeed, if the existing research and writing on moral panics and folk devils illustrates one thing, it is that the link between the demonised individual and the actual focus of public concern is frequently tenuous and often non-existent. Scapegoats are created to act as lightning rods for broader social concerns.

For those offended by any suggestion that the senior staff of the CQC might have been unfairly pilloried, let me be clear about my position. Something clearly went wrong. The regulatory system failed. The three staff at the top of the CQC must be held to account and accept some responsibility. The grit I want to throw into the ointment is a question regarding the apportionment of blame, and the existence of annoying little things called facts and due process.

The facts – if a contemporary social scientist can use such a term – appear to be this: the three senior staff in the CQC are accused of destroying and suppressing a document that outlined the failings in care at the maternity unit of University Hospitals of Morecambe Bay. Yet the document still exists, and all three of the staff deny that there was any attempt at a cover-up. As Ms Finney told BBC Radio 4's 'Today Programme', "There was not a decision [at that meeting] to delete a report nor was there an instruction." Last week's independent report by Grant Thornton created more heat than light in terms of whether a 'deliberate suppression' of an internal CQC memo in Morecambe Bay actually occurred, and even explicitly states 'this allegation has been denied by the person who is alleged to have given an instruction to delete this report.' The report found no 'smoking gun', and Ms Finney has stated on record that the report was 'the first thing' she pointed out to Thornton when they were brought in to conduct an external review. Although redacted in the initial version of the independent review by Thornton, the

CQC quickly caved in to public pressure and identified the women. Unable to contribute to the review or read the report prior to publication, it is hard not to have some sympathy for Cynthia Bower's view that she was "hung out to dry". "The first time I saw the final report was when I read it online on Tuesday night," Jill Finney has stated, "and by Wednesday morning the media feeding frenzy had begun." Could it be that in our rush to apportion blame and claim scalps we have lost our capacity to learn from mistakes and really understand what happened?

In order to begin answering that question, let me throw three more issues into the debate. The first is the issue of complexity. Put very simply, the CQC is expected to regulate an incredibly complex network of institutions but with relatively limited resources. A number of scandals since 2009 have highlighted deficiencies in terms of the CQC's management, resources and regulatory scope – but nothing was actually done. It highlights the manner in which the problems were arguably *systemic* rather than *individual*, and therefore it might be too simple to blame just two or three people.

The second point highlights the political dimension of this scandal and exposes a degree of naivety. The managers of any public sector organisation – be they schools, hospitals, prisons or regulators – will inevitably keep one eye on public perception and media management when dealing with any significant matters. Modern politics is attack politics and public sector organisations now operate in a low-trust/high-blame environment. There is a strong punitive element to any crisis, and for most public servants accountability means blame.

And behind this (and third), lies an implicit level of resentment over the perceived high levels of public sector remuneration at the highest level. Could the price of a senior salary actually be an expectation of total infallibility? This brings us back to the issue of naivety and what has been termed 'the new public service bargain'. The old public service bargain was forged around a job for

life, political anonymity, a relatively low salary but an excellent pension scheme. In the new public service, by contrast, a salary far higher than the Prime Minister's is the price you pay for political visibility, job insecurity and the knowledge that if something goes wrong, the buck will stop with you.

Maybe someone forgot to tell Cynthia Bower about the 'new public service bargain'?

▬▬▬▬▬▬

On reflection

I had no idea that so many of my posts focused on the issues of blame, social lightning rods and complexity. These are themes that flow into 'the problem of many hands' and 'the problem of many eyes'. The former highlights how the more actors contribute to a process, the more links there are in a chain of delegation, the harder it will be to pinpoint the responsibility of any one specific actor; the latter emphasises that too much scrutiny by too many organisations can become incredibly distracting for an organisation to

the extent that it prevents them from focusing on their core tasks. Create more 'eyes' to overcome the problem of many 'hands', and the challenges of governing simply escalate in terms of complexity and bureaucratic costs. Don't create more 'eyes', however, and an increasingly complex and fragmented administrative structure risks becoming unwieldy, uncontrollable and unaccountable. This balance between achieving a proportionate amount of accountability while not impeding organisational performance of flexibility is probably *the* central challenge of modern governance. The flipside, however, is that when things go wrong – as they inevitably will – there is a knee-jerk media-fuelled public clamour for someone to take the blame in a sacrificial sense. Hence the emphasis on lightning rods, sacrificial lambs, scapegoats, etc in a context where 'the problem of many hands' makes blaming any one person for systemic failings a somewhat dubious endeavour. But what is interesting about the years since this post was first written in 2014 is the manner in which the focus of scapegoating has arguably shifted, from an

individualised process based around specific incidents to a collective process based around social challenges. Put slightly differently, in recent years politicians have increasingly blamed (scapegoated or demonised) specific communities or social groups for the ailments of society in order to win public support. Mexicans and Muslims, bureaucrats and bankers, foreigners or fast food producers ... there is something going on that revolves around an odd mixture of blame displacement and guilt reduction, but which offers very little in terms of cultivating collective trust or social solidarity.

Making politics relevant in a post-truth world

The last post

Crockery for sale in the Republic of Stokes Croft, Bristol

52

Explaining political disaffection: Closing the expectations gap

Has political science generally failed to fulfil its broader social responsibilities in terms of cultivating political understanding and stimulating engaged citizenship? The increasing evidence of political disaffection stems from the existence of an ever-increasing 'expectations gap' between what is promised/expected and what can realistically be achieved/delivered by politicians and democratic states. If the 20th century witnessed 'the triumph of democracy', then the 21st century appears wedded to 'the failure of democracy' as citizens around the world (setting recent developments in North Africa and the Middle East aside for the moment) appear to have become distrustful of politicians, sceptical about democratic institutions, and disillusioned about the capacity of democratic politics to resolve pressing social concerns.

Even the most cursory glance along the spines of the books on the library shelves reveals a set of post-millennium titles that hardly engender confidence that all is well (*Disaffected Democracies*; *Democratic Challenges, Democratic Choices*; *Political Disaffection in Contemporary Democracies*; *Hatred of Democracy*; *Why We Hate Politics*; *Democratic Deficit*; *Vanishing Voters*; *Democracy in Retreat*; *Uncontrollable Societies of Disaffected Individuals* etc). And yet, if democracy is in crisis, then it must be said that this has been the dominant narrative for at least half a century. 'Is democracy in crisis?' provided the opening line of the Trilateral Commission's 1975 report into evidence of growing dissatisfaction among the public with political processes, political institutions and politicians. The 'civic culture' so endeared by Gabriel Almond and Sidney Verba had somehow mutated into a 'critical culture' with parallel pessimism about the future of democracy.

In contextual terms the social and political fabric has changed arguably beyond contention in the last half-century. The decline of deference, increasing levels of education, growing levels of mobility in all its forms, the existence and perception of 'new' social risks, an increasingly aggressive media, the impact of ever more immediate and sophisticated forms of communication technology, the influence of three decades of neoliberal dominance have all, in their own ways, increased the demands on democratic political systems.

And yet, the pressures created by the changing context have not generally been matched by related increases in the capacity of democratic governance to deliver. The rise of globalised networks, the transition from 'government to governance', declining levels of social capital and a host of other factors have arguably combined to ensure that the conclusion of the Trilateral Commission's 1975 report – *The Crisis of Democracy* – that '[t]he demands on democratic government grow, while the capacity of democratic government stagnates' – continues to hit a contemporary chord.

The nature of political rule has changed in ways that have generally made the business of government more difficult. This has implications for both the politics and management of public expectations, on the one hand, and for public attitudes toward political processes and institutions, on the other, which scholars have generally been slow to acknowledge.

The politics and management of public expectations

Lying beneath a focus on the changing nature of political rule is therefore a deeper and more basic question concerning the nature of public expectations vis-à-vis democratic politics. My argument here is both bold and sweeping: the politics and management of the public's expectations (regarding lifestyle, healthcare, education, pensions, travel, food, water, finances, the environment, etc) will define the 21st century.

Let me explain this argument by reference to a simple model. Imagine, for a moment, two horizontal bars placed one above the other with a significant gap between them. The upper bar relates to *demand* and specifically to the promises that politicians may have made in order to be elected (in addition to the public's expectations of what politics and the state could and should deliver). The bottom bar relates to *supply* in terms of what the political system can realistically deliver given the complexity of the challenges, the contradictory nature of many requests and the resources with which it can seek to satisfy demand. The distance between the two bars is therefore an 'expectations gap', and recent survey evidence seems to suggest that in recent years the expectations gap has widened. With this simple framework in mind, my argument is straightforward: the increasing evidence of political disaffection stems from the existence of an ever-increasing 'expectations gap' between what is promised/expected and what can realistically be achieved/delivered by politicians and democratic states.

Here are three short observations before moving to the final question. First and foremost, the analysis of public expectations regarding public services and the capacity of politicians appears to represent something of a *terra incognita* for political science. Mass data banks and survey results provide rich data about the state of public attitudes, but provide far less in terms of *why* the public hold such views or exactly *how* their expectations have been shaped, let alone the theories and methods through which political science can generate more sophisticated insights. My argument here is not in line with the advice of Bernard Baruch about 'voting for the man who promises the least as he'll be least disappointing', but it does begin to open up fresh questions about whether democracy really is failing or if society is simply expecting too much. 'If we understood politics rather better,' Colin Hay argues in his award-winning *Why We Hate Politics* (2007), 'we would expect less of it. Consequently, we would be surprised and dismayed rather less often by its repeated failures to live up to our over-inflated and unrealistic expectations.'

Political science and society

A focus on the politics and management of public expectations vis-à-vis democratic politics brings us to the hook, or the barb, or the twist, in this commentary and a questioning of the role of political science itself within the demos. The Trilateral Commission went to great lengths to highlight the *intrinsic challenges* to the functioning of democracy, by which it meant the simple fact that democratic government is not perfect, it does not operate in an automatically self-sustaining or self-correcting fashion, and mechanisms must be put in place, and constantly reviewed, to prevent the abuse of power.

A more subtle intrinsic challenge lies in the straightforward observation that politics (and therefore politicians) is tasked with squeezing collective decisions out of multiple and competing interests and demands (as Gerry Stoker argues in his excellent book *Why Politics Matters*). The political process is therefore inevitably based on compromise,

negotiation and incremental adjustment – Max Weber's 'strong and slow boring of hard boards' – for the simple reason that there are no simple solutions to complex problems. My question here relates to whether political scientists have some form of professional responsibility to the public to stimulate public understanding and debate about the existence of these intrinsic features, and how they play out in relation to a myriad of issues and questions as a counterweight to unrealistic (or what Weber labelled 'infantile') expectations. Put slightly differently, whether political science might play a valuable role in closing 'the expectations gap' or, at the very least, playing a more visible role in public debates.

'Politics is the master science, both as an activity and as a study,' Bernard Crick wrote, '[but] neither the activity nor the study can exist apart from each other.' In making this point, Crick sought to highlight a link between *the health of democratic politics* and *the health of the study of politics*. A quarter of a century later Samuel Huntington would use his Presidential Address to the American Political Science Association to re-emphasise this link in his argument, "Where democracy is strong, political science is strong…where democracy is weak, political science is weak." In making this point Crick and Huntington were attempting to expose the deeper social purpose of political science in the sense of cultivating public understanding and promoting engaged citizenship by daring to emphasise the inescapable moral dimension of politics in both theory and practice. In doing so, Huntington quoted Albert Hirshman's adage, 'Morality belongs [at] the centre of our work; and it can get there only if social scientists are morally alive and make themselves vulnerable to moral concerns – then they will produce morally significant works, consciously or otherwise.'

Political scientists possess a professional obligation not just to each other in terms of disseminating their research findings, but also to the wider public in terms of explaining why their research matters (ie, why it *is* relevant) as a contribution to cultivating active citizenship and political literacy. The discipline must therefore learn to 'talk to multiple publics in multiple ways' – to adopt Michael Burawoy's phrase – in order to not only increase the visibility and leverage of the discipline among potential research funders or to improve levels of public debate and understanding about pressing political issues, but also to improve the overall standard of scholarship.

This is a critical point. As Michael Billig argues in his *Learn to Write Badly* (2013), not only has the general standard of writing deteriorated in the social and political sciences, but scholars also deploy verbose terminology in order to exaggerate, conceal and succeed. Bernard Crick highlighted and warned against exactly this trend in his 'Rallying Cry to the University Professors of Politics', and his complaint about 'all the author's chaff on everything before ever the grain is reached.' My point here is that presenting and testing the findings of research beyond the lecture theatre and seminar room or writing for a public audience offers great potential in terms of stress-testing ideas, assumptions and conclusions. Moreover, in relation to the analysis and understanding of whether democracy really is in crisis, such a model of 'engaged scholarship' may also play a small – but no less important – role in closing the gap that appears to have emerged between the governors and the governed.

On reflection

This was a plea to the university professors of politics to reflect on their wider professional responsibilities to the public in terms of promoting public understanding or encouraging participation. In the three years since this post was first written, I would have to conclude that (overall) my plea has been ignored. This is not to say that political science has not been visible in recent debates about post-crisis politics or climate change, or to deny that new entrants to the profession do seem to possess a far more open and engaged approach to their scholarship. The

problem, however, is more fundamental and revolves around the failure of political science (and the social sciences more generally) to understand the broader political game or how to play it. The election of Donald Trump in the US and the Brexit vote in the UK provide cases in point, and the backlash has already started. Nicholas Kristof has written in *The New York Times* about the 'dangers of echo chambers on campus' and the need for more ideological diversity on campus. There is one thing being anti-Trump, but in presenting an overwhelmingly negative and aggressive stance, the risk is that you simply play straight into the hands of your opponents who want to portray you as little more than part of a self-interested and elite establishment. A similar set of arguments could be made about why academic experts were so easily rejected within the EU Brexit campaign. It remains a worrying truism of modern life that to label something or some comment as 'academic' is to define it as 'irrelevant'. But that's still not enough in terms of understanding the roots of the gap that seem to have opened up between the governors and the governed.

In this regard I was taken by an argument offered by Frank Furedi in the *Times Higher Education* shortly after the Brexit result. 'In years to come, when the post-Brexit dust has settled, I will still remember a comment made to me by a social scientist the day after the Brexit verdict. Still in shock, he expressed his sense of astonishment by noting that he had "never met or talked to anyone who supported Brexit"', Furedi wrote. 'And that's the nub of the problem. It seems that too many academic supporters of the Remain campaign have talked only to people like themselves. They may be "experts", but they are certainly not public intellectuals.' Only a new and more sophisticated politics of political science will change this.

▬▬▬▬▬▬

53

Politics without vision

I've been waiting for this book all my life. Of course, I didn't know that was the case until I'd read it, but now I understand the role that political thought can play in helping me to understand the world around me. All that was once reasonably solid in the world has melted away – across a range of social, economic, technological and environmental dimensions – to the point at which the metaphor of 'liquidity', as the writing of Zygmunt Bauman has revealed, captures a loss of safe harbours or anchor points. Hannah Arendt captured this sense of flux, and the status of and demands on political thought in the modern era, in the phrase 'thinking without a banister' (*denken ohne geländer*). It meant for her that humans could no longer rely on any transcendental grounding to anchor their thinking – be that God, nature, history or technology. She saw this as both an opportunity and a threat. Political thought, she said, could be 'absolutely and uncompromisingly of this world.' Tracy Strong develops this line of thinking by arguing not simply that we have lost our foundational supports in terms of the intellectual scaffolding that helps us to make sense of the changing world around us, but also (and more importantly) by revisiting the past in order to shape the future.

The aim of *Politics Without Vision* is therefore to revisit the work of seven influential thinkers – Friedrich Nietzsche, Max Weber, Sigmund Freud, Vladimir Lenin, Carl Schmitt, Martin Heidegger and Hannah Arendt – to expose new seams of thought and doors left unopened in their work in order to explore new paths and ways of understanding the world.

'The thinkers I consider in this book are neither democrats nor liberals, at least in the Anglo-American sense of those terms,' Strong notes. 'But it is also my conviction that, by examining their thought in a nonrejectionist manner, one can identify what I call *turning points* – points of divergence at which they started down one of several paths.' It is in exploring these untrodden paths that new ways of thinking about the world emerge and, through this, ways of furthering the democratic impulse.

If Strong's aim is to look on the past with new eyes, then he is undoubtedly successful. Every chapter provides a heady mixture of intellectual energy, scholarly passion and fresh perspectives. And, like all good books, it raises as many questions as it answers; it is sure to provoke a strong reaction across a range of disciplines and fields of inquiry. At the core of this book, however, is a double-barbed dimension that left me intellectually more secure and yet at the same time confused.

This is a critical point. We live in strange and troubled times, when a vast number of social variables reflect the day-to-day impact of social dislocations (or social anomie). Initially, I thought this book would deliver new ways of understanding the world around me; new ways of making sense of increasingly ephemeral relationships; and

new ways of thinking about 'the life and death of democracy' (to adopt the title of John Keane's magisterial book). And yet, instead of providing new intellectual frameworks – new signposts, supports, sticks or banisters – Strong rejects the notion of epic theories to fulfil such a role and instead draws on the work of Nietzsche, Weber, Freud and others to almost deify the thinking of those who could step outside existing frameworks 'to do *without* such vision'.

Hence the double barb: there is no doubt that political theory urgently demands a huge injection of fresh thinking and raw ambition – few (particularly young) scholars dare to trespass across boundaries and challenge dominant assumptions in the manner that Strong's arguments imply – and yet, at the same time, surely the role of political theory is, at least in some way, to assist the broader public (the *polis*) to make sense of the world around them by identifying certain boundaries, signposts or landmarks? To put the same point even more simply: surely we need a vision? If we return to

Bauman's emphasis on liquidity, then surely we disappoint ourselves if we ignore the fact that liquids can be channelled, bottled, diluted and even solidified? I also want to look on the past with new eyes, and Strong has certainly allowed me to do this, but I want to look on the future with new eyes that help me to navigate the moral dilemmas and political choices that will have to be navigated.

Strong almost rejoices in the lack of a banister, whereas I'm desperately in search of one.

I make no excuse for the fact that my yearning for a way of making sense of the world may well reflect my own weaknesses and fears. Indeed, to accept this personal weakness – this failure to live up to the challenges that *Politics Without Vision* sets down – is to situate myself within the contours of Nietzsche's statement that, 'He believes in banisters because he believes in his weakness and his fear.' How am I to escape this double bind, this double barb? How can I relearn the art of thinking – even the art *of living* – in an age without banisters? If all handrails and footbridges have fallen into the water, as Nietzsche argued in *Thus Spoke Zarathustra* (1883), then surely the role of social and political theorists is to help build new footings and waymarkers? And it is exactly this sense of provocation and challenge that exemplifies the great beauty and value of this work. This is a book that can be read and enjoyed, by scholars and interested members of the public alike. It is a book that demonstrates Strong's rare gift for discussing complex issues in an accessible manner, and his capacity for bridging 'politics as theory' and 'politics as practice'. This, in turn, flows into the broader significance of this book.

Political thought is (and has been for some time) on the decline because scholars seem unwilling or unable to explain the day-to-day social relevance of their discipline. Ian Shapiro's *The Flight from Reality in the Human Sciences* (2007) provided a damning critique of a field of inquiry that had become increasingly esoteric, isolated and disconnected: 'The flight from reality has been so complete that academics have all but lost sight of what they claim is the object of their study.' Too many academics have become scared of flying (to adopt Shapiro's powerful metaphor) for fear of being ridiculed for being insufficiently specific or rigorous, or rejected by the intellectual gatekeepers who have built their careers on a specific approach to the discipline and now edit journals or chair selection panels. To fly is therefore to feel a heady sort of freedom and manoeuvrability, a feeling that what you write actually matters, and a belief in your capacity to take risks, challenge established idioms and reach out to new audiences.

Strong's *Politics Without Vision* is undoubtedly a book that is not scared of flying; it is a brilliant and provocative work that may just start to reverse the decline that has held back political theory for too long.

On reflection

There is a link between the focus of this post on 'politics without vision' and the previous discussion of the politics of political science. In many ways what I have been arguing for over the past two decades is for those professional students of politics who work within our universities to have a clearer vision about what they are trying to achieve. My starter for ten on this point would be that 'knowledge for the sake of knowledge is not enough' in a world beset by a range of fundamental challenges. This, in turn, leads me to reflect on the lives of two scholars who did approach their scholarship, their politics, with a very clear vision. The first was the leading British economist Sir Tony Atkinson, who did such a huge amount to shape the study of inequality and poverty. Such was his prolific output that he was lovingly known at the London School of Economics as 'The Twins' because it seemed simply impossible that one person could do so many different things at the same time. There was, however, a strong, if not political, then certainly moral, drive behind his scholarship, and he once remarked that 'no theory is worth doing if it is not addressed to a problem that is blighting our world.' Atkinson worked with governments and non-governmental organisations all around the world with a clear vision to understand and alleviate poverty and inequality. Zygmunt Bauman, by contrast, who died just days after Atkinson in January 2017, possessed an equally clear but very different vision that focused on the emergence and implications of what he called 'liquid modernity'. Always unwilling to offer any practical blueprints for a different future, Bauman's work was influential among progressive young activists around the world. His high-level writing provided a broad vision of social change that facilitated social understanding in the manner promoted by C. Wright Mills in his *The Sociological Imagination*. In this regard, Bauman's impact on society was less focused and direct than Atkinson's, but no less important, notably in relation to revealing the potential impact and reach of social and political theory.

54

Dangerous minds: 'Public' political science or 'punk' political science?

The end of another academic year and my mind is tired. But tired minds are often dangerous minds. Just as alcohol can loosen the tongue (*in vino veritas*), for the non-drinkers of this world fatigue can have a similar effect (*lassitudine veritas liberabit*). Professional pretensions are far harder to sustain when one is work-weary, but I can't help wondering if the study of politics has lost its way ... heretical to hear or music to the ears of the disenchanted?

What is the core role of a professional political scientist in the 21st century? Where do our social and professional responsibilities lie within and beyond the discipline? How does political science differ, if at all, from the broader social sciences in terms of defining principles and values? On what criteria should we judge success and failure? How is the external context in which political science operates changing, and what role is the discipline playing in terms of shaping or informing that context? These are the questions that have concerned me

for some years and that I have engaged with in my writing on the concept of 'engaged scholarship'. But Jeffrey C. Isaac's recent editorial 'For a More *Public* Political Science' in *Perspectives in Politics* – in my opinion, possibly the best political science journal in the world – jolted me out of my end-of-semester weariness.

It is an essay that resonates with my concern over professional pretensions: '[as editor] why make believe that I am simply enacting the anonymous and ineluctable requirements of "science"', Isaac writes, 'Everybody knows that this is not the case. And yet we so often pretend. *Why pretend?*'

Pretending is not something that is easy to do when you are tired, and maybe that's why Isaac's arguments hit home with such alacrity at this particular moment in time. The lecture halls and seminar rooms are empty, most academic offices lay vacant, administrators administrate with a lazy summer swagger but in a matter of weeks the whole academic cycle will start again. Maybe that's the problem. Could it be that the whole higher education system has become trapped in a market-led cycle or spiral of its own creation that promotes conformity over difference, results over risk, customers over citizens and 'safe bets' over 'creative rebels'? This question brings me back to Isaac's essay and its 'academic-*political* purpose':

> My purpose is simple: to clarify, defend and expand the spaces in political science where broad and problem-driven scholarly discussions and debates can flourish.

It seems as if something is going on (again) within American political science. That all is not well and that a number of longstanding tensions and schisms that had for some time been managed through the post-*perestroikan* stand-off, within which the creation of *Perspectives on Politics* formed a key element, have once again risen to the surface. In this context Isaac's essay covers a lot of well-worn ground, but then concludes with a distinctive twist, hook or barb. It revisits the debates concerning methodological pluralism, hyper-specialisation and a perceived statistical supremacism that have raged for several decades before then identifying and criticising a resurgent positivism in the discipline, 'which I believe jeopardises what this journal represents.' There is, then, for Isaac, a need to politicise the internal disciplinary debate about which sub-field 'is allowed to claim the mantle of "political science" and to present itself as speaking for the discipline.' The concern is that some of the *perestroikan* energies may have been co-opted or overtaken to the extent that they now threaten the sense of intellectual and methodological value, the belief that qualitative and interpretive approaches produce different but equally valid forms of knowledge to large-N quantitative analysis.

But why do I care? European political science in general, and British political studies in particular, has generally evolved without the same internal divisions and bitter enmities. '*perestroika*-lite' is the way I have described the emergence of similar issues in the European context in recent years, but my sense is that the shadow of exactly those neo-positivist pretensions that worry Isaac are becoming more pronounced. In the UK I am frequently told that the future of the political and social sciences lies in the realm of digital scholarship and its capacity for utilising the increasing availability of mega-data. Now I don't know about you, but 'data-scraping' – let alone debates about data transparency or data analytical techniques – does not float my boat when it comes to thinking about my role as a scholar. However, there is also something slightly disquieting about Isaac's position. Indeed, this is probably where the notion of 'dangerous minds' as a symptom of the end of my 20th year as an academic starts to emerge. Indeed, two naughty little thoughts come to mind.

First, does the notion of *public* political science that Isaac promotes really offer salvation to a discipline that some might see to be in perpetual crisis?

Second, does political science actually have anything to offer the public?

The answer to both these questions is obviously 'yes' and 'yes', but let me play devil's advocate for a few moments in order to contribute to the debate that Isaac has so valuably initiated (or revived).

First of all, the notion of public political science clearly takes its inspiration from Michael Burawoy's influential critique of sociology and his movement for public sociology. And yet my sense is that the ambition and vigour behind the public sociology movement has always been far greater than the vision that Isaac seems to be discussing. Indeed, from my position on the other side of the Atlantic I have always been taken by how internalised the debates within American political science have seemed to be and how little they have focused on the role of the public or the role of the discipline as

an intermediary between the governors and the governed. The Caucus for a New Political Science that was founded as a section within the American Political Science Association in 1967 has, to my mind, always offered a more convincing model of public political science. The Caucus' journal *New Political Science* was established in order to underline the relevance of the discipline and to promote a more problem- and solution-focused form of political science. The notion of *public* political science is therefore not a matter for intra-disciplinary debates but for the ambitious dissemination of research findings into the public sphere and also the engagement of the public within the research process. This latter element is really where the potential lies in terms of demonstrating both 'the trap' and 'the promise' (to borrow from C. Wright Mills) of political science. How might we actively recruit the public as active participants and collectors of data into the research process?

Second, encouraging the dissemination of research findings into the public sphere is all well and good as long as the discipline

actually has something to say. Put slightly differently, engaging in 'the art of translation' whereby the discipline 'talks to multiple publics in multiple ways' (to borrow one of Burawoy's phrases) might actually be counter-productive unless it has something of value to say. This is a critical point as the discipline risks ridicule and reduced funding if the message it promotes is one of limited ambition and limited results. Now this is obviously a naughty and quite scandalous little thought that will be used against me for the rest of my career, but could it be that what we actually need is not *public* political science but *punk* political science? Yes, ridiculous I know, but just stick with me on this. One of the most striking elements of the rise of managerialism and market logic within universities has been the dampening down not simply of the intellectual spirit but also, and more prosaically, the time to think.

Hidden behind Isaac's analysis is the creation of an incentives and sanctions framework within higher education that says, 'This is what a successful scholar should be doing.' But where is the intellectual counter-movement, the restless minds that don't want to follow the crowd, the scholar who rejects the notion of education as little more than a preparation for the workplace and economic growth, the square pegs that cannot be knocked into round holes? Political science just seems to have … lost its political oomph, its vim and vigour; its intellectual 'get-up-and-go' seems to have 'got-up-and-gone'. I'm over-egging the pudding (a very English phrase, I'm sorry), but I wonder how many readers would pretend that this is not really the case. Could it be that what we need is not *public* political science, but a form of *punk* political science that challenges all conventional ways of doing the study of politics, just as the punk movement challenges conventional ways of doing politics? Whether this period of creative chaos could emerge from within given the institutional and cultural restrictions that large sections of the discipline seem to have imbued and accepted is a pointed question. But I cannot help but think it might be one that is worth exploring….

I'm sorry, I did tell you I was tired.

▬▬▬▬▬▬▬

On reflection

Writing while either drunk or tired (or both) is a risky endeavour, but there has to be something in the Latin phrase *in vino veritas*. This is one of those posts – written while tired, not drunk – that allows possibly a little too much deep frustration or disappointment to slip. Suffice to say that the punk political science movement has yet to emerge despite the fact that a little creative chaos is undoubtedly needed to help understand the emergence of what might be termed 'punk populism' in the sense that, when it comes to Trump, there is a clear sense that he has created a new political space that is edgy, carnivalesque, uncertain, volatile and from a certain perspective, punk-like. As James Parker wrote in *The Atlantic* (October 2016), 'Trump-space is not democratic. It depends for its energy on the tyrannical emanations of the man at its center, on the wattage of his big marmalade face and that dainty mobster

thing he does with the thumb and forefinger of his right hand. But it is artistic. Within its precincts, the most vicious and nihilistic utterances retain a kind of innocent levity: They sound half-funny, theatrical, or merely petulant. The scapegoating and bullying are somehow childlike. This is why, so far, no political strategy has succeeded against him. It rolls on, his power grab, his wild Trumpian trundling toward the White House, because he's not doing politics at all. He's doing bad art. Terrible art. He can't go off message, because his message is "Look at me! I'm off message!"' Maybe we need that punk political science after all.

▬▬▬▬▬▬▬

55

Claims of increasing irrelevance of universities are ideology masquerading as evidence

In a recent column[1] in *The Telegraph*, Allister Heath claims that the humanities and social sciences are suffering from increasing groupthink, inwardness and irrelevance – creating an environment in which certain political outlooks are suppressed and academic research rarely resonates beyond the hallowed halls of the university. Such an account simply does not square with the realities of universities in 21st-century Britain. Heath praises the university world of the 20th century, but then neglects the golden rule that drove that work and is still present in 21st-century academia: make sure you have robust evidence to support your arguments. In terms of academic research, the supposed thought police of the left are in little evidence in the pluralistic university faculties that we know across the UK, places in which rich debates over theory and methods take place.

When it comes to Heath's arguments over the narrow reach of academic research in terms of citation, he relies on tenuous evidence. The claim that '98 per cent of academic papers in the arts and humanities are never cited in any subsequent research' comes from a *25-year-old* study that was at the time shown to have been misleading.[2] The very pluralism that Heath argued is absent is what drives the abundance of contributions, and the citation process is the way core arguments and perspectives emerge. In short, we need the plentiful bounty to produce the nuggets of wisdom.

Research impact now plays a central role in the day-to-day life of the modern academic. Emphasis on wider dissemination to public and policy audiences is now integrated into research council funding and the formal assessment of research quality in the government's Research Excellence Framework (REF). The 2014 REF reported that 'research in all UoAs has led to a wide range of outstanding and very considerable social, economic and cultural impacts', with 44% of submissions graded as world-leading and a further 40% as internationally excellent. Social sciences fared well in the REF, with the scores for Panel C[3] and the Politics and International Studies unit of assessment (UoA21)[4] faring well in comparison to the national average – and indeed, above the average score for sciences/engineering (Panel B). This hardly tells a story of irrelevance or a crisis of research impact. There is much evidence of the contribution of social scientists to policy-making in Britain, for example, informing the nudge agenda and more widely providing an important evidence base for Parliament.[5] Claims about the irrelevance of the social sciences are baseless. Big ideas such as those around globalisation, governance and predistribution all had academic starting points. The work of think tanks and other policy advisers relies to a great degree on access to academic

research. To say they, rather than academics, deliver policy advice it is a bit like arguing that all the bills, cards and letters you receive are generated by the postal worker who delivers them to your door.

It is certainly true that the political outlook of universities is to the left of the median voter[6] – regardless of discipline.[7] This arguably reflects the self-selection mechanisms at work in pursuit of an academic career, rather than a suppression of particular political viewpoints. Having sat on more interview panels than we care to remember, we can remember no cases where a candidate's politics mattered. Decisions are driven by pragmatic rather than ideological judgements about the quality of their research, their capacity for academic leadership, their teaching commitment and their ability to raise funds!

More crucially, research in the social sciences has become more rational rather than less. Specifically there has been huge investment in skills and methods training, encouraging a clearer divide between normative and

empirical enquiry. Similarly, emphasis on skills and research methods training has never been more central to the syllabi of degrees in the social sciences and other disciplines. In terms of rigour of method and skill in generating and analysing data, social science has never been in better shape. Initiatives such as the Q-step programme to embed quantitative methods training in undergraduate curricula reflects the increased emphasis on rigour in the production of research, and is just part of a trend towards the importance of causal inference in the social sciences. A quick read of the leading journals of political science would leave Heath in no doubt about the seriousness with which today's academics treat their craft. But then that's the difference between lazy journalism and quality social science research: the former pontificates, the latter takes the time and trouble to create and test the evidence.

On reflection

Re-reading this post in the 'Brexit plus, plus, plus' context of 2017 leaves me feeling somewhat torn about the argument concerning professionalism and the impact being made. In many ways the journalist who prods and pokes the social and political sciences does so with an approach to writing that is designed to achieve just that. As a result, this response brings with it a certain sense of over-reaction and over-defensiveness, which, if the core arguments are true, is probably unnecessary. There is also no doubt that the universities of today are completely different places in terms of professional training, support and procedures to the institutions I began my career in over two decades ago. Back then it was very much a world of 'sink or swim' from Day 1, with very little support or training, whereas today new entrants to the profession are required to undertake a vast number of professional development courses. PhD students are now trained to be rounded social scientists, adept in a number of approaches and methodologies, and not just specialists in the esoteric subject of their thesis. And

yet, there is still a part of me that worries that the journalist might be on to something when he highlights the issue of inwardness and groupthink. One of the unintended consequences of the professionalism that I broadly welcome has been the squeezing out of those eccentric characters, those creative rebels who were not willing to be sculpted into intellectual technocrats. The imposition of a narrow intellectual conformity masquerading as professionalisation is what really worries me. And although I stand by the statement that I have never been on an interview panel where the partisan politics of an applicant has even been discussed, I am also well aware of the self-selection dynamics that lead individuals into one profession rather than another. More worryingly, however, is a growing focus – to the point of being the dominant focus – on not whether a candidate has the intellectual capacity to redefine a discipline or to open up hitherto unexplored intellectual terrain, but on whether they bring with them the necessary prerequisites to satisfy a range of external audit processes. It is this insidious intellectual risk-aversion that is likely to lead to the irrelevance of our universities.

56

The dismal debate: Would a 'Brexit' mean more power for the UK?

'Money, money, money. Must be funny. In a rich man's world'. As an academic I'm highly unlikely to ever have either 'money, money, money' or to live in a 'rich man's world'. But as a long-time student of politics, I've been struck by how the debate in the UK about the forthcoming referendum on membership of the European Union has been framed around just two issues – money and power. The political calculation being peddled in the UK is therefore embarrassingly simple: leaving the EU would mean that the UK had more money and more power.

This really has been a dismal debate. Those in favour of 'Brexit' or 'Bremain' have both engaged in an almost hysterical game of chasing shadows and creating phantoms. Shadows in the sense of making largely spurious claims about the impact of leaving the EU (that is, 'It would be very very bad!' or 'It would be very very good!'), when the truth of the matter is that no one really knows what would happen if the UK left the Union. Predictions must try to grapple with so many variables and uncertainties that the only way anyone would ever really know what would happen would be by the UK actually leaving. And yet, part of this rather childish playground-like debate has been an automatic default to simplistic zero-sum games that are of little value in the real world. Would the UK really save any money if it stopped paying in to the EU budget? Well, at a simplistic level it would, but at a more sophisticated level it may not, because the UK would then no longer receive funding back from the EU or have a seat at the table in major decisions concerning large infrastructure projects.

Would the UK really have more power, and the EU therefore 'less' power, if the UK walked away? There seems to be no understanding of either positive-sum conceptions of power (that is, by pooling some powers with other actors we overall actually gain *more power* and influence in some policy areas than we could ever have on our own) or the real world of global governance or international affairs. Does the UK really think that a small island just 900 miles long off the coast of continental Europe really still remains a global heavyweight with the capacity to 'go it alone'? The seas of contemporary international politics rage like a storm: there is great value in setting sail in flotillas rather than in single small boats, and far better to have safe and secure anchorage points in the middle of a tornado. (And recent years have sent us political and economic storms, tornadoes and hurricanes that really should make the UK think twice.)

In this context, President Obama's recent intervention was a beautiful mixture of charm laced with menace. The UK, was for him, taking a huge step into the unknown, and caution was being urged. But Obama's intervention also raised two issues that have simply not received the attention they deserve, issues that could transform a dismal

debate into something quite different. The first is a shift away from a simplistic focus on power and money and back to a more basic focus on war and terror. To make such a point is not to engage in 'the politics of fear-mongering' that is ripe in the UK at the moment, but to make the simple point that the EU was, from its very inception, framed around the need to ensure peace through collective efforts. From the creation of the European Coal and Steel Community in 1951, the underpinning ideal of the EU knew the *value* of international cooperation and not just its price. In terms of fostering peace and cooperation across an ever-larger union of countries, the EU can only be seen as a success.

This leads me to the second ('Obama-esque') issue: national confidence. I can't help wondering if what is actually driving the Brexit campaign in the UK is a lack of confidence and national belief. This might seem odd in light of the desire to 'go-it-alone', but there is a lot of huff and puff behind the UK's constant position as an 'awkward partner' within the

EU. The missing component – the political 'X Factor' – of the current debate about the UK and the EU is not about leaving but about *re-committing* to the ideals and vision of the EU in a different but positive way. This is not the same as adopting a federal vision or embracing 'ever closer union', but it is about adopting a more positive 'yes we can!' attitude to re-shaping the EU with the UK at its core, and not dragging its feet like a recalcitrant teenager on its periphery. Now wouldn't that make for a more refreshing debate?

On reflection

Unfortunately the referendum ballot paper did not include a choice for 'Remain, but in a reformed European Union' as my sense is that this option would have proved very popular. We'll never know. But what we do know is that for those on the losing side, referendums can appear possibly the worst way of 'doing' politics. We might also draw a number of other lessons and insights from the EU referendum.

Like, for example, the fact that individuals rarely make their decision purely on the specific referendum question. Of course to some extent they do, but at another level the question becomes more of a proxy for a far wider set of questions or social concerns. This was evident in the debate about the UK and Europe, and the manner in which people voted due to concerns about immigration, to bloody the nose of 'the political establishment', and for a range of other interwoven issues. Phrased in this manner the use of referendums can be seen as a blunt tool of democracy due to its binary 'yes'/'no' emphasis, but also due to the manner in which it acts as an umbrella for all sorts of issues (many of which may have little to do with the actual referendum question). Second, although a longer referendum campaign can run the risk of attention burnout on the part of the public and the media, the evidence suggests that levels of public knowledge and understanding do tend to increase over time. Research by the Electoral Reform Society, for example, showed that levels of public 'informedness' about the referendum on the UK's membership of the EU doubled from 16% in February 2016 to 31% by June. These figures might not be very impressive, but they do at least point to the value of longer campaigns in terms of delivering informed public engagement through referendums. Finally, in theory at least, referendums provide a sense of finality or closure on an issue – 'let the people speak!' – but in reality, they rarely close down an issue in a definitive sense. They are a staging post or an important reference point in a political debate but, as the messy business of post-Brexit negotiations has revealed, no matter how dismal the referendum campaign might be, the politics will continue....

57

Post-truth, post-political, post-democracy: The tragedy of the UK's referendum on the European Union

What was the biggest real story coming out of the UK's referendum? Was it the result and its implications for both the UK and the future of the European project? Possibly not. The biggest and more worrying story was the brutal exposure of a new form of 'post-truth' politics in which performance artists pose as politicians and nobody lets the facts or expert opinion get in the way of saying whatever it takes – no matter how disingenuous or deceitful – to win an election. This was democracy deceived, the British public duped.

'Democracy is perhaps the most promiscuous word in the world of public affairs', Bernard Crick suggested in his *In Defence of Politics* (1962). 'She is everybody's mistress and yet somehow retains her magic even when a lover sees that her favours are being, in his light, illicitly shared by many another....

Indeed, even amid our pain at being denied her exclusive fidelity, we are proud of her adaptability to all sorts of circumstances, to all sorts of company.' In the wake of the UK's recent referendum on membership of the European Union it is possible to question whether democracy 'retains her magic' and to suggest that the concept's malleability – its 'adaptability to all sorts of circumstances' – may have been exhausted. This was arguably the first post-truth, post-political, post-democratic election within an advanced liberal democracy.

I used to cringe at the title of John Keane's magisterial book *The Life and Death of Democracy* exactly because of this Crick-inspired belief in the innate flexibility and responsiveness of democratic politics. Now I'm not so sure. There was something about the tone and tenor, the fear and menace of the whole referendum campaign that was somehow tragic. It was a dismal debate but the central defining characteristic was its rejection of basic facts, cold analysis, objective assessments or expert projections. "People in this country have had enough of experts", Michael Gove, one of the leading figures in the campaign to get the UK out of the EU, responded when asked to name one leading economist or financial institution that thought leaving the EU was a good idea for the UK. It was 'post-truth', 'post-fact', strangely almost 'post-political' in the sense that emotive arguments concerning 'control', 'power' and 'sovereignty' were blended and set against 'the other' in the form of 'immigrants', 'foreigners', 'European bureaucrats', etc. The political calculation on which the Brexit campaign was based was alarmingly simple 'emotive claim + identified folk devil = 'leave success'.

The critical issue is not so much the actual result, but the complete failure of the political system to be able to cultivate a balanced and evidence-based public debate. Democracy

was deceived and the public duped because the debate simply never got beyond the level of clichéd sound bites. It created heat but not light, smoke not fire, and noise but certainly no music. As a result the British public took a seismic decision about the future of their county, and their children and grandchildren's future, largely on the basis of a mixture of fantasy, fairy tales and fig leaves. This was an argument that was made in several arenas and with increasing concern as the referendum date drew closer. In its report[1] published at the end of May 2016, the House of Commons Treasury Select Committee complained that 'The public debate is being poorly served by inconsistent, unqualified and, in some cases, misleading claims and counter-claims.' It added, 'Members of both the "leave" and "remain" camps are making such claims.' But the standard of public debate did not improve, and the former Prime Minister, Sir John Major, felt forced to state publicly that he was "angry about the way the British people are being misled." He argued that Vote Leave were running "a deceitful campaign…. They are feeding out to the

British people a whole galaxy of inaccurate and frankly untrue information." Such claims resonate with a public letter signed by over 250 leading academics that suggested that the level of misinformation in the referendum campaign was so great that the democratic legitimacy of the final vote might be questioned.

The final vote has now been taken and it *is* being questioned exactly due to this widespread concern about the veracity of the (publicly funded) information provided to the public by both sides of the campaign.

Within hours of the referendum result being announced, the blame games had begun, with Nigel Farage admitting that the claim that £350 million a week could be saved by leaving the EU and invested in the NHS was "a mistake". The fact that 17 million members of the public had voted to leave the EU in the wake of a campaign that had consistently featured this promise seemed almost trivial. (But possibly not to the millions of people who were at exactly the same time causing

218 WHAT KIND OF DEMOCRACY IS THIS?

the government's official public petitions website to crash with their demands for a second referendum.)

My argument is not therefore with the outcome of the referendum or how each and every person acted when they picked up the rather grubby little pencil in a generally grubby little voting booth and marked the crisp clean voting slip with a simple cross. My argument is with the architecture of politics and its inability to stop politicians spreading falsehoods and lies, its failure to enforce truthfulness. Dissecting this argument into its component elements reveals several dimensions that demand urgent reflection and possibly reform.

The first is the rejection and dismissal of experts. The extent of this stance within the Brexit campaign was almost beyond belief as any expert opinion, considered analysis, objective forecasts, etc that questioned the rationale and claims of the leave campaign were summarily dismissed as part of an orchestrated 'politics of fear'. The paradox

of this position is that, as studies such as Colin Crouch's *Post-Democracy* (2000) or Colin Hay's (2007) *Why We Hate Politics* have illustrated, the dominant shift in modern politics, in the UK and beyond, has been the consistent transfer of functions, powers and responsibilities away from elected politicians to experts and technocrats. Indeed, the short-term, irrational and self-interested 'dysfunctions of democracy' were such that dominant notions of 'good' or 'modern' governance have, for several decades, placed, to some extent and in specific specialist policy fields, the views of 'experts' over those of 'politicians'. This shift in modern governance has stimulated a wide-ranging debate regarding the 'hollowing out' and 'filling in' of democracy that Peter Mair's *Ruling the Void* (2013) surveys with great precision. And yet, the EU referendum campaign cannot be viewed as a successful demonstration of the reclamation of 'democratic space' because 'filling in' democracy is not synonymous with the complete rejection of facts, data, objective analyses or expert viewpoints. 'Filling in'

revolves around the cultivation of a rich and balanced democratic debate in which *democratic voice* is matched by *democratic listening*, and through this, a considered collective position arises. This did not occur on 23 June 2016.

A related dimension of the dismissal of experts in general was the dismissal of academics in particular. The academy was almost unanimous in its support for Remain, offering detailed evidence of the tangible benefits of student mobility, research links, immigration and European grant programmes. Added to this was the sterling work of Anand Menon's 'The United Kingdom in a Changing Europe' project that sought to offer authoritative, impartial and research-based reference points for anyone interested in the referendum debate. But in a 'post-fact', 'post-truth' climate, it was very hard for academics to gain traction, to be heard, and the concern arising from this is whether the result might in some ways be seen as a deeper, cultural defeat for universities. Public confidence in academic expertise, and the relevance of the social and political sciences in particular, may also have been subject to a potentially far-reaching 'hollowing out' effect.

'Scepticism is not the same as outright Gove-style anti-intellectualism, of course', David Matthews wrote in the *Times Higher Education* (22 June 2016). 'But regardless of which way the country votes tomorrow, academics and universities urgently need to ponder why such a significant chunk of the population has come to distrust them.' But – pondering this question – maybe the reason is that the political system itself lacks capacity when it comes to enforcing some basic rules regarding peddling 'inconsistent, unqualified and, in some cases, misleading claims and counter-claims.' Other countries have tighter structures to prevent politicians playing quite so fast and loose with the truth. The options include new legislation, tighter press regulation, a bolstered role for the Electoral Commission or an enforceable code of conduct, but beyond these possible institutional responses what was possibly more worrying about the EU referendum was

the explicit anti-establishment, anti-political, populist position of the Brexit campaign. It was exactly this dismissal of democratic politics that may well come to haunt the UK in ways that have not yet been appreciated.

This point takes us back to Crick's *In Defence of Politics* and his simple argument that democratic politics tends to be slow, cumbersome, inefficient, hard to understand and quite simply messy for the simple reason that democratic politics is an institutionalised form of conflict resolution that must somehow satisfy a vast array of competing demands. Many of the arguments levelled at the EU by the Brexit campaign therefore contained nuggets of truth – its institutions are inefficient, somewhat remote, and its decisions are frequently what economists would define as 'sub-optimal' – but nobody was ever trying to argue that the EU was perfect, especially not the Remain camp. The simple fact is that in the context of 28 very different member states, these 'problems' or 'weaknesses' with the EU can equally be viewed as the strength of the project

in the sense that shared decision-making prevents conflict and generally directs shared resources towards shared risks. The democratic arguments were always secondary to the economic arguments, and even in this regard, all that was achieved was an unedifying public spectacle in which politicians engaged in slurs and counter-slurs, claims against counter-claims and deceit-upon-deceit. Turkey was not about to join the EU, a European Army was not about to be unleashed, and of the £350 million that the UK pays in to the EU each week, it receives well over half of this money back.

And yet, playing 'fast and loose' with the truth cannot be placed at the door of just one person or one side of the campaign. The whole campaign was, to some extent, a case study in how not to do democracy. But there is a dimension of the debate that has not been brought to the fore in relation to why the Remain campaign seemed so lacklustre and the Brexit campaign so vigorously populist – the pressure of the *status quo*. The simple fact was that our membership of the EU acted as a systemic pressure or brake on the claims that the Remain camp could make. Working relationships with European partners had to be retained. Leading figures in the Remain camp were therefore bound by the rather Procrustean realities of political life which left their concessions and pledges appearing rather limited and dry, especially when compared to the rhetoric of the Brexit leads. It was democratic politics in the sense of 'the strong and slow boring of hard boards' – to paraphrase Max Weber – against the populist burning of political bridges.

The problem with populism is that it draws support on the basis that the world would be such a wonderful place if we could simply remove the cumbersome demands of democratic politics. In recent weeks just about every modern ailment has been placed at the door of either European bureaucrats or immigrants (generally both) and a simple solution offered – Brexit. In making such a political offer to the British public Messrs Johnson, Gove and Farage have raised the public's expectations to the

extent that far-reaching failure is to some extent arguably inevitable. What's interesting from the autobiographies and memoirs of former presidents, prime ministers and leading politicians is that electoral success rarely brings with it emotional confidence. Of course, to the outside world it is smiles and celebratory handshakes all round, but inside, the dominant emotion is generally one of dread and a sense of foreboding. 'What have I done?' 'How can I ever deliver what I have promised?' are the questions that keep new leaders awake at night. In this context, John Crace's commentary[2] on the hours after the referendum result was announced in Vote Leave's headquarters takes on added meaning. 'Boris and Gove were looking equally stunned. Neither had either expected to win or Cameron to resign, and what had started out as a bit of a game had become horribly real', Crace wrote. '[Michael Gove] looked like a man who had just come down off a bad trip to find he had murdered one of his closest friends.'

But the truth is that the biggest risk arising from the EU referendum is neither territorial nor economic; it's not even demographic or legalistic … it's the rise of a form of post-truth politics in which performance and personality matter more than the facts. For the large part the EU referendum was a truth-free zone, a post-political referendum of fairy tales, fantasy and fig leaves. Dishonest before the truth means that democracy has been deceived, the public duped.

On reflection

Apologies for the rather depressing tone and conclusion of this post: the black dog must have been upon me. We can at least draw some succour from the previous post's emphasis that referendums very rarely bring an issue to a close, and are best seen as a reference point or an important stage in an ongoing debate. What's really interesting about this post, however, is how quickly the debate about 'post-truth' politics has evolved towards a focus on 'fake news' and

even 'alternative facts'. The latter surfaced in the combative debate between the Trump White House and large sections of the American media about the size of the crowd at the President's inauguration. In a country where it appears size really does matter, the new White House Press Secretary, Sean Spicer, used his first briefing to accuse the media of deliberately playing down the size of the crowd that gathered in Washington to celebrate Donald Trump's inauguration, even claiming that the media were trying to 'delegitimise' the President. Claims that 'This was the largest audience to ever witness an inauguration – period – both in person and around the globe' were met with something close to general ridicule bordering on embarrassment. A White House adviser later explained that Mr Spicer had not been wrong but had given 'alternative facts'. That such Orwellian phrases should be used so openly and early in the presidency takes the debate about post-democracy far beyond the shores of the UK, and raises worrying questions, but what was as worrying was the pugilistic style adopted by Trump's staff to any challenge or questioning. Nevertheless, detailed research by the PolitiFact website concluded that Spicer's 'alternative facts' were simply false, or, as they put it, 'pants on fire'.

58

A talent for politics? The 'great scholar, poor politician' thesis

Sometimes a fragment of a book manages to lodge itself in the back of your mind. An idea, a description, a phrase … just something, and often completely unrelated to the core story,

attaches itself to your mind like an intellectual itch you can't quite scratch. My 'itch' stems from a passing comment towards the end of Michael Ignatieff's *Fire and Ashes* (2013) in which he suggests a certain incompatibility between politics 'as theory' and politics 'as practice', effectively ensuring that successful academics (or political theorists, as Ignatieff more precisely argues) rarely make successful politicians. Cicero, Machiavelli, Edmund Burke, James Madison, Alexis de Tocqueville, John Stuart Mill, Max Weber … all demonstrated huge capacity for writing on the theory and nature of politics, but their forays into the political arena themselves were marred in failure or defined by dissatisfaction. 'Why theoretical acumen is so frequently combined with political failure', Ignatieff suggests, 'throws light on what is distinctive about a talent for politics.'

The candour, rigour, willingness to follow a thought wherever it leads, the penetrating search for originality – all these are virtues in theoretical pursuits but active liabilities in politics, where discretion and dissimulation are essential for success. This would suggest that these theorists failed because they couldn't keep their mouths shut when flattery or partisan discipline required it of them. Equally, however, theorists may have lacked those supreme virtues that separate successful politicians from failures: adaptability, cunning, rapid-fire recognition of Fortuna. (from *Fire and Ashes*, pp 170-1)

This emphasis on 'adaptability', 'cunning' and 'rapid-fire recognition of Fortuna' – what might be termed the 'great scholar, poor politician' thesis – suddenly took on added resonance in the wake of the UK's referendum decision to leave the European Union. Not only had the Leave campaign been founded on the explicit rejection of expert advice, but at a more specific level it had also exposed a gap between academics and the broader public. Writing in the *Times Higher Education*, David Matthews suggested that 'the referendum result revealed that there was amongst universities and those who work in them a profound sense of dislocation from broader society.' James Wilsdon, Director of Policy, Impact and Engagement at the University of Sheffield, suggested that 'we do need to ask ourselves some searching questions about how that [gap between the academy and the public] has grown up.'

To some extent the basic argument that a gap has emerged is open to challenge. The simple fact that most British academics are left-leaning and pro-European, and therefore generally campaigned in favour of 'Remain', is, surveys would suggest, broadly accurate. It is also factually correct to state that 51.9% of those members of the British electorate who voted were in favour of 'Leave'. But to infer from these facts that the academy therefore 'failed' is to adopt a rather simplistic line of

argument. The role of the social and political sciences is to help promote a balanced, accurate and wherever possible evidence-based debate, but if the public decide to disregard or to dismiss that scholarship, then that is not 'failure' but the simple price we pay for living in a democracy.

And yet, Ignatieff's naughty 'great scholar, poor politician thesis' keeps nagging at my mind. By anyone's reckoning the debate about the UK's membership of the EU had to be an opportunity if not to convince the public of the benefits of continued membership, then at the very least to showcase the relevance and value of the social and political sciences. All the aftermath rhetoric of 'soul searching' and 'identity crisis' and the need for experts (including academics) 'to reassert their value to society' left me feeling that maybe, just maybe, we had failed to display exactly the 'adaptability, cunning, rapid-fire recognition of Fortuna' that Ignatieff highlighted. Indeed, if expert research can be so easily disregarded in relation to an issue as important as

membership of the EU, then why bother to fund the social and political sciences?

To make things worse, surveys conducted in the wake of the referendum suggested that levels of public trust in academics had declined significantly and that they were now seen by large parts of society as part of 'the elite' or 'the establishment'.

But *if* – and it is a big '*IF*' – the academy failed in some way and might therefore be expected to shoulder some of the blame for failing to get their message across, *IF* the decision to 'leave' represents something of a deeper cultural defeat for universities as many have suggested, then the rebuilding of public trust in academic experts represents a far-reaching challenge. Indeed, as the work of Sir Bernard Crick repeatedly attempted to emphasise, it is the role of scholars, intellectuals and the universities to 'speak truth to' both 'power' and 'the public', and to act as a counterweight to the embedded position of elites, markets and other dominant institutions. The question then is what –

specifically – might have gone amiss in the relationship not between the governors and the governed, but between the professors and the public? And at the root of any answer to this question has to be a focus not so much on the evidence or data, but on the basic skills of political communication and social engagement. If there was a 'problem' that demands reflection – and possibly some strategic response – it has to focus on 'the art of translation' when it comes to the framing and provision of academic knowledge.

A slightly bolder argument might suggest that in many ways the social and political sciences displayed a failure to learn from the core insights of the social and political sciences in recent decades, especially in relation to the link between emotion and fact. Studies have repeatedly revealed how firmly held beliefs tend to be incredibly resilient in the face of conflicting 'facts' or 'evidence'. Indeed, the more you bombard an individual, community or section of society with 'data', 'facts' and 'research', the more likely they are to hold on to preconceived

ideas and assumptions. The 'problem', then, for academics within the Brexit debate was that they – quite understandably – adopted a facts-based approach that may well be the dominant idiom within higher education but that possibly failed to find any traction in the emotive sphere of cultural politics and national identity. The 'facts' were not grounded and the projected 'risk scenarios' meant little to large sections of the public who thought they had little to lose or put at risk anyway. Although irrational from an objective scientific perspective, spurious claims to 'take back control', 'regain power' and put the 'Great' back into all sorts of things including 'Great Britain' offered powerful emotional triggers that scholarship appeared unable to challenge or dissect. As a result, academics in favour of remaining were rapidly defined by the Leave campaign as part of an elite that benefited from exactly the 'gravy train' that Brexit was intended to bring to a halt.

Returning to Ignatieff's naughty little thesis, might it be that academics really did fail to display exactly that mixture of adaptability

and cunning – 'those supreme virtues' – that might allow them to have slightly more traction in the political sphere?

There are no simple answers to complex questions, and this is certainly a complex question, but we can at least use Ignatieff's 'great scholar, poor politician' thesis as a useful intellectual reference point from which to make at least three observations. First, there is something to be said for academics receiving more professional training on 'the art of translation' and 'engaged scholarship'. How do we engage 'with multiple audiences in multiple ways' without over-simplifying, dumbing-down or compromising our academic credibility? There is (second) an anti-thesis that legitimately questions the role of academic experts within political debates and campaigns. Far better, some might say, not to risk dirtying one's hands within the grubby world of politics, especially if it involves locating research findings within emotive language. The tricky context for this 'dirty hands, clean research' argument is that 'society' seems to be demanding more of academics in terms of evidence that publicly funded research is a worthwhile public investment. Squaring the circle need not involve dirtying one's hands or 'selling out' in terms of risking the credibility of one's research, but a more sophisticated and subtle understanding of the need to ground or frame the available facts and research within the 'everyday lives' of the public. This would involve a more granular analysis, more refined prescriptions and an acceptance that issues that may be 'positive' in terms of aggregated effects across time can also be 'negative' when viewed from the short-term and immediate position of local communities. In short, maybe the Brexit campaign suggests that academics need to display just a little more adaptability and social awareness – possibly even a dash of non-partisan political cunning – otherwise the gap between the professors and the public is only likely to grow.

On reflection

There is a sense in which the academy feels trapped. Pushed to demonstrate its relevance and impact *vis-à-vis* major social debates, challenges and controversies, academics feel vulnerable to both partisan attacks and partisan co-option, to accusations of 'dumbing-down' or self-aggrandisement, and to a pressure to skew their research towards issues that may lend themselves to direct engagement with potential research users rather than the questions they really think need to be explored. Some research has no policy relevance or public engagement potential. Even where some direct relevance can be identified, the relationship between research and public impact is rarely direct or linear but generally fuzzy, contested and indirect. This is why – deep down, if we are honest – most social scientists feel very uneasy about putting their name to the sort of impact claims demanded by the current external audit processes. As the social, economic, technological and environmental challenges grow in terms of scale, potential impact and complexity, and where the media

space for mature evidence-informed debate shrinks, so the capacity of scholars to exert influence within the public political spheres also shrinks. It is possible to identify a new academic political class of left-leaning scholars who have stepped into the arena, particularly in Southern Europe. Leaders of the new left in Europe, such as Pablo Iglesias Turrión[1] of Podemos[2] in Spain and the former Greek finance minister Yanis Varoufakis, are cases in point. In Portugal, where the left gained power in November 2015, there are now academics serving as ministers in the government, such as Mário Centeno[3] and Manuel Heitor, but overall there is little evidence that many academics have a talent for politics for the simple reason – as Ignatieff suggests – that the demands of the role arguably pull in very different directions. This is not to be defeatist but it is to accept the fact that 'politics' will always trump 'evidence' – is that not the core finding of over two decades of research on evidence-informed policy?

59

Standing up and shaping the agenda: Rejecting discrimination, embracing difference

Worrying signs of an increase in abuse and intolerance towards non-UK staff and students demands an urgent response. The integrity of the UK's world-class universities is at risk, and yet the government resembles a cabal of sleepwalkers that doesn't really know where it is going or why. British universities are, as a result, sailing on … without a map or compass, into unmapped waters. The time has come for university leaders to stand up and shape the agenda, notably in relation to protecting the position and future of European staff and students.

Although it has been less than a fortnight since the EU referendum in the UK, I have already received a significant number of worrying accounts about not only the increased insecurity felt by non-UK academics and students, but also of open abuse and racism directed at foreign staff

and students. The instability and intolerance unleashed by Brexit could hardly have been predicted with any certainty, but the outlook is gravely worrying for a number of reasons. Long held as a 'jewel in the crown' of the UK's continued global significance – as a leader in terms of cutting-edge research, innovative and high-quality teaching, and in relation to positive social impact – British universities are now sailing into unchartered waters. At this time, clear leadership, certainty and global ambition are most needed. The government's position is one of 'steady as she goes' and offers a simple re-statement that 'the UK remains a member of the European Union, and we continue to meet our obligations and receive relevant funding.' But beneath the rhetoric is a more telling reality that looks more like a government of sleepwalkers that doesn't really know where it is going or why. The mantra is the same irrespective of the topic – from the status of EU staff and students through to European access to the Student Loans Company, and from Erasmus+ through to Horizon 2020 research funding – 'no immediate changes … a matter for future discussions.'

If a vacuum exists in relation to political leadership, then it is up to the broader academic community (vice chancellors, learned societies, scholarly academies, etc) to seize the agenda and to plot a positive course of action. The question then becomes one of the values and principles that should inform that agenda and what practical steps might be taken. In this regard three issues demand brief comment.

The first is an emphasis on *tolerance* as a central and defining feature of the British higher education system. Throughout the 20th century British universities helped several thousands of academics who were in immediate danger in their home countries find safety and refuge in the UK. The Academic Assistance Council was formed in 1933 to

coordinate efforts, and today, the Council for Assisting Refugee Academics (CARA) works closely with Universities UK to continue this work. The UK academic community is therefore a global community. It is one in which those members who require support and assistance are not defined as 'problems', but as the source of new experiences and ideas to enrich those institutions that take them in. The challenge here is that the Brexit vote arguably projects a global image of *in*tolerance on the UK in ways that are unlikely to enhance its global reputation or student recruitment. A powerful campaign to protect and enhance the UK's global image as a welcoming and friendly place to work and study is therefore urgently required.

Standing up for higher education in this time of political instability might also emphasise the public *value* of higher education. Not simply in economic or financial terms, but also in relation to the value of learning for learning's stake, for the role of education in terms of promoting active and engaged citizenship, and for encouraging individuals

to look beyond their own community and to reflect on their role in the broader world. It is at this point impossible to ignore the educational divide that was revealed by those who voted either for or against continued membership of the EU. Nor should universities be embarrassed to trumpet the fact that anyone who has studied at a university in this country tends to have an international outlook. But the hidden risk at the moment is that universities undermine their reputation and credibility if they accept, however unintentionally, discriminatory practices (such as an unwillingness to appoint EU citizens or to offer anything more than a temporary rolling contract) that will hollow out exactly that international diversity and intellectual tolerance that makes universities such special places.

If *tolerance* and *value* form the first two pillars of what an agenda-shaping strategy for British universities – a shared vision – might look like, then *duty* provides a third. Duty in the sense of a civic and professional obligation to speak out against the current climate of fear and insecurity on the basis of a fairly simple fact: it is impossible to undertake world-class research unless you are a member of a world-class network that provides access to the necessary international experts, facilities and research groups. Shared resources, shared facilities, shared data, shared risks … all lead to shared benefits and truly transformational research in a way that is simply impossible to achieve on a national basis. British universities cannot be – and do not want to be – independent of the world around us. Collaboration and mutual stimulation combined with a willingness to trespass across national and professional boundaries are the drivers of discovery and growth, and we need to make this case louder and clearer.

So what next for British universities? They cannot be allowed to drift like some flotsam or jetsam in increasingly choppy political seas. 'We must keep damn close together as a community', Sir Keith Burnett, Vice Chancellor of the University of Sheffield, recently argued, 'remembering our purpose' – to which I

would add *our tolerance*, *our value* and *our duty*. Irrespective of whether the EU leaves the EU in the wake of the Brexit vote, there is no reason why the UK cannot negotiate to remain a partner in Erasmus+ or Horizon 2020, and there is no reason why the Student Loans Company might not offer its services to European citizens who want to study in the UK in the future. There is certainly no reason why European staff and students should not feel secure within the British higher education system. It is possible. But the time has come for universities to stand up, to take control and to shape the agenda.

▬▬▬▬▬

On reflection

Even in this 'post-fact', 'post-truth', 'fake news' world of 'facts' versus 'alternative facts', it seems legitimate based on the analysis of available data to argue that hate crimes soared in the UK in the wake of the Brexit vote. In July 2016, police recorded a 41% increase compared to the same month the year before, according to a Home Office report. Data from

31 police forces showed that 1,546 racially or religiously aggravated offences were recorded in the two weeks up to and including the day of the referendum on 23 June.[1] But in the fortnight immediately after the poll, the number climbed by almost half, to 2,241. In September 2016, the National Police Chiefs' Council released figures that showed the number of incidents rose by 58% in the week following the vote to leave the EU. Many of these incidents have involved students from abroad who are visiting the UK and in some cases academic staff. Despite the attempts of universities to support all students and staff members, a worrying anti-intellectual and anti-foreigner sentiment appears to pervade the continuing debate, not just about future relationships with the EU, but in relation to 'protecting' the UK's borders more generally. The Prime Minister's 'hard Brexit' stance combined with a refusal to provide details about the UK's negotiating position have added to this worrying atmosphere within higher education.

▬▬▬▬▬

60

Welcome to the year of living dangerously – 2017

I am not usually a worried man but today – New Year's Day 2017 – I am a worried man. Gripped by an existential fear, my mind is restless, alert and tired. The problem? A sense of foreboding that the impact of the political events of 2016 will shortly come home to roost on a world that is already short on collective good will or trust. There is also a sense that games are being played by a new über-elite of political non-politicians who thrive on the vulnerabilities and fears of the masses – the great non-über-elite (if that is not too many hyphens and too few umlauts).

And yet to suggest that this new elite thrives on vulnerability and fear is not quite correct. I am doing them a disservice. They do not *just* thrive on vulnerability and fear: they create and manufacture vulnerability and fear.

Don't believe me? Think I am wrong?

Haven't you noticed the new statecraft of 'divide and rule' that has arisen across large parts of the world? Have you not noticed the rise of national populism with its simple rhetoric of 'us' against 'them'? When Trump says 'Let's make America great again!' he isn't just acknowledging the decline of a superpower; he is also implicitly blaming certain parts of society for that decline. When the Brexiteers campaigned for the UK to leave the European Union, the debate was viciously polarised to the extent that anyone who dared to even question the benefits of a British departure risked being hanged, drawn and quartered as a traitor. I exaggerate for effect … but only slightly. Across the world there is a more of a hint and a kink of a psychological warfare in which sections of the precariat are pitted against other sections of exactly the same broad body of people who exist in a socioeconomic state of uncertainty. These are the workers of the 'gig economy' – the apex of Bauman's 'liquid modernity' – who exist in a hinterland of self-employed temporary employment. Employment protection, workers' rights, unions … little more than quaint phrases from a long-forgotten phase of economic development.

It is the precariat – a phrase and focus of analysis originally developed by Guy Standing – who are living dangerously, and their numbers are growing. As this slice of society grows from a thin seam to a major layer of the social structure, then so, too, do the opportunities for abusing the existence of obvious social fears and frustrations. It is easy to divide a vulnerable class, a hope*less* class, a hope*ful* class and for false prophets to promise the world in return for a vote. Too easy, and this is the problem with democracy that has now emerged.

I don't want a red cap or a union jack. I don't want to be told there are simple solutions to complex problems. I don't want to be told that foreigners, immigrants and 'others' – those demonised souls – are *the problem* when I know that the problem is really one of 'us', not 'them'. My foreboding is therefore based on a sense that the public (or really 'the publics' of the modern world) have been manipulated

by false fears that will only generate new fears and isolationism at a historical moment when the fears and risks that really matter can only be confronted through united collective action.

I may be completely wrong. The year 2017 may go down as one defined by a move towards broad, sunlit uplands, or one defined by a new dark age made more sinister by the perils of populism unconstrained and misunderstood. So let us brace ourselves for a rough ride and tough times that will go far beyond Trump and Brexit. General elections this year in the Netherlands, Germany and Italy may lead to significant gains for the Party for Freedom, the Alternative for Germany and the Five Star Movement, respectively. But it is in France where the real test will come. This is a country where the standard of living has not fallen and where levels of social inequality have generally been kept in check and yet, where the right-wing National Front may also gain significant support in the presidential elections. How? Through the manufacture and manipulation of fears and vulnerabilities.

During 2016 complacent governments around the world created a political void that was quickly filled by populist parties. In 2017 war and poverty will continue to drive displaced peoples towards Europe – the most precarious of the precariat – but national populism will splinter and fragment the shores on which the tired and hungry collapse. Sand and blood, sand and blood, such an ugly phrase that captures my sense of foreboding…. Listen to my chronicle of a death foretold. Welcome to the year of living dangerously.

▰▰▰▰▰▰

On reflection

The ink on this post has hardly dried and it is far too soon to reflect on the prescience of my thoughts concerning the year of living dangerously. Let us hope my fears, my chronicle of a death foretold, remain little more than the existential anguish of a simple scholarly soul. The problem is that my worries have now been amplified by the fact that without my knowledge just about

every global political or social commentator has also labelled 2017 the 'year of living dangerously'. My point in admitting this apparently obvious nomenclature is that I can no longer console myself that my worries are probably way out of line with those of the majority of 'real' experts. Moreover, the global pace towards nationalist populism shows little sign of waning. In this regard whenever I close my eyes I see the face not of Donald Trump, Nigel Farage or Marie LePen, but of the nearest thing the social sciences have to a punk political philosopher – Slavoj Žižek. This may well be the most curious and embarrassing admission I have ever made, and I beg the reader not to tell another soul, but Žižek's face haunts my mind. Do you see him as well? Is it just me? His mannerisms reflect the existence of another tortured soul: the constant twitching of the head, the continual licking of lips, the unceasing rubbing of the face, the flaying hands that often appear beyond his control ... all combine to give the impression of a creature almost fighting to escape the confines of their body. (Close your eyes ... do you see him?) The psycho-

analytical philosopher, cultural critic and Hegelian Marxist is famously idiosyncratic, he roams and trespasses across intellectual and disciplinary borders like no other scholar, but he scares me, and the echoes of this fear – I have just realised – are inscribed across this post. In 2011 Žižek published *The Year of Dreaming Dangerously* and this book must have unconsciously shaped my writing when reflecting on the future. The problem is that we are no longer *dreaming dangerously*; we really are *living dangerously*. (Close your eyes ... do you see him now?)

A special delivery: 'So, what kind of democracy is this?'

Life can sometimes deliver the most ironic little twists. As I sit here to reflect on 'the politics of postcards', what should happen to fall through my letterbox but a personal and handwritten little note from my local MP, Nick Clegg. 'Dear friend', the letter begins in a scrawl that suggests a rushed message. 'I wanted to drop you a quick note to wish you and your loved ones all the best for the Christmas period and the New Year.' The phrase 'all the best' somehow irks in my mind as a phrase that has been carefully chosen, possibly *too* carefully chosen, to reflect the desperation of someone who craves the acceptance of a post-industrial northern community. The personalisation of the note in terms of both style and content is striking: cheap, informal notepaper, blue ink, faux handwriting including smudges. 'For me, Christmas is an opportunity to relax with Miriam and our three boys, who seem to be growing up so fast', the note continues in a manner that increasingly resembles a plea for social acceptance: 'I have children', 'My kids are growing up quickly', 'I want to relax at Christmas', 'I'm just like you'. 'I work extremely hard', he tells the reader, his 'friend'; he has tried to save 'a lovely pub' and to 'protect our historic healthy trees', and as a result, 'our area has so much to be proud of'.

The problem is that much of the area feels it has little to be proud of. The 'historic healthy trees' are a case in point. In 2016 the local population erupted in anger at plans by the local council to fell them; petitions were signed, protests were organised, court cases were held, and neighbourhood watch schemes even organised to sound the alarm at the first sign of an axe. The problem was the axes came at night and came silently, bolstered by the support of police riot vans and officers. Those protestors who raced to the scene in pyjamas and dressing gowns were immediately arrested, and by breakfast, all that was left was a pile of sawdust and a hastily made sign on a sad little stump that reads 'Democracy RIP'. The dawn raid on the centurion lime trees of Sheffield was 'something you'd expect to see in Putin's Russia, rather than a Sheffield suburb', Nick Clegg told the world's media, but it's not something he deigns to mention in his Christmas note to constituents. The truth of the matter is that in a world in which public services are delivered by a vast range of arm's-length or private sector bodies, the local MP and former Deputy Prime Minister had not even been able to obtain a full copy of the contract between the local council and the private provider to whom responsibility for the trees had been delegated. What kind of democracy is this?

The case of Sheffield's trees would make a wonderful topic for a postcard or short letter simply due to the manner in which it is *rooted* (please excuse the pun) in the day-to-day lives of people who rarely take such a direct interest in politics. Neither does politics frequently take such a direct interest in them. It provides a snapshot of a very localised and relatively straightforward issue where the outcome is a frustrated and angry local community that now believes that even when the public speaks, politicians don't listen. This, in turn, takes us back to the great value of postcards as brief snapshots of life in the sense that they are used as *an expressive act* and as *a form of expression*. Put slightly differently, it is through this short-form writing process that the author

attempts to make sense of the world and their place within it, on the one hand, and the recipient receives an account of that world that may also make them reflect on the changing dynamics of modern life. The specific focus – be it sharks, trees, forks or festivals – is therefore secondary to the broader sociopolitical context with which it connects. Phrased in this manner, the value of the 60 posts presented in this book lies not simply with their commentary on a disparate sets of issues or themes, but with what they combine to tell us about the changing nature of democracy. But what do they tell us about the kind of democracy we have at the end of the second decade of the 21st century? If you were to reduce all 60 posts down in order to reveal a certain core essence, what would that be, and why would it matter? What might that core essence tell us about 'why we hate politics' or the drivers of democratic disaffection? The need to answer these questions can hardly be greater. The election of Donald Trump in the US, the UK's decision to leave the European Union, the rise of neo-fascism in Eastern Europe and populist

'insurgent' parties in the West all point to a rejection of the current 'kind' of democracy and a desire for something quite different. The issue is therefore one not just of *what kind of democracy we have*, but also what *kind of democracy we want*. Pushing this line of questioning back towards the seam of writing presented in this book, the great value of such an overview is not so much what the collective insights of the posts might be, but also what they have missed. There is, then, a certain sense of intellectual embarrassment on the part of the author at the narrowness of the arguments, of the indulgence of the analysis, and of the distance that each post inevitably brings with it from the worldly art of politics itself. But in terms of drilling down into these questions of '*what we have*' and '*what we want*' it is possible to sketch out just four core pairs of issues that are not only interrelated but that also allow us to expose what I would suggest is at the core/heart/ root of 'the problem with democracy'. These issues can be summarised as follows and form the structure of this final reflective essay:

- ▶ The trap and the promise
- ▶ Populism and emotion
- ▶ Democracy and solutionism
- ▶ Inequality and 'thinking big'

The trap and the promise

Possibly the most striking conclusion offered by this book – both as a set of fragmentary posts and as a coherent whole – is that Wright Mills' 'trap' has become more intense. The research and data on democratic disillusionment and disengagement is therefore a symptom of the ensnaring of an ever greater proportion of the public within *a social context that is as increasingly intense as it is increasingly shallow and unfulfilling*. It is for exactly this reason that Zygmunt Bauman's work on 'liquid modernity' casts a long shadow over many of the posts in this book, but to capture the true essence of 'the trap' one only needs to read Salman Rushdie's *Two Years, Eight Months and Twenty-Eight Nights* (2015), and his description of a 'peripatetic world' in which,

People easily became detached from places, beliefs, communities, countries, languages, and from even more important things, such as honour, morality, good judgement and truth; in which, we may say, they splintered away from the authentic narratives of their life stories and spent the rest of their days trying to discover, or forge, new synthetic narratives of their own.

In this simple statement Rushdie captures the essence of Wright Mills and Bauman and Crick, while at the same time capturing many of the themes and emotions that characterise the posts in this book. Uprooted but not yet re-rooted. All that was solid appears to have melted away, and hence Bauman's focus on liquidity ('liquid love', 'liquid hate', 'liquid times', 'liquid fear', 'liquid life', 'liquid water', etc) and the fragility, temporariness, vulnerability and inclination to constant change that appears ever-present across all social domains. In this context individuals must attempt to find meaning, secure anchorage and impose at least some kind of order. And yet, to some extent, it is too easy to regurgitate Wright Mills' classic work

because to do so not only fails to dismember 'the trap' in order to expose its sustaining and perpetuating roots, but also because it fails to explore exactly how the nature of social alienation and social anchorage has itself altered. In this regard I cannot help but think that the election of Trump, the Brexit vote and 'the populist signal' (to adopt the title of an excellent report by Claudia Chwalisz) is not simply the latest phase of a long-running pattern of democratic decline, but is, in fact, indicative of a more threatening and dangerous social shift.

The demographic analysis of those who voted for Trump and for Brexit reveal a clear link with the existence of a social underclass who felt almost disowned and abused by a dominant economic order that treated them as little more than flexible goods. Guy Standing was therefore correct in his analysis that *The Precariat* (2013) were 'a new and dangerous class', and to some extent the danger of having a large section of the public who felt 'left behind' has come to the fore. Although the white working class in the US is shrinking, it remains the largest voting block in that country, and was to some extent sympathetic with Trump's attacks on an East Coast establishment that was blamed for destroying jobs and communities across large swathes of the Midwest and South; in the UK the Leave campaign's attacks on 'the establishment' and immigration policy tapped into similar sentiments. And yet, what has received less attention is the manner in which the social sweep of 'the precariat' has widened in recent years in North America and Western Europe to include large sections of the middle class. This is a critical transformation of the political economy. The precariat is no longer restricted to the unemployed or uneducated, but has expanded into the professional classes where part-time, short-term contracts are becoming the norm for doctors, teachers, professors and a host of other careers, where mobility has been emphasised and professional collective capacity dismantled.

To explain Brexit and Trump as the actions of angry, white, uneducated young men is therefore wrong and is actually related *back* to the dismantling of those deeper institutions of social solidarity. An additional trap – 'a-trap-within-a-trap' – is to view the rise of social alienation and frustration as simply an economic or institutional issue when, in fact, it has far deeper psychological implications. The rise of the 'über-generation' or the 'gig economy', whereby workers are increasingly self-employed on highly flexible short-term engagements (agency work, outsourcing, etc), has powerful and pathological impacts on mental wellbeing. For those working in the gig economy the likelihood is that they will undertake a large amount of work that is neither recognised nor remunerated, they will often be educated to a level far beyond the needs of their actual role and have to work increasingly long hours in an environment devoid of non-age benefits or a sense of professional community. In the gig economy it is only the individual that counts. The result of this distinctive shift, a global shift, is that not only have a wider range of individuals entered the precariat to undertake a wider range of roles, but also those individuals have been 'precaritised' in the sense of their approach to life and broader social relationships. This frequently involves a sense of being out of control of time, and lacking any clear occupational identity or narrative that offers meaning and shape to their lives. They have been commodified, which gives rise to a constant sense of existential insecurity. God help the Deliveroo generation with their 'bits-and-pieces-lives', but the simple point is that Wright Mills' 'trap' is not only more intense and possibly deeper than it was when first outlined in the late 1950s, but also that a wider sweep of society have (and are) falling or being pushed into it. The *kind of democracy we have is a precarious democracy* because it has lost its capacity to counter-balance market forces and market logic, and as a result, an angry and disillusioned precariat has emerged.

But I want to go further in terms of the analysis and dissection of the current state of democratic distemper for the simple reason that I believe we are entering a transformative phase of human history. If 'the trap' has really deepened and become more ensnaring to millions of educated people who cannot get jobs, to millions of women who feel abused, oppressed and trapped in the labour market, to millions of people labelled as 'disabled', and to hundreds of millions of migrants who are constantly carried on the ebb and flow of economic tides with little chance of finding safe port or firm anchorage, then two further linkages must be explored. The first is what happened to the 'the promise' of the social sciences and 'the precariat', and the second is the link between the precariat and populism.

It would be far too easy to bemoan the social and political sciences for failing to deliver on 'the promise' of these disciplines in terms of empowering the public to understand how and why the world is changing in certain ways and, through this, to allow individuals to regain at least some element of control over their lives. To put the same point slightly differently, 'the promise' of the social sciences in this context was to help men and women understand their position

in the world and their capacity to act and shape their relationship with a broader social system that could too often appear remote and uncontrollable. But for Wright Mills, 'the promise' of the social sciences would only be achieved when scholars moved away from the 'abstracted empiricism' and 'grand theory' that had, in his opinion, undermined the social relevance of the social sciences. The simple 'fact' – if such foundational terms can be used with any credibility – is that the social and political sciences have not delivered on their 'promise'. The intellectual history of many social sciences, from political science through to sociology, economics and many others, is one of a professionalisation process that, if anything, incentivised ever greater levels of 'abstracted empiricism' and 'grand theory'. (As one of the few academics who stimulated a record-breaking 'Twitter spike' for using the term 'methodological masturbation' no less than six times in one keynote address, I feel strangely confident about discussing such issues.) And yet, once again, there is a 'trap-within-a-trap' in the sense that recourse to the almost constant flaying of academics risks

overlooking the existence of two interrelated and distinctive shifts in the wider context that has, in turn, significant implications for the potential role or credibility of academics. The first shift was the emergence of 'expert rejection', the second the emergence of 'post-truth politics'.

> *Expert rejection* [noun] – the popular rejection of independent, objective analyses provided by academics or actors with credible expertise claims by politicians, policy-makers, communities or the public as a whole.

It is impossible to explain the sociopolitical roots of the contemporary concern regarding 'expert rejection' in any simple or linear fashion. It is also far too simplistic to link the rise of this phenomenon solely to the EU referendum or the election of Trump; for some time, concerns have been voiced about public trust in experts, the tension between fact- and emotion-based arguments, the impact of social media on the credibility and reach of academic knowledge, the science of scientific advice and – at it broadest level

– the changing relationship between science (broadly conceived) and democracy. And yet it is possible to identify a broad global trend over the last 20 years within the policy-making process *towards* evidence-informed policy. This is reflected in the creation of a whole range of bridge-building networks and institutions such as the 'What Works?' centres in the UK, the new Scientific Advisory Mechanism within the European Commission, new global assessment mechanisms such as the Intergovernmental Platform on Biodiversity and Ecosystem Services and in 2014, the International Network for Government Science Advice was established with a remit to strengthen and facilitate the exchange of lessons and best practice across different advisory bodies and national systems. And yet, a key feature of both the Brexit referendum in the UK and the US presidential election was the manner in which academic findings were so easily dismissed and sidelined. For one reason or another the academy failed to connect with the public.

One response might be to return to the 'great scholar, poor politician' thesis, and to focus on the need for academics to better understand the art of translation in the sense of grounding their data and research in the lived everyday experience of ordinary men and women. It might even be correct to suggest that academics need just a touch more political cunning and adaptability, a willingness to risk dirtying their hands or burning their fingers in the rough world beyond academe. But even here such arguments appear somewhat underpowered vis-à-vis the scale of a social challenge that poses more fundamental threats to the credibility of knowledge and the capacity to cultivate balanced debates. Indeed, the capacity of academics to deliver on 'the promise' of the social sciences that Wright Mills so majestically promotes seems confounded by the emergence of 'post-fact' or 'post-truth' politics.

Post-truth [adjective] – relating to or denoting circumstances in which objective facts are less influential in shaping public opinion than appeals to emotion and personal belief.

There is, of course, a distinguished body of scholarship on the mendacity of politics and the mendaciousness of politicians, and to some extent it would be too simple to say that the problem was that politicians lied in 2016 – politicians have lied, and to some extent always will lie, for the simple reason that politics is a worldly art – something more subtle and possibly far more dangerous has happened within democratic dialogue. The *Washington Post's* fact-checker blog has awarded its maximum dishonesty rating – four Pinocchios – to nearly 70% of the Trump statements it has vetted. The problem is that even the other 30% don't turn out to be true but instead are found to be extreme distortion rather than outright lies (ie, just three Pinocchios). Brexiteers toured the UK in a big red bus with the slogan emblazoned along its side, 'We send the EU £350 million a week'. It was a great slogan despite the fact that it was untrue because it fails to acknowledge the British rebate or the proportion of funding that is actually immediately redistributed back to the UK. The problem is that the experts who raise such boring issues risk immediately being labelled as bores and spoilsports. As such experts were rejected, fairy tales and fig leaves were promulgated, the public was undoubtedly duped, but the deeper shift was undoubtedly the dominance of emotions above rationality. Not only did academics appear unable (or unwilling) to frame their research in a manner that the public could set against their day-to-day lives in a meaningful manner, but they also seemed incapable of understanding why their generally pro-European or pro-Clinton messages were not getting across. Worse than this was the slight whiff that academics and experts alike slipped into an arrogant state of denial in which 'the public are stupid' argument was implicitly deployed. And yet, to make this argument is to badly under-estimate the intelligence of the public and the power of the populist.

Populism and emotion

The issue of populism unites the previous discussions about both 'the trap' and 'the promise'. I would argue that populism is itself a dangerous 'trap', and yet I can understand why many people appear seduced by its simple promise. The simple fact is that populism promotes an emotional signal that is very attractive to those in search of control, clarity and order in an increasingly disordered and complex world. This is exactly why the rational arguments of experts and academics had little impact when set against the emotive assertions of Trump or the Brexiteers. To be part of 'the precariat' is to inhabit not just a physical world but also to live within a psychological world of uncertainty and constant threat. The precariat – the unemployed youth, the disabled adult, the migrant families, the hyper-mobile zero-hours self-employed worker – are both physically and metaphysically 'unanchored'. Human nature craves stability, meaning and a sense of being valued within a community, but such characteristics are an anathema to the precepts of liquid modernity and the gig economy. This mismatch fuels stress, anxiety and fear, emotions that can too easily be focused not on the roots of the ailment but on other sections of society that exist under exactly the same pressures. The precariat therefore brings with it a tendency to vent its anger internally, thereby simply fuelling and sustaining a sense of insecurity. As Guy Standing notes, 'the precariat is easily lured by the sirens of populism.'

This is democracy turned inside out and upside down. Populists offer simple solutions to complex problems and hold out the promise of control, stability and social meaning – the claim to offer both safe port and firm anchorage. The problem is, however, that the price that is paid is that of democracy because democracy is too often viewed as 'the problem' – 'If we could only get rid of those bums in Washington!', 'If we could just release ourselves from those parasites in Brussels!', 'Let's drain the swamp', 'If we could just find some way of buttressing our borders!', 'If we could just remove those democratic safeguards and do what we know needs to be done!' For those wanting clarity and order there is the simple Crick-ian fact to contend with that democratic politics is inevitably messy. As a crucible of compromise democratic politics tends to grate and grind, its processes tend to be slow and cumbersome, its decisions can be inefficient and hard to understand from the outside – think of every criticism that has ever been levelled at the EU – which, in turn, makes fast-paced responsiveness very difficult. In this context it is easy to understand the attractiveness of populist parties and their simplistic promises of far-reaching change to those who may feel they have little to lose. The problem is that they have the most to lose.

As Mark Mazower's *Dark Continent* (1998) makes clear, Europe in particular enjoys a particularly fragile relationship with democracy. Although the 20th century is often hailed as the democratic century, the years 1912-49 were defined by war, destitution and at least three sustained and partly successful attempts to destroy and exterminate whole populations. There is no joyous tale of progressive social, economic or political development during these decades, but a horrific account of killing, imprisonment, torture and dislocation involving hundreds of millions of people. The fact that the UK voted to leave the EU just days before the centenary anniversary of the Battle of the Somme, one of the largest and bloodiest battles of the First World War, was therefore a poignant reminder that the EU's origins in a post-war 'peace project' seemed largely to have been forgotten. In terms of understanding the type of democracy that is currently emerging, the spectre of populist nationalism cannot be denied, and the problem with nationalism is that it has the unfortunate habit of 'assuming that human beings can be classified like insects and that whole blocks of millions or tens of millions of people can be confidently labelled "good" or 'bad'", as George Orwell wrote in his essay 'Notes on Nationalism' in 1945. The global shift that was signalled by Trump's victory and the UK's decision in relation to European membership was one defined by the emergence of populist nationalism and possibly the end of the dominant liberal order that was constructed very much as a response to the disorder of the first half of the 20th century. As Francis Fukuyama wrote in *The Financial Times* (11 November 2016), 'The risk of sliding into a world of competitive and equally angry nationalisms is huge.' The pattern of political posturing and growing public support is relatively clear as anti-establishment candidates utilise a fairly simplistic brand of populist nationalism (think Erdoğan in Turkey, think Orbán in Hungary, think Putin in Russia, think, think, think, etc).

But what is driving this global shift? The root answer is the dysfunction of the liberal order and the growth of inequality (discussed below), but a more subtle response would be to focus on the role of emotions and emotional intelligence. The uncomfortable truth is that the populist politicians and insurgent parties – such as the Freedom Party in Austria, the Danish People's Party, the Alternative für Deutschland, Syriza in

Greece, Fidesz in Hungary, the Latvian National Alliance, the Party for Freedom in the Netherlands, the Law and Justice Party in Poland, etc – have all managed to tap into an emotional landscape that conventional politicians and parties seemed to have overlooked for too long. 'Let's put the "Great" back into "Great Britain"', 'Let's make America great again' and 'We're taking back control!' are, at one level, meaningless political slogans but, at another level, they resonate with broader concerns regarding social equality and identity politics. Moreover, with the estimated size of the precariat reaching almost 40% in the US, parts of Western Europe, East Asia and Australasia, the political appeal of national protectionism and the implicit, sometimes explicit, attack on non-nationals (those defined as 'bad' by 'the good', to paraphrase Orwell) taps into a powerful source of emotive desire, the desire to feel bonds of association with a solid physical community. These emotions are compelling and to some extent were epitomised by the competition between Donald Trump and Hillary Clinton. The

former projected a simple set of emotional signals and combined this with a rather lose relationship with the truth, while the latter was constantly perceived and portrayed as 'poker-faced', dispassionate and as someone who needed to 'lighten up'. In the wake of the presidential elections the Democrats are still struggling to explain their shocking loss, but one explanation was the failure to connect with large sections of the public at an emotional level. This, in itself, forms one element of the broader populist narrative about the existence of a disconnected, cosmopolitan and privileged elite who no longer understand the everyday lives of most people.

And yet, even the populism struggles to explain exactly what is going on in a post-Brexit, pre-Trump world. The emotions that tend to drive populism – anger, frustration, alienation and a yearning for hope – only go so far in explaining recent developments, and if anything, the situation is far more complex and takes us *back to*, rather than *away from*, a focus on liquidity and social change.

Whatever type of democracy is emerging it is driven by a new emotional architecture that seems to reject conventional labels. It is what Gavin Sullivan describes as 'complex hybrid emotional identity politics' characterised by 'hopeful nihilism' in the sense that when Trump declared 'The forgotten man and woman will never be forgotten again. We will all come together as never before', he gave renewed optimism to those sections of society that felt *trapped*. Trump-ism might therefore be seen as a form of emotional release. A release of long-standing and growing socioeconomic tensions combined with the ability to openly discuss previously off-limits social issues. The simple fact is that for some years ordinary men and women in small towns across the US and Western Europe had been concerned about swelling immigrant populations that were perceived as draining public finances and limiting job prospects for local people. Fearful of being branded as racist, many people suppressed these concerns until the emergence of populist nationalist parties provided a lightning rod. This was less about 'left' and 'right' or rational, evidence-based evaluation, and more about subjective social status and felt emotions. The traditional institutions of mainstream democratic politics seem unable to respond. Clinton's emphasis on the need for tolerance, economic reform and national unity did little to assuage a large social base that felt it had been tolerant enough for too long already. There was also a clear sense of psychological statecraft in the campaigns of Trump and Brexit due to the manner in which they both invoked claims of former 'greatness', a strange nostalgia for a solid mythical past that offered control. What they did not offer was any real vision of a new and democratic society that brings us to a focus on our third pairing, a brief discussion of democracy and solutionism.

Democracy and solutionism

The focus of this concluding essay is trying to reach across the 60 posts presented in this book in order to tease out some common themes or innovative insights that help us understand not only 'what kind of democracy is this?', but also 'what kind of democracy do we want?' The nature of the answers that are emerging appear more than a little worrying – 'the trap' is not only deeper, but more people seem to have fallen into it, and this has fuelled growing political disenchantment that has been exploited by populist nationalist parties. Added to this is the rise of 'post-fact', 'post-truth', 'fake news' – driven politics and an almost complete lack on the part of established politicians or political parties to understand exactly why emotions, feelings and sentiments matter. If anything, the liberal elite fell straight into a trap of their own making by thinking they could counter emotion with facts and, through this, convince the public that they were wrong and everything was far better than large sections of the public seemed to think it was. Facts never trump emotions. Indeed, one of the most excoriating and destructive emotion-based criticisms of academics, experts and politicians was delivered not by a gloating populist but by an award-winning artist. When collecting the Arts and Culture Award from the UK Political Studies Association in November 2016, the Turner prize-winning artist Grayson Perry made a statement that merits quoting at length:

> I'm so honoured to be given this award by a room full of experts…. I'm not an expert. I'm an artist and I always feel like the academics are hovering behind me when I pontificate on anything … like they are going to catch me out. But I think the word "truth" is really interesting as we often talk about truth in terms of academic truth, statistical truth, empirical truth, scientific truth but very little do we actually talk about emotional truth. And I think that if the one thing that all the experts need to [improve] is their emotional literacy because what the liberal academic elite has done it let us down because they are not emotionally literate enough to understand what 52% of the electorate was thinking – or *feeling*, should I say [when they voted to leave the EU]. There is a whole world out there that we need to have more empathy with even if we don't like the results of what those kinds of feelings bring about. But I thank you for this award … from *the experts*!

Never has a professional punch on the nose been delivered with such eloquence and precision, but Grayson Perry's point can only be fully examined against a more considered discussion, not of 'expert rejection', but of what might be labelled 'democratic rejection' in light of the simple fact that not only is populist nationalism spreading geographically, but it is doing so on the basis of, as the paleoconservative Pat Buchanan has noted, an explicit platform that rejects many of the 'niceties of liberal democracy.' The answer to the question 'what kind of democracy is this?' can only therefore conclude that it is a type of liberal democracy that not only seems socially and intellectually exhausted, but also appears besieged on two sides. On one flank exists a disparate range of extremist, nationalist and populist parties that appear, rhetorically at least, to endorse radical change; on the other flank the traditional parties and existing liberal elites appear to be questioning not the political economy of capitalism but the merits of democracy. The former wants a deeper more engaged and participatory type of democracy; the latter think that democracy allows the uneducated to make bad decisions and should therefore be restricted. This is clearly a broad-brush analysis of a complex topic, and simple binary frameworks should always be, like sharks or smart forks, approached with caution. But at a basic level democracy does appear to be under attack from all sides which, in itself, demands at least some discussion, and in this regard the posts contained in this book offer a number of insights.

First and foremost, the institutions and processes of democracy have arguably failed to keep pace with the speed of social change. It is not, therefore, large sections of the public, those disparate social groups that share the core characteristics of the precariat, that have been 'left behind', but it is the institutions of democratic politics that have also been 'left behind' by the transfer of powers above and beyond the purview of the nation state. Whether viewed as 'post-democracy' or the 'end of democracy' is secondary to the simple fact that the spheres of global governance and the private world of international finance exist largely beyond democratic control. This is exactly the 'disconnect' or 'deficit' about which so many people from North America to Australasia are aware of and angry about. It is not that voting doesn't matter, but it is that voting matters far less when so much power exists beyond the control of elected politicians. Moreover, there is a clear '*politics of*' democratic reform that acts to prevent the closure of this gap – or this 'void', as Peter Mair describes it – in the sense that there are few incentives for those elites that currently benefit from the status quo to want to institute far-reaching change. (Hence the seductive quality of nihilist populist parties.)

A second issue focuses on the relationship between populism and democracy, and the need for at least some sense of proportionality or balance between the participation of the public and the capacity of representatives to govern. This is exactly the delicate balance that A.H. Birch discussed in his classic *Representative and Responsible Government* (1964), and that has remained something of a touchstone for more recent analyses that have suggested that a situation of representative *versus* responsible government has emerged with the latter dominating the former (and in the process, fuelling disengagement), through to works – such as Simon Tormey's *The End of Representative Politics* (2015) – that suggest contemporary democracy is defined by *neither* representative *nor* responsible government. This relates to an argument that is to be found within a number of posts and focuses on the emergence of 'hyper-democracy' and the suggestion – heretical though it might at first glance appear – that the problem with democracy might not be that we have too little, but that we have too much – too much of the 'wrong kind of democracy' (shallow, fast, loud, aggressive, etc) and too little of the 'right kind of democracy' (deep, slow, listening, constructive, etc). But could the risk of the populists lie in their impatience with convoluted democratic procedures and safeguards that exist to restrict and scrutinise political power? Populists generally claim that representative institutions perform worse

than direct democracy because they allow self-interested politicians and officials to subvert the public interest in favour of narrow self-interest. Research by the European Council on Foreign Affairs published in June 2016 found that insurgent parties across the EU were campaigning for at least 34 referendums on issues such as EU membership, Eurozone membership, refugee relocation figures, constitutional reform, immigration and limitations on the further transfer of sovereign powers. And yet the risk is less about the use of referendums as a tool of democracy and more about the capacity of a charismatic leader to impose an artificial but emotively powerful definition of who is 'good' or 'bad' within society, or to manipulate the public into supporting the centralisation of power and the removal of those meddlesome 'niceties of liberal democracy'.

This brings us to a third issue and the flipside to the *politicisation* that populism ultimately seeks. The wrong response to the populist signal would be denial, retrenchment and further attempts to simply depoliticise policy

areas by putting them beyond the reach of elected politicians. Long before the events of 2016, scholars and commentators were provocatively asking whether the problem with democracy is that it too often tended to give the public what they wanted but not necessarily what they needed, as well as having little concern for intergenerational justice. Jason Brennan has gone further in his book *Against Democracy* (2016) by promoting the concept of 'epistocracy' (meaning government by the knowledgeable) to launch a challenging critique of democracy. In doing so he draws on works such as Ilya Somin's *Democracy and Political Ignorance* (2013), which would itself resonate with works such as Bryan Caplan's *The Myth of the Rational Voter* (2007), Christopher Achen and Larry Bartel's *Democracy for Realists* (2016) and even David van Reybrouck's *Against Elections* (2016), which all in their own ways attempt not to undermine the concept of democracy but to explore its inevitable weaknesses and frailties. But is the problem with democracy actually a problem *with* democracy or more of a reflection on the emotional and arguably unrealistic needs of individuals for control and certainty? Democracy works – as many posts seek to illustrate through different topics – in a fairly rough and ready manner. It is an institutionalised form of conflict resolution that emphasises the showing of hands and the placing of crosses above and beyond the fixing of bayonets and the marching of boots. It is therefore inevitably slow and cumbersome, it grates and grinds, it produces decisions that tend to satisfy no one for the simple reason that democracy is based on compromise, on the collective over the individual. Democratic politics is the art of imperfection because it is driven by human nature and emotion. And yet, at the root of contemporary discussions and much scholarly analysis seems to be an assumption of what has been termed 'solutionism' as a starting point from which democratic politics can only ever be judged as failing.

Solutionism [noun] – The belief that all difficulties have benign solutions, often of a technocratic nature. The providing of a solution or solutions to a customer or client.

The folly of solutionism and the peril of perfectionism is that there are no simple or pain-free solutions to complex sociopolitical challenges. The development of social media and personal technology seems particularly focused on eliminating anguish or uncertainty from modern life. 'Smart glasses' take a series of photos throughout each and every day to relieve the wearer of the need to worry about not capturing special moments for posterity. This is a long way from the folklore notion of the 'Kodak moment', but it feeds into a contemporary sense that everything has a solution. And yet is solutionism really the solution? Could solutionism actually be creating more problems? Such oxymoronic questions form the focus of Evgeny Morozov's excellent book *To Save Everything, Click Here* (2014), but what is less developed is our understanding of how the strong social pressure for 'solutions' has an impact on democratic politics. This theme takes us back to a focus on populism, on the role of emotions, but also on the limits of politics and the dangers of a technocratic and depoliticised approach to social dilemmas. Maybe solutionism risks becoming a dangerous political ideology in its own right.

Writing at around the same time as Bernard Crick's *In Defence of Politics*, the Polish philosopher Leszek Kołakowski penned a superb essay that – like Crick's work – seems incredibly prescient. 'In Praise of Inconsistency' sought to underline the fact that given that we are regularly confronted with equally valid choices where painful ethical reflection is in order, being inconsistent is the only way to avoid becoming a doctrinaire ideologue who sticks to an algorithm. Absolute consistency was, for Kołakowski, synonymous with fanaticism, which brings the discussion back to the innate dysfunctions of democracy and why politicians are so frequently lampooned for being ... inconsistent. The high price of Western intervention in Iraq – the loss of life, the financial cost, the controversy, etc – is now refracted through concern about the price of not intervening in Syria. Nevertheless, when judged against illiberal regimes, the performance and achievements of liberal democracy should not be underestimated. As the economist Amartya Sen has illustrated, democracies never have famines, and other scholars have highlighted how democracies almost never go to war with each other, rarely murder their own populations, nearly always manage the transition of power without the shedding of blood or the breaking of bones, and tend to respect human and political rights. Which brings us to a final focus and to the roots of not only what kind of democracy this is but also what kind of democracy we want – that is, on the growth of inequality and the failure of our political imagination.

Inequality and 'thinking big'

I started this book by arguing that as a written form postcards provide a particularly powerful medium due to the manner in which they force the sender to adopt a rather sparing attitude to the use of text. Not only do they operate along the mantra of 'less is more', but they also tend to be written at a time when the author is temporarily based beyond their day-to-day lived experience. This element of distance combined with the paucity of space creates honest fragments of knowledge – glimpses of the soul – that can often say a great deal about an individual's view on a range of issues (their life, their job, their relationships, their future, etc). The most perceptive reader of these will often infer far more from what is left unsaid than what is actually written, which is why postcards and handwritten personal correspondence of any kind generally convey the essence and existence of a very personal relationship. Nick Clegg's little 'Christmas note' therefore matters less for its specific content and more for what it represents about the nature of contemporary politics. I can't help remembering speaking at a public event in the North East of England some time ago, at which a very old and frail-looking woman dared to speak out in defence of politicians. "Politicians do care!" she told the audience, and proceeded to explain that only recently she had received a handwritten note from her MP about a number of local issues. "Would somebody who did not care really take the time to write me a letter?" she announced, and how crestfallen she looked when nearly every member of the audience explained that they, too, had received exactly the same letter. They did not laugh, they did not need to, the letter had been designed to deceive – mass communication elaborately styled as a personal note.

So let me end this essay (and this book) by returning to a swifter style of writing and by focusing on what I consider to be the main central driver of political frustration – disaffection and distrust and the central defining characteristic of the kind of democracy we actually have and which seems to be under such intense pressure. We have, for want of a better term, a *deranged democracy* that is fatally undermined by its tolerance and perpetuation of increasingly stark levels of inequality. From social inequality to educational inequality, and from financial inequality to inequality of opportunity, the evolutionary trend is towards an ever-growing gap between the 'haves' and the 'have nots'. This is linked directly to the gap (chasm or gulf) between the governors and the governed in many parts of the world that have formed the dominant focus of the 60 posts in this book. The crisis of democracy is a symptom of the deeper malaise of unbridled global capitalism, and as the inequalities become more stark, as the number of 'losers' far outweighs the number of 'winners', and as an ever-greater proportion of the public feel trapped and increasingly desperate in an economic system they perceive to be unfair, then pressure for change will inevitably build. As Danny Dorling's *Inequality and the 1%* (2014) illustrates, since the great recession occurred in 2008, the most wealthy 1% of the population (the 'super-rich') have actually grown richer during exactly the time that the remaining 99% was expected to endure an 'age of austerity'. And yet this body of research also reveals the manner in which inequality is not just about money – being born outside the top 1% is also highly likely to reduce your life expectancy, your educational opportunities, your capacity to express

yourself politically, your work prospects and even your mental health.

Democratic disaffection is a complex social phenomenon that has many layers and elements, but stripped down to the core what one finds is a focus on rising inequality. Disaffection is a symptom; inequality is the ailment.

This argument helps us pin down not only an answer to 'what kind of democracy is this?' but also to 'what kind of democracy do we want?' In some ways the answer to the first question is now easier to classify – it is a market-driven liberal democracy that is increasingly riven by social fragmentation fuelled by rising levels of social inequality. The second question is trickier due to the simple fact that different people will want different things. Those in the top 1%, the top 10% or even the top 50% may have different views on the specific nature of the problem that needs to be solved, let alone the nature of viable solutions to those problems. Some people will argue that the existence

of extreme inequalities is itself not a 'bad' thing, or if it is 'bad', then it is for the market and not the for state to intervene or correct it. Such piffle simply reflects the views of an embedded elite who have little incentive to radically reconstitute an economic order that serves them so well. And yet democracy is not about 'them'; it is about 'us'. It is a collective, not individual, endeavour. But the bigger issue that paradoxically has received far less attention is the question of *what we want*. Political science has for a long time been a problem-focused field of endeavour when what has arguably been needed is a more solution-focused mode of thinking. My final point is therefore a provocation to you, the reader. It is a provocation to 'think Big' – returning to C. Wright Mills' approach to scholarship and even Bernard Crick's 'A Rallying Cry to the University Professors of Politics' – by thinking about a new project.

This is also the key failure in my own writing that this book so clearly exposes. The posts exist very much within a critique of what might be termed the enlightened social democratic model of liberal democratic capitalism. The dominant characteristic is therefore a tendency to focus on a specific issue or events as little more than yet another example of political exhaustion. What they completely fail to do is step outside this framework in order to consider *new* ways of organising social life. They therefore reflect a scarcity of thinking that actually has little to do with the size of the paper and more to do with the intellectual limits of the author. Nevertheless, what many of the posts in this book have charted is the manner in which a model of liberal democracy that appeared triumphant towards the end of the 20th century has succumbed to a range of pressures. There was a relatively short-lived period associated with Fukayama's 'End of History' thesis in which a broad consensus revolved around the existence of a liberal democracy with elements of state control and intervention to soften the sharp edges of capitalism. This was, for a decade around the turn of the millennium, certainly not 'the end of history' but accepted as the least-worst 'type' of democracy by a broad sweep of the political

spectrum. The Keynesian welfare state needs a strong nation state with the capacity to impose fiscal rules, but global markets have eroded that capacity. Furthermore, the events of 9/11 and the economic performance of non-democratic regimes like China destroyed the notion that liberal democratic capitalism was either universally accepted or particularly efficient. Moreover, since then global capitalism has arguably become ever more brutal and predatory, inequalities have grown, a dangerous precariat class has emerged and in a rather odd way capitalism no longer needs democracy. They have become un-coupled, de-coupled, divorced.

This is not a new argument, and Slavoj Žižek's *Living in End Times* (2010) provides a scintillating analysis of this thesis. The question posed by this book is therefore less about *what we have* and more about *what we want*; as such the problem with democracy is less about the failings of what we have now and more about our failure to articulate any clear vision of what a re-imagined 'type' or 'model' of democracy might

actually look like, how it might operate, or where power should ultimately reside. What is absent at the moment is any evidence of a collective capacity to 'think Big', and what is in evidence is a constant retreat to tinkering with a social democratic model of controlled capitalism that was a 20th-century construct. The result is two features of modern life that seem little more than intellectual cul de sacs or distractions from the need to think afresh about the bigger picture. From the right is a cunning process of individualisation that delegates guilt and culpability away from the core structural drivers to those individuals who will ultimately pay the price. Environmental risks are met by an emphasis on individual recycling, public health depends on the capacity of the individual to live like a monk, the erosion of the welfare state leads to an emphasis on personal financial management ... political activism is redefined as little more than a consumer choice or lifestyle decision. The result is that collective challenges are viewed through the lens of individualised and granular responses. The potential of collective action and collective responsibility are denied, blame is devolved, and the private sphere even manages to create new markets in guilt reduction by charging higher costs for products that claim to offer an ethical choice.

To some extent this is exactly the profit-driven, rational behaviour of the market, and the real failing when it comes to 'thinking Big' about how to counter increasing inequalities is the failure of the left to offer a viable alternative of a different sociopolitical model. To many on the left the answer lies in a new project based around the far-reaching devolution of powers to the local level and the emergence of a highly decentralised polity in which decisions are taken through deliberative or communitarian processes. This approach has the benefit of shifting the focus from individuals back towards institutional structures and the value of collective action, but it fails at the issue of scale. The 21st century and the ultimate success or failure of democracy will rest on its capacity to manage those facets of the global commons. From water wars to fish stocks and from clear air to global warming, it is hard to see how hyper-localism could actually offer a viable model. It is in the design of large-scale solutions that focus on major global challenges that the left really needs to offer a new model that is seductive enough to forge an emotional connection with those who feel 'left behind' but robust enough to actually forge a less unequal society.

Notes

1st post

2 Down and out in Bloemfontein

[1] *Daily Mail* (2013) 'The shanty town holiday where the rich get to pretend they are living in lean-to like millions of Africans (but with running water, electricity and even Wi-Fi)', 19 November (www.dailymail.co.uk/news/article-2509857/Emoya-Estate-holiday-rich-pretend-living-poverty.html).

3 Reveries of a solitary fell runner

[1] Rousseau, J.J. (2011) *Reveries of the Solitary Walker*, Oxford: Oxford University Press (https://global.oup.com/academic/product/reveries-of-the-solitary-walker-9780199563272?cc=gb&lang=en&).

[2] Oxford Index, 'Sigmund Freud, 1859-1939' (http://oxfordindex.oup.com/view/10.1093/oi/authority.20110803095835377).

4 Feral politics: Searching for meaning in the 21st century

[1] English Oxford Living Dictionaries, 'Feral' (https://en.oxforddictionaries.com/definition/feral).

[2] Monbiot, G. (2013) *Feral: Searching for Enchantment on the Frontiers of Rewilding* (www.monbiot.com/2013/05/24/feral-searching-for-enchantment-on-the-frontiers-of-rewilding/).

[3] World Health Organization, Health topics, 'Depression' (www.who.int/topics/depression/en/).

[4] Mental Health Foundation, 'Suicide' (www.mentalhealth.org.uk/a-to-z/s/suicide).

[5] Oxford Index, 'Émile Durkheim, 1858–1917' (http://oxfordindex.oup.com/view/10.1093/oi/authority.20110803095736538).

[6] English Oxford Living Dictionaries, 'Anomie' (https://en.oxforddictionaries.com/definition/anomie).

[7] Oxford Index, 'Max Weber, 1864–1920' (http://oxfordindex.oup.com/view/10.1093/oi/authority.20110803121529170).

5 Sharks, asylum seekers and Australian politics

[1] Oxford Index, 'Matthew Flinders, 1774–1814' (http://oxfordindex.oup.com/view/10.1093/oi/authority.20110803095824279?rskey=s0sREm&result=1).

[2] Wikipedia, 'Greg Hunt' (https://en.wikipedia.org/wiki/Greg_Hunt).

[3] Oxford Index, 'Shark' (http://oxfordindex.oup.com/view/10.1093/oi/authority.20110803100459630?rskey=rba888&result=2).

6 The smart fork and the crowding out of thought

[1] Cameron, S. (2013) 'Battle lines drawn in Whitehall's phoney war', *The Telegraph*, 16 January (www.telegraph.co.uk/news/politics/9806136/Battle-lines-drawn-in-Whitehalls-phoney-war.html).

[2] Raines, T. (2013) 'Britain's EU future: Cameron's gambit', Chatham House, 25 January (www.chathamhouse.org/media/comment/view/188785).

[3] Kelion, L. (2013) 'CES 2013: Intelligent cutlery and other smart phone innovations', BBC News, 7 January (www.bbc.co.uk/news/technology-20932073).

[4] Lanchester, J. (2012) 'What Money Can't Buy by Michael Sandel – review', *The Guardian*, 17 May (www.theguardian.com/books/2012/may/17/what-money-cant-buy-michael-sandel-review).

[5] Quoted in de Botton, A. (2010) 'The limits of freedom', *The Guardian*, 24 February (www.theguardian.com/commentisfree/2010/feb/24/morality-motivation-dogmatism-judgement).

[6] English Oxford Living Dictionaries, 'Leitmotif' (https://en.oxforddictionaries.com/definition/leitmotif).

[7] Quoted in Dillon, B. (2010) 'Living in the End Times by Slavoj Žižek: review', *The Telegraph*, 30 July (www.telegraph.co.uk/culture/books/bookreviews/7916506/Living-in-the-End-Times-by-Slavoj-Zizek-review.html).

8 Saints and sinners, politicians and priests

[1] BBC News (2013) 'Justin Welby is enthroned as Archbishop of Canterbury', 21 March (www.bbc.co.uk/news/uk-21875199).

[2] Oxford Dictionary of National Biography, 'Ronald Stuart Thomas', 1913-2000 (www.oxforddnb.com/public/dnb/74584.html). Thomas, R.S. (1985) 'Threshold', in *Poems of R.S. Thomas*, Fayetteville, AR: The University of Arkansas Press.

2nd post

11 The problems with democracy – continuing the conversation into a new year

[1] Flinders, M. (2015) 'The problem with democracy', *Parliamentary Affairs*, vol 69, no 1, pp 181-203 (https://academic.oup.com/pa/article-abstract/69/1/181/2472983/The-Problem-with-Democracy?redirectedFrom=fulltext).

[2] Baldini, G. (2015) 'Democracy, golden ages and balancing acts – Comment on Flinders, M. (2015) The Problem with Democracy', *Parliamentary Affairs*, vol 69, no 2, pp 451-63 (https://academic.oup.com/pa/article-abstract/69/2/451/1940988/Democracy-Golden-Ages-and-Balancing-Acts-Comment?redirectedFrom=fulltext).

[3] Gillan, K. (2015) 'Reflections on "The Problem with Democracy"', Movements@ Manchester blog, 15 December (www.movements.manchester.ac.uk/flinders-problem-with-democracy/).

[4] Flinders, M. (2008) *Delegated Governance and the British State: Walking Without Order*, Oxford: Oxford University Press (https://global.oup.com/academic/product/delegated-governance-and-the-british-state-9780199271603?cc=gb&lang=en&).

12 Do we have too much democracy?

[1] Wikipedia, 'The Life and Death of Democracy' (https://en.wikipedia.org/wiki/The_Life_and_Death_of_Democracy).

14 Look beneath the vote

[1] See www.turnup.org.uk/

[2] English Oxford Living Dictionaries, 'Disengagement' (https://en.oxforddictionaries.com/definition/disengagement).

[3] See www.crickcentre.org/

15 Democracy is about more than a vote: Politics and brand management

[1] Chwalisz, C. (2015) 'An Athenian solution to democratic discontent', Policy Network, 19 February (www.policy-network.net/pno_detail.aspx?ID=4845&title=An-Athenian-solution-to-democratic-discontent).

16 Beastly Eastleigh and the 'None-of-the-Above' Party

[1] Wikipedia, 'Eastleigh' (https://en.wikipedia.org/wiki/Eastleigh).

[2] English Oxford Living Dictionaries, 'Benny Hill' (https://en.oxforddictionaries.com/definition/hill,_benny).

[3] Mitchell, B. (2013) 'Now naked rambler Stephen Gough is covered by a nationwide Asbo', *Independent*, 28 February (www.independent.co.uk/news/uk/crime/now-naked-rambler-stephen-gough-is-covered-by-a-nationwide-asbo-8515548.html).

[4] English Oxford Living Dictionaries, 'UKIP' (https://en.oxforddictionaries.com/definition/UKIP).

[5] English Oxford Living Dictionaries, 'Populist' (https://en.oxforddictionaries.com/definition/populist).

3rd post

18 What a mess! The politics and governance of the British constitution

[1] English Oxford Living Dictionaries, 'Anomie' (https://en.oxforddictionaries.com/definition/anomie).

[2] See www.parliament.uk/business/committees/committees-a-z/commons-select/political-and-constitutional-reform-committee/inquiries/parliament-2010/constitutional-convention-for-the-uk/

21 Looking beyond the Scottish referendum

[1] Grossman, R.S. (2014) 'The economics of Scottish Independence', OUPblog, 3 September (https://blog.oup.com/2014/09/economics-scottish-independence/).

[2] Crawford, R. (2014) 'Why Scotland should get the government it votes for', OUPblog, 12 September (https://blog.oup.com/2014/09/scottish-independence-debate/).

[3] Berry, D.H. (2014) 'The Scottish referendum: where is Cicero?', OUPblog, 11 September (https://blog.oup.com/2014/09/scottish-referendum-cicero/).

[4] Mitchell, J. (2014) 'Should Scotland be an independent country?', OUPblog, 13 September (https://blog.oup.com/2014/09/scotland-independent-country/).

24 Let the people speak! Devolution, decentralisation, deliberation

[1] Goodin, R.E. (2012) *Innovating Democracy: Democratic Theory and Practice After the Deliberative Turn*, Oxford: Oxford University Press (https://global.oup.com/academic/product/innovating-democracy-9780199650552?cc=gb&lang=en&).

[2] Dryzek, J.S. (2002) *Deliberative Democracy and Beyond: Liberals, Critics, Contestations*, Oxford: Oxford University Press (https://global.oup.com/academic/product/deliberative-democracy-and-beyond-9780199250431?cc=gb&lang=en&).

[3] Nabatchi, T., Gastil, J., Leighninger, M. and Weiksner, G.M. (2012) *Democracy in Motion: Evaluating the Practice and Impact of Deliberative Civic Engagement*, Oxford: Oxford University Press (https://global.oup.com/academic/product/democracy-in-motion-9780199899289?cc=gb&lang=en&).

25 Raw politics: Devolution, democracy and deliberation

[1] See https://global.oup.com/academic/search?q=John+Dryzek&cc=gb&lang=en

[2] See https://global.oup.com/academic/search?q=Frank+Fischer&cc=gb&lang=en

[3] See https://global.oup.com/academic/search?q=John%20parkinson&cc=gb&lang=en

4th post

27 After the storm: Failure, fallout and Farage

[1] Oxford Index, 'United Kingdom Independence Party' (http://oxfordindex.oup.com/view/10.1093/oi/authority.20110803110725792).

[2] Oxford Index, 'Front National' (http://oxfordindex.oup.com/view/10.1093/oi/authority.20110803095836626).

[3] Oxford Index, 'Liberal Party, Austria' (http://oxfordindex.oup.com/view/10.1093/oi/authority.20110803100103843).

[4] Oxford Index, 'Nigel Farage' (http://oxfordindex.oup.com/view/10.1093/ww/9780199540884.013.U15437).

[5] Oxford Index, 'Spitting Image' (http://oxfordindex.oup.com/view/10.1093/acref/9780199916108.013.7493).

28 Tony Benn was a true man of the people

[1] Crossman, A. (2014) 'Tony Benn, conviction politician and old-Labour stalwart, dies', *The Conversation*, 14 March (https://theconversation.com/tony-benn-conviction-politician-and-old-labour-stalwart-dies-23336).

29 Dear Russell Brand: On the politics of comedy and disengagement

[1] See www.newstatesman.com/staggers/2013/10/weeks-new-statesman-russell-brand-guest-edit

[2] Wikipedia, '24-hours news cycle' (https://en.wikipedia.org/wiki/24-hour_news_cycle).

30 Foolish, but no fool: Boris Johnson and the art of politics

[1] See www.conservativehome.com/

[2] Oxford Index, 'Max Weber, 1864-1920' (http://oxfordindex.oup.com/view/10.1093/oi/authority.20110803121529170).

[3] English Oxford Living Dictionaries, 'Statecraft' (https://en.oxforddictionaries.com/definition/statecraft).

32 Trump that: The failure and farce of American politics

[1] Brooks, D. (2016) 'The Governing Cancer of Our Times', *The New York Times*, 26 February (www.nytimes.com/2016/02/26/opinion/the-governing-cancer-of-our-time.html?_r=1).

[2] MacWilliams, M. (2016) 'The one weird trait that predicts whether you're a Trump supporter', *Politico Magazine*, 17 January (www.politico.com/magazine/story/2016/01/donald-trump-2016-authoritarian-213533).

33 Mad politics

[1] *Science Daily* (2015) 'New report finds 43 percent increase in ADHD diagnosis for US schoolchildren', 8 December (www.sciencedaily.com/releases/2015/12/151208150630.htm).

[2] Lee, B.Y. (2016) 'The one thing to do to stop the obesity epidemic', *Forbes*, 12 October (www.forbes.com/sites/brucelee/2016/10/12/the-one-thing-to-do-to-stop-the-obesity-epidemic/#4cd117531bdf).

5th post

35 DIY democracy: Festivals, parks and fun

[1] See www.glastonburyfestivals.co.uk/

[2] See www.parkrun.org.uk/

[3] Wikipedia, '*Runner's World*' (https://en.wikipedia.org/wiki/Runner%27s_World).

37 The body politic: Art, pain, Putin

[1] Flinders, M. (2015) 'Raw politics: Devolution, democracy and deliberation', OUPblog, 1 November (https://blog.oup.com/2015/11/raw-politics-and-academia/).

38 It's just a joke!

[1] Wikipedia, 'Aristophanes' (https://en.wikipedia.org/wiki/Aristophanes).

[2] Wikipedia, 'Aristotle' (https://en.wikipedia.org/wiki/Aristotle).

[3] Wikipedia, 'Niccolò Machiavelli' (https://en.wikipedia.org/wiki/Niccol%C3%B2_Machiavelli).

[4] See www.youtube.com/watch?v=0WptW-LulBM

[5] See www.cc.com/shows/the-daily-show-with-trevor-noah

[6] See www.cc.com/shows/the-colbert-report

[7] See www.bbc.co.uk/programmes/b006mkw3

[8] See www.mocktheweek.tv/

[9] See www.cbc.ca/22minutes/

[10] Jones, J.P. (2007) '"Fake" news versus "real" news as sources of political information: *The Daily Show* and postmodern political reality', in K. Riegert (ed) *Politicotainment: Television's Take on the Real*, New York: Peter Lang.

[11] Baumgartner, J. and Morris, J.S. (2006) 'The Daily Show effect: Candidate evaluations, efficacy and American youth', *American Politics Research*, vol 34, no 3, pp 341-67 (www.npr.org/documents/2006/jul/dailyshow.pdf).

[12] Kalin, M. (2006) 'Why Jon Stewart isn't funny', boston.com, 3 March (http://archive.boston.com/ae/movies/oscars/articles/2006/03/03/why_jon_stewart_isnt_funny/).

[13] English Oxford Living Dictionaries, 'Thermometer' (https://en.oxforddictionaries.com/definition/thermometer).

[14] English Oxford Living Dictionaries, 'Thermostat' (https://en.oxforddictionaries.com/definition/thermostat).

[15] Wikipedia, 'The Clouds' (https://en.wikipedia.org/wiki/The_Clouds).

[16] See www.cc.com/

40 Why Parliament matters: Waging war and restraining power

[1] BBC News (2013) 'Syria vote: Political reaction', 30 August (www.bbc.co.uk/news/uk-politics-23896042).

42 Democracy Day: We need to break free

[1] BBC News (2015) 'As it happened: BBC Democracy Day', 20 January (www.bbc.co.uk/news/live/30876658).

[2] See www.flickr.com/photos/voteforachange/3682027242/

6th post

43 Attack ads and American presidential politics

[1] English Oxford Living Dictionaries, 'Democrat' (https://en.oxforddictionaries.com/definition/democrat).

[2] English Oxford Living Dictionaries, 'Corrosive' (https://en.oxforddictionaries.com/definition/corrosive).

[3] Zeleny, J. and Rutenberg, J. (2012) 'GOP "super PAC" weighs hard-line attack on Obama', *The New York Times*, 17 May (www.nytimes.com/2012/05/17/us/politics/gop-super-pac-weighs-hard-line-attack-on-obama.html?_r=2&ref=politics).

[4] English Oxford Living Dictionaries, 'Demonize' (https://en.oxforddictionaries.com/definition/demonize).

44 Dante and the spin doctors

[1] See www.youtube.com/watch?v=GgvXniTz7D8

[2] Dobson, A. (2014) *Listening for Democracy: Recognition, Representation, Reconciliation*, Oxford: Oxford University Press (https://global.oup.com/academic/product/listening-for-democracy-9780199682454?cc=gb&lang=en&).

45 Democratic realism

[1] Zelinsky, E. (2012) 'The likely failure of Obamacare after "National Federation", OUPblog, 2 July (https://blog.oup.com/2012/07/failure-obamacare-national-federation-scotus/).

[2] Woodruff, P. (2012) 'What Pericles would say about Obamacare', OUPblog, 2 August (https://blog.oup.com/2012/08/what-pericles-would-say-about-obamacare/).

47 Fig leaves and fairy tales: Political promises and the Truth-O-Meter

[1] See www.politifact.com/truth-o-meter/

[2] Crick, B. (1962) *In Defence of Politics*, Chicago, IL: University of Chicago Press (http://press.uchicago.edu/ucp/books/book/chicago/I/bo3637614.html).

50 Dear Maria Miller, it really wasn't all your fault

[1] Watt, N. and Wintour, P. (2014) 'Maria Miller quits as culture secretary in blow to David Cameron', *The Guardian*, 9 April (www.theguardian.com/politics/2014/apr/09/maria-miller-quits-culture-secretary-david-cameron).

[2] See www.theguardian.com/politics/video/2014/apr/03/maria-miller-expenses-apology-video

[3] Dominiczak, P., Watt, H., Swinford, S. and Newell, C. (2014) 'Maria Miller's behaviour is shocking, claims former chairman of Standards Committee', *The Telegraph*, 5 April (www.telegraph.co.uk/news/newstopics/mps-expenses/conservative-mps-expenses/10746387/Maria-Millers-behaviour-is-shocking-claims-former-chairman-of-Standards-Committee.html).

[4] Hardman, I. (2014) 'Will reforms to self-regulation of MPs be enough to distract from Miller row?', *The Spectator*, 7 April (http://blogs.spectator.co.uk/2014/04/will-reforms-to-self-regulation-of-mps-be-enough-to-distract-from-miller-row/).

5 IPSA (Independent Parliamentary Standards Authority) 'MPs' business costs and expenses' (www.theipsa.org.uk/mp-costs).

The last post

55 Claims of increasing irrelevance of universities are ideology masquerading as evidence

1 Heath, A. (2015) 'A refusal to think freely is making universities increasingly irrelevant', *The Telegraph*, 2 December (www.telegraph.co.uk/education/universityeducation/12030100/A-refusal-to-think-freely-is-making-universities-increasingly-irrelevant.html).

2 Pendlebury, D.A. (1991) 'Science, citation, and funding', *Science*, vol 251, pp 1410-11 (http://garfield.library.upenn.edu/papers/pendleburyscience1991.html).

3 See www.ref.ac.uk/results/analysis/sectorandmainpanelaverageresults/

4 See www.ref.ac.uk/media/ref/results/AverageProfile_21_Politics_and_International_Studies.pdf

5 Select Committee (2015) *Building Public Engagement: Options for Developing Select Committee Outreach* (www.publications.parliament.uk/pa/cm201516/cmselect/cmliaisn/470/47002.htm).

6 Morgan, J. (2015) 'Almost half of sector to back Labour, THE election poll suggests', *Times Higher Education*, 30 April (www.timeshighereducation.com/news/almost-half-of-sector-to-back-labour-the-election-poll-suggests/2019944.article).

7 See www.timeshighereducation.com/sites/default/files/Attachments/2015/04/29/q/e/n/voting-intentions-by-disciplinary-area-new.pdf

57 Post-truth, post-political, post-democracy: The tragedy of the UK's referendum on the European Union

[1] House of Commons Treasury Committee (2016) *The Economic and Financial Costs and Benefits of the UK's EU Membership* (www.publications.parliament.uk/pa/cm201617/cmselect/cmtreasy/122/122.pdf).

[2] Crace, J. (2016) 'Over to you, says puffy-eyed Cameron as the Brexit vultures circle', *The Guardian*, 24 June (www.theguardian.com/politics/2016/jun/24/over-to-you-says-puffy-eyed-cameron-as-brexit-vultures-circle).

58 A talent for politics? The 'great scholar, poor politician' thesis

[1] Wikipedia, 'Pablo Iglesias Turrión' (https://en.wikipedia.org/wiki/Pablo_Iglesias_Turri%C3%B3n).

[2] See https://podemos.info/

[3] See www.portugal.gov.pt/en/ministries/mf/the-team/minister/mario-centeno.aspx

59 Standing up and shaping the agenda: Rejecting discrimination, embracing difference

[1] Staufenberg, J. (2016) 'Brexit: Cartoonists around the world react to EU referendum result', *Independent* (www.independent.co.uk/news/uk/home-news/brexit-cartoon-eu-referendum-results-latest-reaction-live-updates-a7099856.html).

Sources

1 Fire and ashes, OUPblog, 6 December 2015.

2 Down and out in Bloemfontein, OUPblog, 8 January 2014.

3 Reveries of a solitary fell runner, OUPblog, 9 January 2013.

4 Feral politics, OUPblog, 2 October 2013.

5 Sharks, asylum seekers and Australian politics, OUPblog, 6 August 2014.

6 The smart fork and the crowding out of thought, OUPblog, 6 February 2013.

7 'Vape', Sir Bernard Crick Centre Blog, 20 November 2014.

8 Saints and sinners, politicians and priests, OUPblog, 1 May 2013.

9 Why satire is no joke any more, *Yorkshire Post*, 4 November 2013.

10 In our name, *Parliaments, Estates & Representation*, vol 34, no 1, pp 114-15, 2014 (www.tandfonline.com).

11 The problems with democracy, OUPblog, 3 January 2016.

12 Do we have too much democracy?, OUPblog, 2 July 2014.

13 Calming the storm, *Teaching Citizenship*, 2014.

14 Look beneath the vote, OUPblog, 5 March 2014.

15 Democracy is about more than a vote, OUPblog, 1 March 2015.

16 Beastly Eastleigh and the 'None-of-the-Above' Party, OUPblog, 6 March 2013.

17 Where next?, OUPblog, 4 October 2015.

18 What a mess!, OUPblog, 3 April 2013.

19 The Dis-United Kingdom?, OUPblog, 3 September 2014.

20 A new and fair constitutional settlement?, *Yorkshire Post*, 19 September 2014.

21 Looking beyond the Scottish referendum, OUPblog, 3 December 2014.

22 The culture of nastiness and the paradox of civility, OUPblog, March 2017.

23 Learning to love democracy, OUPblog, 5 November 2014.

24 Let the people speak!, OUPblog, 1 February 2015.

25 Raw politics, OUPblog, 1 November 2015.

26 Vote Jeremy Clarkson on 7 May!, OUPblog, 5 April 2015.

27 After the storm, OUPblog, 4 June 2014.

28 Tony Benn was a true man of the people, *The Conversation*, 14 March 2014.

29 Dear Russell Brand, OUPblog, 30 October 2013.

30 Foolish, but no fool, OUPblog, 5 June 2013.

31 Remembering Margaret Thatcher, OUPblog, 8 April 2013.

32 Trump that, OUPblog, 3 April 2016.

33 Mad politics, OUPblog, 5 February 2014.

34 Shake your chains, OUPblog, 6 March 2016.

35 DIY democracy, OUPblog, 5 July 2015.

36 Participatory arts and active citizenship, OUPblog, September 2014.

37 The body politic, OUPblog, 4 September 2016.

38 It's just a joke!, OUPblog, 30 April 2012.

39 Left behind?, OUPblog, 2 June 2016.

40 Why Parliament matters, OUPblog, 4 September 2013.

41 Rip it up and start again, OUPblog, 7 January 2015.

42 Democracy Day, Sir Bernard Crick Centre Blog, 28 January 2015.

43 Attack ads and American presidential politics, OUPblog, 19 June 2012.

44 Dante and the spin doctors, OUPblog, 7 May 2014.

45 Democratic realism, OUPblog, 3 August 2012.

46 Bang, bang – democracy's dead, OUPblog, 7 February 2016.

47 Fig leaves and fairy tales, OUPblog, 3 May 2015.

48 Disengaged Britain, UK Parliament Week Blog, 20 November 2013 (www.ukparliamentweek.org).

49 The blunders of our governments, *Governance*, 13 March 2014.

50 Dear Maria Miller, it really wasn't all your fault, *The Conversation*, 9 April 2014.

51 Bring me a scapegoat to destroy, OUPblog, 3 July 2013.

52 Explaining political disaffection, British Politics and Policy, LSE Blog, 27 January 2014.

53 Politics without vision, *Times Higher Education*, 17 May 2012.

54 Dangerous minds, OUPblog, 2 August 2015.

55 Claims of increasing irrelevance of universities are ideology masquerading as evidence, Political Studies Association Blog, 15 December 2015.

56 The dismal debate, OUPblog, 1 May 2016.

57 Post-truth, post-political, post-democracy, OUPblog, 3 July 2016.

58 A talent for politics?, OUPblog, 7 August 2016.

59 Standing up and shaping the agenda, Political Studies Association Blog, 7 July 2016.

60 Welcome to the year of living dangerously – 2017, OUPblog, 8 January 2017.

INDEX